American Examples

American Examples

New Conversations about Religion

volume 5

Edited by
RACHEL E. C. BECKLEY, JACOB LASSIN, ANDREW
KLUMPP, AND MICHAEL J. ALTMAN

THE UNIVERSITY OF ALABAMA PRESS   TUSCALOOSA

The University of Alabama Press
Tuscaloosa, Alabama 35487–0380
uapress.ua.edu

Typeface: Scala Pro

Cover design: Sandy Turner Jr.

DEPARTMENT of
RELIGIOUS
STUDIES
THE UNIVERSITY OF ALABAMA®

*Published with the support of the University of
Alabama Department of Religious Studies*

Cataloging-in-Publication data is available from the Library of Congress.
ISBN: 978–0–8173–6257–7
E-ISBN: 978–0–8173–9596–4

Contents

CONTENTS

The Cryptic Dramaturgies of Christian Performance

Illustrations

American Examples

Introduction

A New Conversation about Religion

RACHEL E. C. BECKLEY, JACOB LASSIN, AND
MICHAEL J. ALTMAN

*Disclaimer: The views expressed in this introduction are those of the author and do
not reflect the official policy or position of the US Air Force, Air University, the Department of Defense, or the US Government.*

As we reach the fifth edition of the American Examples anthologies, the editors discussed the possibility of a new form of introduction for the book. In
the experimental spirit that has defined American Examples, this introduction
is more of a conversation. Indeed, as our subtitle insists, American Examples
brings new conversations about religion. In what follows, editor and director
of the American Examples program, Michael J. Altman, asked two of the editors and participants in the 2022 AE program, Jacob Lassin and Rachel E. C.
Beckley, to offer their thoughts about American Examples and the study of
American religion more broadly.

MICHAEL J. ALTMAN: The American Examples program started in 2019 and
now we are introducing our fifth volume of *American Examples*. From where
we sit now, after five cohorts of the program, what themes or ideas do you see
motivating the field, or what do you find less apparent in the study of religion
in America?

RACHEL E. C. BECKLEY: As I see it currently, US religious history is still dominated by description or a narrative of diversity. Don't get me wrong—I don't

see that as necessarily a bad thing. It's been a long time coming! This focus on the diversity of the American religious landscape has begun to enter our teaching, as well. For example, when I first started teaching the one-hundred-level Religion in American Society course, I inherited a syllabus that focused on comparative religious practices. So, I tried to fill the syllabus with more and more nonwhite, nonmale, and nonorganizational voices. I diversified. Yet, even as I added more description of US religious diversity, I felt the need to ask: "So what?" How does adding diverse experiences help us understand "religion" in "America"?[1] It is a first step, but it can't be the last step. So many times, religious historians of the United States are so preoccupied with describing diversity that they ask only what those diverse experiences entailed rather than what they formed, created, or coconstructed.

So, what happens when we look to Harry Hosier, Jarena Lee, or Samson Occom rather than Francis Asbury or George Whitfield to examine religious revival in the colonial eighteenth century? What did "America" mean to the adherents of the Moorish Science Temple, and how did they shape that identity? What if "scripture" referred not only to organized texts but also to any constructed canon? Beyond just adding "alternative voices" to a picture of America as a hegemonically Protestant nation, these types of questions can shine a light on how that hegemonic status has always been contested.

These types of questions also challenge us to look to interdisciplinary methodologies. Rather than bind ourselves to unshifting, disciplinarily held methods, instead we can embrace other ways of forming knowledge. How can we draw from Latinx studies, Black studies, scriptural studies, Indigenous studies, material religion, space/place studies, queer and trans studies, to name only a few?[2] Interdisciplinary, or transdisciplinary studies, is readily evident in this American Examples volume.[3] For example, Mihee Kim-Kort uses critical race and postcolonial studies, Kit Hermanson brings queer theory and museum studies, Dustin Gavin looks to embodiment and aesthetics. This sort of transdisciplinary work is exciting and vibrant!

How can we bring together different methodologies like ethnography, oral history, and digital humanities to widen and enliven the traditional historical archive, to tell different stories about what someone somewhere calls religion?

JACOB LASSIN: Along with crossing those interdisciplinary lines, the study of religion in America should also cross national borders. American exceptionalism looms large over much academic discourse and the study of religion is no exception. Too often religious phenomena in the United States are viewed as sui generis and without analog in other places. Moreover, Americans often suffer from "main character syndrome," believing that their country and experiences are the main driver in world affairs and the central focus for the world's population. These related issues tend to lead to a blinkered understanding of religion in America. As a result, I believe that more attention must be paid to transnational and comparative studies of religion.

Understanding how religious ideas and practices emerge, circulate, are transposed, and develop around the world is necessary to study religion in America. Greater attention to the international connections of religious groups, practitioners, and ideas in America provides for richer, more comprehensive interpretations. The study from American religion could benefit from de-emphasizing the notion that religious developments in the United States are unique and that the country's experiences and religious experiments set the agenda for the rest of the world.

ALTMAN: Those are a lot of the issues that motivated us to create American Examples in the first place. I think that we've started to push the field toward those questions you both raise but there's always further we can go. To that end, what themes or ideas should shape American Examples right now or in the future?

BECKLEY: American Examples brought up the question of the "third thing." I think something vital for American Examples in moving forward is dealing with the predictable barriers that scholars face in searching for this "third thing." Particularly, the risks and barriers that face early-career and contingent faculty scholars, as well as those scholars working "beyond" the academy.

If American Examples pushes us to challenge traditional US political history and US religious history, then how do early-career scholars network at the American Academy of Religion (AAR), so nicely sliced and diced by discipline and category? Where does an early-career scholar who is doing interdisciplinary research publish? And, speaking as a historian, how do we access diverse methodologies represented in other area studies especially when—and I will speak for myself here rather than at large—I don't always talk the theoretical language, trained as a historical empiricist. How do we train ourselves to do digital humanities while also doing the research that we want to express with those new digital platforms?

The community of American Examples is fantastic. I do, however, see a future in which more established scholars within American Examples can make headway to carve out institutional space in our current systems, so that early-career faculty and contingent faculty with less power and more precarity can

work safely. I look forward to more listservs that advise publications in journals that are willing to take on a change to interdisciplinary methods, rather
than well-known flagship journals that so carefully gatekeep "the field."

Lassin: The structural challenges are certainly real and getting more difficult.
In many institutions of higher education around the United States there appears to be less and less support for the study of religion. Often the topic is
viewed as laden with potential pitfalls and opportunities to offend or become
embroiled in controversy. At the same time, university administrations tend
to favor fields of study that seem to have more direct connections with the
job market for students after they graduate. But the work in American Examples and realities in American society show that the place and role of religious
thinking and practice remains a cornerstone of our social lives. How then can
we as educators and researchers overcome these issues? I believe that American Examples helps to point toward some models or, not to be too cute, examples. What this initiative shows is the multiplicity and ubiquity of religion in
every facet, every community, and every time period in America. Expanding
our courses and our outreach to show students that religion is not just the de-
bates over belief and divinity or questions of dogma or the histories of movements and denominations then, we will make a strong step away from the
parochialization of religious studies and move it more into the center of understanding social life broadly.

I think we see that expansion in the chapters in this volume. Kit Hermanson's study of gender in the Oneida Community takes an example that is
well known in American religious history and brings a new set of theoretical questions to it. Similarly, Ryne Beddard's account of the Dismal Swamp
includes Nat Turner, a familiar historical figure in American religious history, but does so through the theoretical lens of myth and the context of the
swamp. Sarah Hedgecock uses youth camps to find a new way into an analysis of twentieth-century American evangelicalism. But this volume also moves
away from things typically categorized as religion. Dustin Gavin examines majorette dance at historically Black colleges and universities while Mihee Kim-
Kort argues for the religious significance of H Mart supermarkets. Similarly,
Judith Ellen Brunton turns "energy" like a multifaceted diamond in her chapter as she investigates the layers of meaning and history surrounding energy
extraction. All of these chapters offer examples of how we might expand our
thinking about things called religion (or not) in America.

But to return to your question about the future of American Examples,
underlying American Examples is a desire to document and analyze the

pervasiveness of religious thinking and religious forms in all aspects of American life. It may seem cliché to say things like "this or that is like a religion." However, the reality is such that religious thinking and behavior is a staple of nearly all aspects of American life. The value that American Examples provides is in how it reveals the expressions of this religious impulse both historically and contemporarily. American Examples captures this in research that either can show how a category of religious practice fits into a phenomenon that is not necessarily always seen as religious or in how more traditionally religious endeavors in America speak to larger political and social questions and are not merely the purview of a single community, tradition, or denomination.

ALTMAN: You both have training in other disciplines outside of religious studies and American Examples has tried to include scholars from a variety of training and disciplinary backgrounds since the beginning. How can AE continue to move ahead methodologically?

BECKLEY: One way to do different methodologies and learn from interdisciplinary studies is to dive in. It takes curiosity and it takes bravery, recognizing that we won't have all the answers—and that we may even get it wrong! But transdisciplinary studies also requires the one thing that none of us has—time. How can I do my teaching and service, my research, all while keeping up with my own field plus another interdisciplinary field, especially a field that speaks a different theoretical language than I know? Who has time to learn a new methodology?

I think that, in order to ask the big questions American Examples calls us toward, we must slow down a bit. Can we spend more time writing shorter pieces of literature—blogs, reflections—putting ideas and questions out there and seeing what comes back to us? Is there a way that we can open our fields so we can mutually engage? Can we recognize that scholars outside of traditional academia have a great deal to offer?

This is what I see as the greatest impediment in the field of American religion. It is the necessity to shift not only the way we think about things but also how we produce that knowledge. American Examples provided the space to break not only disciplinary boundaries by asking new questions using interdisciplinary methodology but also "traditional scholarship"—the way it is produced, the speed at which it is produced, and the way it is discussed.

We are looking at an uncertain future as religious studies departments across the nation contend with fewer majors and fewer advanced degrees while also weathering current national rhetoric surrounding the devaluation of the humanities.[4] In times of uncertainty and transition, I am reminded of the words of Octavia Butler in *Parable of the Sower*. In describing that God is change, Lauren Olamina, the main character, states the following:

> *All successful life is*
> *Adaptable*
> *Opportunistic*
> *Tenacious,*
> *Interconnected, and*
> *Fecund.*
> *Understand this.*
> *Use it.*
> *Shape God.*[5]

AE attempts to do this: to be tenacious and adaptable, because everything around us is shifting. I don't think we can do "business as usual" anymore. The stories we tell about our past have deep impacts on the way we see our present. The pages of this volume represent research that is fecund. We can shape change as it comes, but it means tearing down what we know and opening ourselves to new possibilities.

ALTMAN: I agree that scholars of religion in America, and really scholars of all sorts, need to experiment with new methods and new forms of scholarly production. At the writing of this introduction, American Examples has completed its last cohort of participants in its workshop series. We are at the cusp of a new era for American Examples where we want to maintain the community we have built and celebrate the innovative research we have done but also look ahead to what the future might be. As American Examples moves toward a new era in the next few years, I can imagine a turn toward more digital methods and scholarly products. This is where the Department of Religious Studies at the University of Alabama, AE's home, is headed already. What sorts of podcasts, digital exhibits, and digital projects could continue the work of American Examples? How can we use computational methods, text analysis, large language learning models, AI, and other digital tools in research on things someone called religion somewhere someone called America? These are the questions guiding where American Examples is headed, and it is very exciting.

We would not be headed in these new directions, however, if it was not for the support we have received to get this far. We are so grateful to the Luce Foundation for the grant that has made American Examples possible and to

Kristen Hop at the University of Alabama Press for all of her work on this anthology series. Last, we are grateful to our colleagues in the Department of Religious Studies at the University of Alabama, particularly Vaia Touna and Steven Ramey. They both read these papers and offered feedback as part of the 2023 American Examples Research Workshop. American Examples is a remarkable community because it is made up of excellent scholars and people.

NOTES

1. Michael J. Altman, "Introduction: Something Someone Calls Religion Somewhere Someone Calls America," in *American Examples: New Conversations About Religion*, vol. 1 (Tuscaloosa: University of Alabama Press, 2021), 10–13.

2. For an example from Latinx studies, see Jacqueline Hildago, *Revelation in Aztlán: Scriptures, Utopias, and the Chicano Movement* (New York: Palgrave Macmillan, 2016); from Black studies, see Bettye Collier-Thomas, *Daughters of Thunder: Black Women Preachers and Their Sermons* (San Francisco: Jossey-Bass, 1998); from scriptural studies, see Vincent Wimbush, ed., *Masquerade: Scripturalizing Modernities through Black Flesh* (Lanham, MD: Lexington Books, 2023), and Richard Newton, *Identifying Roots: Alex Haley and the Anthropology of Scriptures* (New York: Equinox, 2020); from Indigenous studies, see Tisa Wenger, *Religious Freedom: The Contested History of an American Ideal* (Chapel Hill: University of North Carolina Press, 2017), and Joel W. Martin and Mark A. Nicholas, eds., *Native Americans, Christianity, and the Reshaping of the American Religious Landscape* (Chapel Hill: University of North Carolina Press, 2010); from studies in material religion, see Sonia Hazard, ed, "Religion and Material Texts in the Americas," special issue, *Material Religion* 17 no. 2 (2021); from trans studies, see Natasha L. Mikles and Joseph P. Laycock, eds, *Religion, Culture, and the Monstrous: Of Gods and Monsters* (Lanham, MD: Lexington Books, 2021).

3. Vincent Wimbush, *White Man's Magic: Scripturalization as Slavery* (Oxford: Oxford University Press, 2012), 7.

4. For resources and data, see the AAR website.

5. Octavia Butler, *Parable of the Sower* (1993; New York: Grand Central, 2019), 124–25.

"I'm a Darned Sweet Woman, and You Know It"

On the Majorette Strut

Dustin Gavin

The dance begins before it is danced. With a gesture, Airielle Brooks, the 2022–2023 captain of the Southern University Fabulous Dancing Dolls, signals to her troupe the pattern of the catch-on she will soon throw.[1] Raising both arms to the sky, she breaks her wrists in perfect sissy indication and elegantly flutters her hands.[2] This cue, among a list of others, directs how her movements are passed and picked up by those behind her. These signals work similarly to those between the catcher and the pitcher in the American game of baseball. However, for the dancers, the roles are reversed: it is the pitcher, the captain, who signals how the dance should be caught by the dancers who chevron up the risers of the stadium. The lead's stylized waves are the first call to how the dance troupe behind her knowingly responds. With this, the dance commences.

Airielle gracefully removes her white cape and rises according to the band's beat. She throws her right arm across her torso, a sort of snap that orbits around her bevvied stance. The movement isn't released until that cast arm has reached behind her; its whip, then pull, directs her torso, placing her body in profile. Her face and eyes remain pressed forward as the hurled arm reaches down and finds itself parallel to the arm left by her side. That meeting is swiftly shadowed by a smooth swoop of both arms over and above her head. She turns, then rocks into her right hip before propelling her blade-like limbs outward, sweeping her arms and twisting her torso into a windmill that returns her body forward. In that arrival, the rhythm is stalled, softened. Those arms, once blades, become wings, rushing across her chest, then skimming up and over her face and head. In the next moments the element shifts, and the movement is made liquid. She melts her hands down her nape, slinking and curling her body all the while. Then hands brush past hips, setting up the return of the eight count's original orbital snatch. As she repeats the series of movements, a subset of the dancers behind her—those instructed by Airielle's first organizing gesture—stand and join in her dance.[3] This structural following continues throughout the song's duration: Airielle leads; her chorus follows. Though each eight count is choreographically different, all danced moves meet and extend ritualized embodied standards and proclivities of a Fabulous Dancing Doll.[4]

A Dancing Doll of the Southern University Jaguars doesn't grind. Her preference is a catlike groove; her movements hiss and purr. She pounces on the beat, then kneads it. You will never see her throw that ass in a circle. No. Her dance is sassy, then soft sissy, melded into something quite sensual. Her dance is a tease. A Fabulous Doll's liquid moves, punctuated with limp wrists and a flourish of a hand say: "Leave—wait, no. Stay." "Look. Don't touch." It draws the viewer's attention with a gurgling femme-ness. Its audacity plays coy. Its softness bites.

A Doll's delicate outstretched limb gesturally whispers and beckons the commands of the late Venus Extravaganza: "Touch this skin, darling. Touch this skin, honey. Touch all of this skin," while also dancing a repulsion to the mere idea of that request being met.[5] A Doll can't be touched. She can't be bothered. She dances a Black woman and femme queen who wants you to know that she noticed you noticing her, while reminding you that noticing her should have less to do with her than it has to do with you. She conjures something demanding yet suggestive. Honey sweet and bitingly sour. Her aesthetic is a strategy, a sacred erotic embodiment managed by respectable Blackness. Her steps are ordered, and one can't help but notice that those steps are ordered by prescripts of class and etiquette. Though clad in bedazzled unitards and leotards, a Doll's quiet postures—her sway, her glare, her sitting—meet the conventions of women who lunch. Dr. Akai Smith, former coach of the Fabulous Dancing Dolls, makes their commitments and philosophies clear: "The one thing you can say about Dancing Dolls is that they are a respectable and classy and talented group of women who display the art of dance."[6] However, this acknowledgment only speaks to/of the Dolls and their signature style. There are other stylistic formulas that make up the idiom and genre that is majorette dance.[7]

This chapter demonstrates that historically Black college and university (HBCU) dance extends our conceptions of Black religiocultural performance practices by focusing on its militaristic affects. I argue that majorette dance theorizes long histories of Black performance techniques, Black gender formations, and adaptations of nationalistic militarism.

Take, for example, the progenitors of HBCU majorette dance: The Golden Girls of Alcorn State University Sounds of Dyn-O-Mite Marching Band. They have come to conjure a pageantry grittier than the belle-like flaunt of the Fabulous Dolls from Baton Rouge, Louisiana. Pleasantry, a Doll's sassy civility, is not the mode a Golden Girl (GG) embodies through her practice of majorette dance. One could notice this divergence in how a Golden Girl sits. She does not cross her legs and assume a flirtatious aloofness, as the Southern Dolls do. Golden Girls sit erect. Her hands don't exactly rest on her thighs; they are placed with intention: a kinetic steadfastness. The GGs rarely give sign or signal to the start of their dance; we know them for their elements of surprise, for their ability to shock and awe. The formalism of their physicality stages ritual drama in which the Golden Girls surprise through precision. As Alcorn State's Sounds of Dyn-O-Mite strike their first note, the Golden Girls pop to their feet and land in a pose with their heads cocked and arms folded. It occurs in rhythmic succession beginning with the back row of the four staggered rows of dancers and ripples its way down to Dayjasia Wright, the captain of the 2022–2023 Golden Girls squad. It's danced like a battle call. It screams: "Wassup?! Get Buck!"[8]

To "get buck," a phrase repeated among majorette squads, is to show oneself prepared for battle. This mode of bucking states its preparedness while simultaneously beckoning opposition and competition. But a buck—to buck, to get buck, bucking—invokes multiple valences within Black vernacular cultures. To begin, bucking has implications across histories of Black dance and minstrelsy in the United States.[9] It, too, has a life within US popular culture that frames its contemporary usages. In 2024, one might first think of bucking alongside Beyoncé's "SWEET*HONEY*BUCKIIN'" and its choreographic application on the popular social media platform TikTok.[10] Beyoncé's track begins sweetly with talks of "Jiffy cornbread [and a] booty cornfed" but ends with some "buckin' like a mechanical bull"—a description that names movement that is boisterous and attention-seeking and -grabbing. Crime Mob's 2004 single "Knuck if You Buck" also comes to mind. Crime Mob's song (and battle cry) names a buck as an explicit challenge. Here the term suggests that one is prepared for war, "ready to fight," (to quote rapper Princess) upon approach.[11]

A buck (provocation), in both verbal and physical application, implies that

one is prepared to knuck (fight). Bucking invites and instigates battle, and bat-
tling is constituent to the ritualistic nature of HBCU band culture (see "Battle
of the Bands"). Bucking, a component of HBCU majorette dance, exists as its
own idiom within Black culture, but might also be an embodied interpolation
and extension of Black diasporic movement vocabularies, a sort of embodied
Afro-fabulation that imagines a future with different kinds of resistance than
known armies.[12] Majorette dancers such as the Golden Girls assume bucking's
prescriptions with their bodies and movement, in formations that replicate
militaristic fanfare. With arms folded and heads cocked, the Golden Girls invoke a buck's forms and calls. While the Fabulous Dolls milk—slink, pour, and
even curdle—the Golden Girls buck—pop, sock, and drop.

In unison, the Golden Girls whip their hair and roll back to a seated position while tracing their hands down their breasts and midsection. For their
song and dance, the Golden Girls perform a prepared stand routine, one that
doesn't utilize the improvisatory call-and-response structure of the catch-on.[13]
After rolling to the seated position, the Golden Girls hop back up, then cast
their hands, hips, and heads left then right. These forceful throws of the body
are accented with smacks of the thighs. They part their legs to position their
bodies with the full bend of grand plié; however, in this plié hips are pushed
back, not forward. These postures are the makings of bucking. Loud, gaudy,
and virtuosic.

The protrusion of the buttocks is an important accent. With ass pushed
back, the Golden Girls bring their hands to their knees, then swoop their upper torso and head around the negative space before them. They turn left,
bend over, and meet nose to knees before snapping their heads and whipping
their face and eyes to the viewing audience. With heads down and posteri-
ors up, they steal a glare. Every moment that follows is brassier than the one
that precedes it. Hands are placed on hip as they pop so hard one could imagine they're testing the hinge of the hip's socket. A buck: they pop, dig, hunch,
and thrust the pelvis, suggesting with each move that thighs and loins are the
grounds for which a GG moves and breathes.[14] Their lower parts move with
the rolling tension of a crank; the locomotion is palpable. In this dance and
many others of theirs, the pop, grind, and throw of the ass is the medium and
message. A Golden Girl bucks, she chucks her body with control and intention. In her dance, she squats low enough to scrub and muck up the grounds
of respectability.

Much like (yet quite different from) the Fabulous Dancing Dolls, Golden
Girls can't be touched. A Golden Girl can't be bothered. She dances a Black
woman and femme queen who understands that her dance may force some

eyes to avert, that vulgarity might be the lens for which audiences craft her doing and being, while simultaneously dancing with a tenacious and conscious
power that commands attention and acknowledgment for its virtuosity. Her
loudness conjures something beyond approach and reproach: the sheer force
of her wingspan and meticulous play with bawdy movement keep audiences at
arm's length.

Beginning in 1968 with the Golden Girls of Alcorn State University, the
majorette dance style announced its presence through its particular forms of
embodiment.[15] However, the lands of TikTok trends and primetime television
have now caught wind of its charismatic force.[16] From a recent profile in *Essence* magazine and *Good Morning America* to its featuring at Vice President
Kamala Harris's 2021 inauguration, majorette dance—the southern-born Black
femme dance idiom—has quickly attracted the attention of middle America.[17]
In light of this, we have come closer to naming what *is* majorette dance. Their
featuring on *Good Morning America* suggested that "majorette dancers mix
multiple styles of dancing, including jazz, hip-hop, ballet, burlesque, cabaret,
kick lines and more." Sydney Clark, a 2023 member of North Carolina A&T
State University's Golden Delight majorette team, defines the dance and its
dancers through an inability of being defined: "I think if you can define [a majorette dancer], it's a dancer who cannot be defined."[18] For Clark, indefinability
marks the idiom and its practitioners, but her definition should not be con-
flated with indecipherability. There is no question that HBCU majorette dance
is discernible. Its rise on social media platforms and its naming in light of this
rise demonstrate that there are characteristics to its form that make the idiom
stand-alone. It is a form of dance whose styles and influences can be detected
even when danced outside of the institution of the HBCU marching band.
Sydney Clark's response suggests that we are asking the wrong questions.

In his text *Poetics of Relation*, Édouard Glissant suggests that we "reverse
the order of questions and begin . . . by shedding light on the relations of
language-culture-situation to the world."[19] Definition isn't this work's end; in
many ways the following is an argument for an opaque look at HBCU majorette dance, as this project's interests lie in illuminating the languages, cultures, and situations that *made* and *make* HBCU majorette dance's forms. I do
not wish to clarify what the form *is*. The idea of such specification risks suffo-
cating the form into stagnancy. Majorette dance—at once social, ceremonial,
and technical—is an idiom made manifest via its relations and movements
across time. I evaluate these moves and relations to speculate what HBCU
majorette dance might be saying and what longer histories can be gleaned
from its aesthetic formations and applications. Across different institutional

and regional histories, HBCU dance troupes turn ideas and indexes of Black femme figurations into aesthetic and choreographic techniques. Each team invokes an embodied philosophy to their dance. Each team has traditions and commitments they transform into embodied ritual and ethic. And each team commits to structures in volley with respectable codes of ethics. Their dance is a complex history, theory, and poetry in motion. Audre Lorde reminds us that poetry is not a luxury, that it is "the way we give name to the nameless so it can be thought."[20] HBCU majorette dance compels thought through its unique application of multiple languages and forms. With a whip of the neck, a layout, and undulating hips, HBCU dance lines extend and complicate the liminality of the sacred and profane and Black cultural hybridity.

Herein I speculate some of what this dance names in its doing. In illustrating the breadth of histories and historiographies majorette dance theorizes, I engage anthropologist Zora Neale Hurston's canonical 1934 essay "Characteristics of Negro Expression" as a theoretical compass for understanding the relationship between Black religion and Black culture. Alongside deep engagement with Dr. William Patrick Foster's 1968 handbook *Band Pageantry: A Guide for the Marching Band*, I focus on one element of HBCU majorette dance, the majorette strut. In the spirit of the guides that inspire it, this chapter episodically explores the majorette, the drum major, band pageantry, and the strut as characters, characteristics, and techniques that make up what we now call HBCU majorette dance.

MAJORETTE

Majorette dance cites the choreographic movement and gestures of all dance lines and those queer performers who have been central to its production. The term *majorette dance* is a catch-all that indexes the structure and styles of a southern-born, femme performance culture. Its primary constant is a multilayered attendance to formation and alignment—alignment of bodies, frames, and sequences paired with virtuosic and ostentatious movement. These gestures and movements form the idiom's signifying vernacular. The form does not dictate its content; it possesses unique relational histories and genealogies relative to respective dance troupes. Regional/local style and sensibility shape each dance team's movement structure.

HBCU majorette dance is an embodied turn of phrase. It expresses ideas and indexes of Black femme figuration and performance with and against the historical misnaming of Black womanhood and turns Black brass band's militaristic architecture into Black femme choreographic techniques and aesthetic formations. The majorette strut is a great sight/site to explore a few of the dance's historical retentions and dimensions.[21]

In her canonical essay "The Race for Theory," literary and feminist theorist Barbara Christian argues for theory rooted in practice. Her frustration in the article is palpable as she announces her annoyance with contemporary theory's affinity for prescription over pleasure.[22] She writes that she is "appalled by the sheer ugliness of the language, its lack of clarity, its unnecessarily complicated sentence constructions, its lack of pleasurableness, its alienating quality."[23] What stands out in this essay is Christian's beckon to writers to be sensitive and to refuse the impetus to create new theory that takes for granted the intelligence that accompanies sensuality. Her musings focus on literature, but her lens is useful as I understand dance to be an ephemeral hieroglyphic and mode of writing that uses space and time as its tableau. For Christian, literature is a way of knowing that whatever she knows and feels *is*, and that sensual language is language that *makes* sense. HBCU majorette dance (majorette dance) is a sensual language that *makes*, as in *creates* or *develops*, sense. HBCU majorette dance makes meaning. My reading of majorette dance is motivated by how its body language compels my understanding of its fabrication. Majorette dance's meaning does not occur in a vacuum; it is a pas de deux with historical and cultural (mis)understandings of Black womanhood. I therefore speculate its stylistic ingenuity through historiographies of Black femme-ness and Black womanhood. As I know, feel, and see it, majorette dance is a manifestation of much more than the moment in which it arises: it indexes a longer past; however, let us begin by naming the form and how the form's historians detail its emergence.

The majorette form announced its presence with a feature article in *Ebony* magazine. Noticing that women dance lines were becoming integral to Black college and university marching band aesthetics, *Ebony* made "dancing girls" their January 1972 cover story.[24] Titled "Beauty—and the Beat: Black Colleges Feature Pretty Girls, Jazzy Bands at Football Halftime," the article chronicles the utility of this new "beautiful" edition to Black college and university marching bands. The cover story notes: "The 'blow' is in the marching bands. The 'show' is in the beautiful girls."[25] This article argues that HBCU majorette dance's material story begins in 1968. "Founded in July of 1968 by the late Samuel Griffin . . . the Golden Girls, aka GG's were the first dance line to perform as a featured squad with choreographed movements to an HBCU's marching band's live tunes."[26] This is understood as majorette dance's inception within the HBCU marching band system and is relevant to its mythmaking enterprise. The story of majorette dance's initiation and its initiators takes on legendary iconicity and its telling uses the language of lore. "According to records, no one had ever seen a female dance team perform during halftime of a Historically Black College and University (HBCU) football game," but upon witness, "a silence fell upon the crowd as the original eight regal,

African-American ladies took the field." This is the story of the Girls. The story of
the Dolls differs.

The same year the Golden Girls of Alcorn State declared themselves the
first all-female Black dance line of a Black college marching band, Gracie
Perkins founded the Southern University Dancing Dolls. Instructed by then
band director Dr. Isaac Greggs, Perkins was tasked to create a dance troupe
for the Southern University marching band that would take inspiration from
the Rockettes he'd once seen at Radio City Music Hall. The "high kicks, ex-
travagant outfits, and the glitz and the glam" of the Rockettes captivated
Greggs; he wanted the Southern University's Human Jukebox first all-female
dance troupe to possess a similar flare. Specifically, he indicated to Perkins
that he didn't want "majorettes" because they had "the little short boots and
the dresses." For Greggs, these sartorial elements lacked the "pizazz" evident
in the Rockettes' costumes and performance aesthetics.[27] However, it is the
Prancing J-Settes of Jackson State University's Sonic Boom of the South, established in 1971, who pride themselves on "initiat[ing] the concept of the majorettes abandoning their batons and dancing to popular musical selections."[28]
Their influence was so dynamic that many refer to the majorette dance style as
"j-setting," understanding j-setting as an umbrella term for HBCU majorette
dance.[29] These competitive claims of origin abound in the promotional language of dance teams.

These assertions of difference ("abandoning their batons" and "often im-
itated but never duplicated") use the syntax of mythology. They don't clearly
articulate what is original about this culture of dance or what draws others to
borrow from its expressive work. They instead overstate. The promotional and
historical accounts of HBCU dance troupes work much like myths: they con-
tort. As theorist Roland Barthes suggests, myth "distorts; myth is neither a lie
nor a confession: it is an inflexion."[30] The form is justified in and through excessive language, and, in turn, this excess works to ground these stories of
majorette dance. Because majorette dance uses mythic language to natural-
ize its history and forms, it makes its interweaving histories matters of fact.
Each troupe finds itself and its origin in the other's cross hairs. Each group
cites their inspirations as something native to its own imagining of itself; however, their separate histories trip over one another: they conjoin even as they
work to stylistically and linguistically distinguish themselves. The myths of
HBCU majorette dance and its troupes, through its annual renewals, make
themselves and their accompanying traditions both natural occurrences and
telltales as old as time.

Participants cite the Golden Girls and 1968 as the idiom's forming. Such specificity is true to majorette dance's mythmaking endeavor but not to the historical arc I argue began in the Reconstruction. The year majorette dance supposedly discovers itself, the nation is amid major shifts defined by protests informed by the tenuousness of American citizenships. By the fall the Golden Girls premiere at the 1968 Orange Blossom Classic, Martin Luther King Jr. and Robert Francis Kennedy have been assassinated, inciting respective protests, antiprotests, and riots across the country; the Fair Housing Act has been signed and Students for a Democratic Society at Columbia University are demanding a right to demonstrate; North Vietnam's Tet Offensive has launched and succeeded in dismantling US support for the war effort, and police riots have broken out in the midst of antiwar protests at the Democratic National Convention in Chicago; and, as a protest to the Miss (white) America Pageant, the Miss Black America Pageant launches at the Ritz-Carlton in Atlantic City, New Jersey, just weeks before the Miss (white) America Pageant will meet Women's Liberation Movement protests led by New York Radical Women in that same New Jersey city at Boardwalk Hall.[31] In chronicling these American beauty-(un)defining events, anthropologist Maxine Leeds Craig links these events through the lens of protest when she writes: "In September 1968, a panel of beauty experts prepared to select the forty-eighth consecutive white Miss America, two protests were under way. One protest denounced beauty contests. The other *was* a beauty contest."[32] The events of 1968 converge within a framework of reconstructed racial and national identities, which are arguably shaped by militaristic and nationalistic ideals of Americanness that emerged during the Reconstruction era.[33] A less immediate history of HBCU majorette dance might provide a historical account that first considers Black performances of these ideals in the United States. The historical aesthetics and sensibilities of Black military and Black brass bands seem to form majorette dance's signifiers. A longer history of these Black and American adaptations suggests that sensibilities of Black (American) pride began much earlier than the years of Black Pride's—and subsequently, HBCU majorette dance's—officiating and embellishing.

MAJOR

The HBCU majorette dancer is a derivation and femme deviation of the drum major. She belongs to militaristic histories that inform her aesthetic configurations. Within Black band histories, the drum majorette also finds herself in racial, religious, and cultural flux.

The term *majorette* derives from the Dutch word *dansmarietje*, a carnival dancer who twirls batons.[34] *Brewer's Dictionary of Modern Phrase and Fable* defines her as "a girl or young woman who marches at the head of the procession, twirling and tossing a baton. Her uniform and prominent position to some extent mirror those of a drum major, who commands the corps of drums of a military band."[35] In this configuration, the majorette is tangential to the drum major. The majorette's prominent position and sartorial styling put her in direct conversation with the performance of the drum major, and, according to the above definition, she reflects the pageantry of the band's drum major. This ideation is not unique; it follows in the construction and presentation of the HBCU majorette dancer. Except, she reflects the aesthetics of Black band pageantry and its drum major, then translates those forms and foundations to meet, make, and suit her majorette dance. Her steps can be understood as augmentations of the march of a Black band's drum major.

A drum major is a noncommissioned officer commanding the drummers of a regimental band.[36] He is the leader of the band, and his responsibility is to keep time with baton in hand. In this figuration, he is not the show, he commands it. Tracing as far back as 1861 and the American Civil War, when brass instruments and drum lines were used among military bands in the United States, each Black regiment of the United States Colored Troops had their own band. Following the Civil War—by the last quarter of the nineteenth century—"well-trained ex-military musicians" and their performances were becoming a standing trend within most towns and cities across the United States.

These bands could be heard everywhere. They performed at "political rallies, circuses, minstrel and medicine shows, carnivals, picnics, dances, athletic contests, reunions, seasonal parades, serenade fairs, and holiday gatherings."[37] The brass band had become an integral component of sociality and began to develop its own forms of pageantry. In 1865 the United States began seeing its first permanent all Black minstrel troupes. By 1896, composer W. C. Handy, member of the Mahara's Minstrels, began to take note of the movement methods and practices created within these shows. For example, for Handy, the drum major of minstrel shows didn't keep time, he stole it: "The drum major— not an ordinary drum major beating time for a band, mind you, but a performer out of the books, an artist with the baton. . . . The drum major in a minstrel show was a character to conjure with; not infrequently he stole the parade."[38]

More than a leader and timekeeper, the drum major Handy describes assumed the role of both military musician commander and conjurer. Here, W. C. Handy introduces an evolving brand of (Black) pageantry and showmanship, one still upheld by contemporary drum majors (and majorettes) of Black college and university bands. In his writing, Handy demonstrates that the "universal" role of the drum major as timekeeper is extended within the performance of the Black band drum major. For the Black brass band, the drum major was timekeeper, artist, and spectacle. His movements and gestures were (and are) not intended to merely direct the band, but also "conjure" a spirit significant to the performance, one that could affect his audience. Handy rhetorically places the drum major's movement and gestures in religious domain and implies that the drum majors do we now call affective labor.

It has been concluded that affective labor produces collective subjectivities and ultimately society, but consider affective labor's productive capacity within terms of conjure.[39] In her text *Black Magic: Religion and the African American Conjuring Tradition*, Yvonne P. Chireau builds on the work of Charles Long and his elucidation of the critical and creative import of "extrachurch orientations" within Black communities. To assist in Long's expansion of common concepts of Black religions, Chireau writes that religion "not only pertains to the formal creeds, doctrines, and theologies of a church-based faith tradition but includes beliefs that are embedded in the ordinary experiences and the deeply held attitudes, values, and activities of members of a group or community."[40] Religion and its affective registers were seen in unlikely institutions, in realms of the secular. Adding David D. Hall's conception of "lived religion" to this equation, Chireau goes on to state that "African American religion . . . not only embodies ecclesial formations of faith but also encompasses noninstitutionalized expressions and activities."[41]

There are a couple things here to consider. First, ecclesial formations are not conjure-deficient. In her anthropological discoveries, Zora Neale Hurston wrote that "all hold that the Bible is the great conjure book in the world," so we need not imagine Christian faith and its practices outside of at least tangential degrees of conjure.[42] The contentious relationship between Christianity and (its attendant) secularism is what obfuscates views of the religious potential in secular dance and communion.[43] The adaptation of Africana ritual forms— their structure, process, contexts, dress, kinetic patterns—into the religious, the mundane, the secular, even the militaristic fabrics of the Black brass band allows for the aesthetics of mingled African religious traditions to hide in plain sight. In *The Sanctified Church*, Hurston spends time with the moving potential of dance within the Black cultures she observed. She writes that Black dance forms are "dynamic suggestion" and "compelling insinuation." She continues: "The Negro is restrained, but succeeds in gripping the beholder by forcing him to finish the action the performer suggests."[44] Hurston's account names a force, a pull, enacted by the dancer, where the dancer is the opening clause and the audience is that same phrases conclusive punctuation. The drum major's work within the Black band is ritual and communal causation. Conjure, then, might be an appropriate description of the drum major's step and dance. The term *conjure* is generally understood under the notion of spells, witches, and incantations, but a focus on its effect and affect makes it a useful term to capture the feelings felt by onlookers of the Black drum major and band. The drum major's movements grip the beholder by forcing him to finish the action, an action he finishes in ways both ecclesial—familiar in re-peated form—and noninstitutional. Something about the drum major seems subject to strong rule and surprising. Shock and awe.

W. C. Handy does not name an ecclesial formation in his writings on the Black band's drum major nor does he name religion is his evaluation of specta-cle of the drum major. What he does name is a spiritual exchange between the drum major and his audience, and writes that this conjuring was made man-ifest through the drum major's swagger and dance. We must remember that dance and religion have been intertwined in various ways through the centu-ries.[45] Historian Albert J. Raboteau speaks of the "African styles of worship, forms of ritual, systems of belief, and fundamental perspectives [that] have re-mained vital on this side of the Atlantic" and how these were preserved and transformed within and without Africana religious practices.[46] Distinguish-ing between the sacred and secular is not an inheritance of many Africana religious practices. P. Sterling Stuckey reminds of this in his article "Chris-tian Conversion and the Challenge of Dance" when he writes: "The sacred for slaves, as for Africans, was not demarcated by time: Threads of spirituality—of art itself—were woven into the fabric of everyday life."[47] There are Africana religious retentions and tensions in Black expressive cultures. It appears that Handy bore witness to this.

If Handy is taken at his word and not belied by Western thought's rigid di-chotomies of religious experience (or even by the vision that conjuring is al-ways a matter of material brew), one could imagine that a measure of con-juring occurs in this communal space of band pageantry. Audiences feel something in visually absorbing the strutting, prancing drum major. They might be, even for a moment, changed from the experiences of participation and witness. Black social subjects are moved by and through the drum major's movements. In this vision, the drum major could be seen as an extension to/of the band who holds and conjures the sonic on a visual plane, an authority figure somatically preaching or teaching something about Black authority, cre-ativity, autonomy, and play. Musical composition is explored and articulated in his limbs, in his strut, in his pageantry. The drum major, as well as the band, represent moments of cultural organization—a pattern and articulation of space and style. The point, then, of the Black band might be to communally gather and tell visual, sonic, and visually sonic embodied tales. These tales can certainly be presumed when viewing the majorette and her dance.

PAGEANTRY

Majorette dance is a Black, femme, and often respectable articulation and extension of Black band pageantry.[48] The HBCU majorette dancer's aesthetics are formed and informed through intermingling militarism with a seesaw sexual and racial parody of middle-class (white) womanhood and respectable Black womanhood.

There is no nonracial, nongendered history of American band performance; it was (and is) a look and sound of certitude within racial and cultural histories. Dance scholar Jacqui Malone makes these racial and cultural distinctions clear in her metaphorical comparison of white and Black regiments. In her rendering, white soldiers "ardently strove to march like well-oiled war machines, like battle-ready robots," while Black regiments "introduced both melody and foot-stomping syncopation into military cadence."[49] The Black band and drum major married flamboyant excess to military precision. Militaristic fidelity remained a foundational element of the brass band, and as Black brass bands continued to develop, embodied aesthetics continued to reflect southern religiocultural commitments.

Black brass bands were always in religious and secular flux. Syncopated steps, stomps, and struts were choreographed "not from the white man's stock of patriotic sheet music, but from church and secular songs," writes historian Frederic Ramsey Jr.[50] Ramsey goes on to describe the rhythms and styles of the Black brass band. They didn't have a "tight, regular march step."[51] Their movements were larger, and fluid, "more of a flowing, anticipatory emphasis and counter-emphasis, ideally suited to a free style of dance."[52] Ramsey describes not a freestyle dance but a dance styled free. Not tight—loose—potentially a step and dance contained in its loudness; these are not movements outside of control. The drum major's balancing act of timekeeper and showstopper and the Black band's queering of its militaristic foundation created an aesthetic formation that provided productive scaffolding for the Black college and university marching band. The Black brass band (and later, the HBCU marching band) combined military precision with loud, Black and proud showmanship.

The aesthetic, communal, and cultural commitments of the Black brass brand are clear throughout Dr. William Patrick Foster's 1968 guidebook, *Band Pageantry: A Guide for the Marching Band*, the text that defined college band pageantry in the mid-twentieth century. Foster writes: "Band pageantry is an elaborate and spectacular performance, executed by a marching band, and designed for the entertainment of the public at pre-game, half-time and post-game periods of football games. . . . Underlying the pageant should be a philosophy that is exemplified in terms of music as well as in the maneuvers by which the drama is portrayed."[53] Foster made spectacular drama the bedrock of the Black marching band's pageantry and used this tenant to create "a social environment" that was made material through the band's "structuring of space, architecture, [and] ritual performance." In effect, these structures induced bodily sensations.

Riffing on Benedict Anderson's notion of an imagined community, religious studies scholar Birgit Meyer extends his concept of community and suggests that an "aesthetic formation" might better encapsulate the process of creating community. Key to her argument is a turn toward a focus on style rather than meaning. She writes: "Style is at the core of religious aesthetics exactly because the adoption of a shared style is central to the processes of subjectivation, in that style involves particular techniques of the self and the body that modulate—and, indeed, 'hone'—persons into a socio-religious formation."[54] Distinctive style, according to Anderson and Meyer, is central to creating religious communities. Their work suggests that particular techniques of the self and body produce and mediate. Dr. Foster transformed these styles into a record of standard techniques for the HBCU marching band and its auxiliary performers.

Marching band drama, for Foster, was a technical occasion. A section in his guidebook entitled "Special Formations in Band Pageantry" laid out the structure of its program—such as entrances, animated formations, intricate steps, and dance steps—and provided a subsection detailing the qualifications and expectations of the drum majorette.[55] These included twirling ability, marching ability, neatness, leadership qualities, harmonious personality, and military bearing.[56] In Foster's detailing of the pageantry expected of the drum majorette, "neatness" and "harmonious personality" stand out. These principles of pageantry are undoubtedly gender specific. Of note, while William Patrick Foster founded the Marching 100 in 1946, women did not infiltrate his corps until 1974, with band members Carmena Fennel, Carla Wilson, and Debra Hines.[57] This is to say, Foster's address to band members within his band pageantry text is an address to male members only. His expectations of the men of the Marching 100 did not require they possess traits relative to their personality. Said another way, there was a separate, conservative form and expectation of pageantry from the "show": the drum majorettes.

Foster lists these expectations quite rigidly. In part of his didacticism, he writes that the "old-fashioned, rear-back strut and hip-swinging walk" should not be tolerated and that majorettes "should march and strut with the same graceful body alignment that dancers exhibit."[58] He goes on to detail the three elements that make the drum majorette "outstanding in appearance." Under his purview, she must wear high white boots, a colorful shako, and a short skirt, but on the other hand, these uniforms should not have "low neck lines and those featuring other aspects of a burlesque costume."[59] This for Foster was unacceptable. In his detailing, Foster is not merely naming band pageantry for drum majorettes, he is naming a pageantry expected of Black women in the South. Not only this, he standardizes unspoken rules of respectable Black womanhood.

In her work *Pageants, Parlors, and Pretty Women*, historian Blain Roberts contends with the ways southern women experimented with sexualized femininity against the US South's expectations and ideals of female behavior. Roberts's work focuses on how women's bodies did important racial work, highlighting how their bodies came to represent the modern in both economic and cultural terms.[60] Black and white women represented the state and times of the region. Roberts writes that "beautiful white women were transformed into symbols of white supremacy and, eventually, massive resistance, [while] beautiful black women . . . personified racial uplift and racial progress and, later, Black Pride."[61] The concern of representation was greater for Black women: there was more at stake and therefore more prescriptions. In her text, Roberts notes that Black southerners would often "prescribe the appropriate parameters of [Black women's] self-presentation—to dictate what items of clothing to buy and how to wear them."[62] Respectability—a politic used by Black women as a weapon against discourse that wrote Blackness and Black womanhood as innately deviant—was a matter of manners and morals, which was read and concluded through ocularity.[63]

We see these prescriptions in Foster's *Band Pageantry*. We can also see a similar dogma in Dr. Isaac Gregg's instructions to Gracie Perkins when forming the Southern University Dancing Dolls. Majorette dancers exist in institutions with a complicated theologically informed relationship to gendered freedom and belong to a gendered and racialized history and region that limit their choreographic and sartorial choices. Their dance has never been entirely liberatory, so the erotic potential of their bawdy language remains liminal. Gendered and racialized anxieties, effects of anthropological pathologies that framed Black women as a stand-in for deviant sexuality, have shored up that constriction.

In the preface of her collection of essays *The Black Interior*, scholar and poet Elizabeth Alexander reminds us that Black people have been imagined through "sociological and fantasy discourses."[64] Alexander's mention of what is seen and imagined bespeaks the artifice of the sociologically constructed and historicized Black figure. We find truth to her reflection in the works of canonical sociologists such as Gunnar Myrdal and Daniel Patrick Moynihan, who ascribed hegemonic meaning to Black culture.[65] Scholar Roderick A. Ferguson captures the (canonical) sociological discourse Alexander names when he writes that "at the base of sociological arguments about African American cultural inferiority lay questions about how well African Americans approximated heteronormative ideals and practices embodied in whiteness and ennobled in American citizenship."[66] Ferguson uses his text to critique canonical sociology's assumptions about Black culture, about sexual difference, and how these marked differences pathologize(d) Black culture because it did not well mimic Western civility. Prominent sociologists such as Myrdal and Moynihan helped color the fictions and fantasies of Black life, and those fantasies crafted vis-à-vis their sociological records find themselves within HBCU band's structure and hierarchy. Those hegemonic expectations and deployments of femme comportment were inherited by the HBCU marching band. Foster's paternalism around HBCU majorette dancers and their stylings was also a cultural and historical inheritance. When we add to this that Foster is working under a southern rubric of correctness (he is working at FAMU in Tallahassee, Florida), there is no surprise that "hip-swinging" and "low necklines" were deemed unbecoming.

Invocations of "Peaches," "Brown Sugar," "Sapphire" and the like were to be avoided by southern Black women.[67] Religious studies scholar Tamura Lomax unpacks these mythological images of Black womanhood and Black female sexuality in her work *Jezebel Unhinged*. She writes that the "discourse on black womanhood recognizes the sociopolitical and cultural work of race-sex-gender-class-specific mythology as an essential American and diasporic project [that] foregrounds the cross-penetration of meta-narratives on Black Venus, Jezebel, and Black-woman-as-whore/ho/thot (that ho over there)."[68] She goes on to suggest that there are notable parallels in ideas of Blackness and femaleness ("as object, primitive, immoral, other, accessible, hyper, simultaneously titillating") to the biblical Jezebel, who is "commonly interpreted as wicked, immoral, and seductress."[69] Let's hold on to this idea of the immoral seductress for a moment, keeping in mind that "majorette dancers mix multiple styles of dancing, including jazz, hip-hop, ballet, burlesque, cabaret, kick lines and more."[70]

Burlesque performances are sutured to minstrelsy, and burlesqued portrayals by white actors in blackface associated Blackness to sin and deviance.

In the United States, burlesque is commonly defined as a "disreputable form of . . . titillating dances."[71] Regarded as "a form of sexual objectification of women," a formal dance structure created by Black women (and Black queer men) would attempt to avoid a dance possessing designations of "disreputable" and "titillating." Considering the commonplace and routine objectification and abjection of Black women, we might imagine Black female lasciviousness a clear faux pas. However, if we understand the history of the burlesque stage as a space for self-gratification, the choice to include its tenets within majorette dance performance culture appears less strange.[72] As scholar Jayna Brown writes in *Babylon Girls*, Black burlesque women used the stage to both dramatize and satirize the "decorative fantasies of African American affluence." These burlesque acts "parodied the pretenses of the African American middle classes" and "resisted the strictures put upon the mixed-race female protagonists of uplift literature."[73] The burlesque stage and dance was/is a critical one.

What Brown makes clear in her work is that Black burlesque dancers were able to annotate with their bodies, and I contend that majorette dance provides similar, contemporary commentary through their erotic embodiment. With their bodies, majorette dancers write with and against history and complicate hegemonic ideas of polity and civility. The dance proclaims and embodies its own unique script of beautiful, "classy," femme performance. Across troupes, majorette dance names class and beauty politics through movement and dress.

In their feature article on majorette dancers, *Ebony* makes clear that majorettes were the "beauty" to the "beat" (the college marching band), and Blain Roberts reminds us that nearly every conversation about beauty in the US South (the region where majorette dance begins) was underscored by anxieties around morality and sexuality. There was a damning correlation between the body and soul.[74] Jim Crow politics begot the Black Pride era, and in southern regions of the United States, Black southerners were making sense of the legacies that preceded a new era of Black beauty politics that treated Black beauty as reputable and integral to itself.[75] Foster's book on band pageantry was published in 1968, the same year that majorette dancers appear within the HBCU marching band's paradigm. It isn't until 1971 with the Prancing J-Settes that it became standard for majorette dancers to perform without batons. These events happen in occurrence with the development of a Black Pride era that declared Black beautiful. Undoubtedly moved by this Black Pride movement, majorette dancers dropped the baton and began to instrument their bodies as producers of discourse on the play between Black beauty, erotic performance, and respectability. One might notice this easiest in their sitting. In their sitting, majorette dancers flirt with ideas of "class" and "grace."

Sitting, with bodies at perceivable rest, is alive with dynamic suggestion within majorette dance's many performative acts. As if plotted for the occasion, piercing glares seep out the side of their eyes, demure glances are placed over the shoulder, and flips of the hair act as gestures of practicality and announcements of brassy presence. With necks long and backs erect, majorette dancers graze French-manicured hands ever-so-presumptuously across their thighs.

Every moment seems a reflection of allure, modest vanity, and seductive drama. Watching their supermodel-like stature, we are again brought to an iconic scene in *Paris is Burning*—this time articulated by Octavia St. Laurent as she ogles her supermodel idol Paulina Porizkova: "I look at [Paulina] here and she's seductive and alluring. I look at her there and she's sexy and provocative. I look at her here and think she's childish and little girl type."[76] These well-managed expressions, all intentional in their excessive lightness, are marks of model-like elegance that majorette dancers assume as they sit.[77] Every quiet gesture is a serve; every moment is commentary on proper presence. In their sitting, majorette dancers' bodies act out negotiations of performed moral correctness. Majorette dancers sit within long histories of citizenship and womanhood, but their sitting is always in direct relation to the prescripts of its time and place. They become models of their time and space, and sitting is political, especially for models.

Elspeth H. Brown's work on models teaches us that the work of the model was instrumental in achieving this "rapprochement between bourgeois morality and commercialized leisure. [A model's] posing represented a critical site for the intersection of new public modes of looking: part aesthetic, part desire, and wholly commercial, the model tied together discourses of sexuality, the body, and the market in new ways during the 1920s," and these discourses exist presently and locally for HBCU majorette dancers.[78] Their sitting is a dialectic that maps out past and present forms of civility and etiquette.[79]

The pageantry and pleasantries of the majorette dancer, much like but distinct from her precursor, the drum major, are shaped by a cunning historical and cultural balancing act. Majorette dancers' bodies became their primary tool of expression and their performances potentially began to provide truer words of prescripts within Black femme performance—not necessarily Black femme sexuality. With time, burlesque aesthetics slowly edged their way into the cultural practice.[80] In his band pageantry guide, William Patrick Foster condemned "burlesque" elements within drum majorette's signifying repertoire. Today, that burlesque element is elemental to the idiom. Majorette dance's form exists as historical commentary on modern embodiment.

The modern (Black) woman, especially as it contends with female embodiment, was a challenge to traditional gender norms. Majorette dance finds itself caught within this affront. Dr. Shawn Zachery, director of the Prairie View A&M University Black Foxes, announces to *Essence* magazine that what impresses and captivates him about majorette dance is "the showmanship, style, and glamour" and how these forms of entertainment have changed and evolved over the years.[81] These evolutions morph around the commodification of beauty. Women's bodies and beauty have done important work on behalf of racial conceptions, and male band directors still use majorette dancers to do race work.[82]

Paternalism belongs to that history and its fancy, and majorette dancers have been sat down when dancing outside of the liminal space crafted by their board of (generally male) band directors. Majorette dancers were (and remain) under the watchful eyes of Black male band directors, but as batons were ditched, there was a noticeable shift in the dancers' emerging applications of erotic forms in their walks of *grace*. Batons were abandoned, but the marching band's militaristic instruction and influence were not. Majorette dancers picked up and femme-ed up the drum major's exaggerated strut. William Foster writes that "strutting, an exaggerated graceful walk, is one of the main [technical] ingredients," for the marching band's drum major, and majorette dancers developed that strut into an aesthetic all its own.[83] The hip-swinging strut became an important element in majorette style's syntax.

STRUT

Majorette dance belongs to longer histories of Black expressive techniques and cultures. We see this most clearly in its strut. The majorette dance idiom is presented across three primary categories within the HBCU band tradition: the strut (parade procession/march-ins), stand routines, and the field show.[84] Across these categories, the majorette dance straddles ceremonial, social, and concert dance forms. The strut is the majorette dancers' march and is seen in their processions at parades, as they enter and exit the stadium and its risers, and as they march onto the field. These struts often apply eight-count or sixteen-count choreographed interstitials within their march. The stand routines (or "stands") are performed in front of the band. Majorette dancers banner the band and perform at its head. Stand routines are the choreographic sequences traditionally performed on the bleachers (or "the stands") of a stadium. The field show is where majorette dancers perform choreographed numbers during the halftime show of the college football sporting event. Across and within these categories of majorette dance, themes such as Black femme expressive culture(s), the diversity and prowess of dance techniques, and the spirituality of erotic, "cool" power are explored, organized, and theorized. Let us explore the strut.

The strut is of great significance for majorette dancers of HBCU bands, but no team struts alike. The march of majorette dancers "is a choreographed sequence meant to travel the dance line forward in space with a stylized strut, walk, march, prance, or glide," but these marching forms take shape to meet each dance line's ideas of itself.[85] A troupe's strut must declare itself as one of its identifying components. A troupe's strut is signature, but not singular. Their struts are many, but have similar ends: to move forward in style. Moving forward in Black femme style has its own history outside of the majorette dance idiom.

Strut is an intentional term. "You know the band march. We strut," proclaims Kyre Walker, 2021–2022 dancer of the Fabulous Dancing Dolls.[86] While majorette dancers meet their respective band in its militaristic formation, they depart from that band's collective march and instead execute a signature collective strut.[87] Central to a strut are the ways it embodies an arrogance in its gait. A strut generally possesses a stylistic and gestural comportment of conceit. Pedestrians walk, models strut. And majorette dancers are meant to embody contours of model behavior.[88]

In "Characteristics of Negro Expression," Zora Neale Hurston writes about the saunter of a southern Black girl rounding a corner; it's a stroll that directs, then commands, the attention of a corner lounger. The walk described uses a "hippy undulation below the waist" as its accent. It is a fully embodied stroll in which the "whole body pang[s] and pos[es]." The techniques of this walk are not held in one section of the body. The stride possesses "a slight shoulder movement that calls attention to [the] bust." As Hurston recounts, these gestures are the embodied formations of a dare. In this walk the body talks. It announces "a sheaf of promises tied with conscious power." In her writing, Hurston names these intentional poses "drama," disrupting any notion that these bodily enunciations are indexes of being. She instead suggests that these pangs are expressive and dramatic ways of doing.

These pangs do not suggest who the southern Black girl is; they showcase what she can do, the ways she has learned to move, the ways in which she has learned to use her body. Said differently, the girl is displaying some techniques of a Black femme body, a social choreography of sorts.[89] French sociologist and anthropologist Marcel Mauss theorizes techniques of the body as an

expression of how different societies learn to use their bodies.[90] "Every tech-
nique," he writes "has its own form," and "each society has its own special
habits."[91] In his analysis, he, like Hurston, makes note of a girl walking and
compares the gait of American girls to that of French girls. He noticed that
the "positions of the arms and hands while walking form[ed] a social idiosyn-
crasy" and that both culture's techniques of walking were "not simply a product of some purely individual, almost completely physical arrangements and
mechanisms" but instead socially constructed applications. Mauss describes
methods and designates them to the societies to which they are formed. In
the essay, he argues that different groups apply their own moral standards to
their embodiments. The distinctions Mauss names are important for our purposes, especially in light of what Hurston observes in/of the walking Black
girl. Because Hurston evaluates within the vernacular of southern Blackness,
the pinging and panging is not demonized but celebrated. The movement is
read, then rendered, through Hurston's Black and southern feminism. Victorian sensibilities do not infect how she speaks of the strolling girl.

For Hurston, the dramatic indication and suggestion of swindling hips are
expressions of conscious erotic power. These acts and moves adorn; they do
not disfigure. With Mauss and Hurston in tow, we might then conclude that a
Black femme strut is, perhaps, an "ornament [that] does not attempt to meet
conventional standards" but instead "satisfies the soul of its creator" and its
knowing audiences.[92] This feels even more apparent if held within the poetics
and being of a Black world and its worldmaking. The dramatic embodiment
of a "panging and posing" stroller is an embellishment, an act of accessoriz-
ing, a choreographic intention. We can only speculate what this Black strolling
girl felt as she walked under Hurston's watchful eye, but I would like to imagine that Hurston bore witness to "rampant and unfetishized black beauty," the
concretization of the Black imaginary that Elizabeth Alexander bespeaks.[93] The
girl's walk is commentary. It might, too, be an embodied performance of folk-
loric Blackness.

The "girl" Hurston describes is not a woman whose walk requests the
onlooker's touch; this is a woman who cannot and should not be bothered.
Through her walk, she demonstrates what she knows of herself. "She's acting
out 'I'm a darned sweet woman and you know it.'"[94] These undulations, poses,
slight maneuverings of the shoulder's blades that direct attention to the bust
and clavicle—the performative contortions deemed Black feminine expressive tradition within Hurston's text—show up as characteristic flourishes held
across the struts of majorette dance teams. One could speculate that these sul-
try contortions say something of Black and femme gender performance within

Black southern cultural traditions, or that Hurston's detailing of the conscious power of a darned sweet woman begins Audre Lorde's theorizations of erotic power. "In touch with the erotic," writes Lorde, "I become less willing to accept powerlessness, or those other supplied states of being which are not native to me, such as resignation, despair, self-effacement, depression, self-denial."[95] Both Hurston and Lorde speak of a power felt within and carried throughout the body. This power is recognizable in the majorette strut and each team's struts talk across modes of erotic power in their execution.

For example, the Prancing J-Settes, the premiere dance line of the Jackson State University Sonic Boom of the South, are most known for three forms of strut: the salt and pepper, the tiptoe, and the J-Sette walk. The "salt and pepper" is "kinda where you throw your arms back and forth," states Kayla Gordon, 2018–2019 captain of the Prancing J-Settes.[96] In this walk, knees are lifted to meet the hip's level, mimicking the style of the marching band, but the march diverges in subtle swings of the hip. Alternating arms are pulled in, then thrown forward. When reaching the length of the extended and cast arm, the wrist is flicked—a gesture that parodies the dashing of salt and pepper—to meet the rhythm of their marching feet touching ground. In another signature, the "tiptoe," the J-Settes, with upper bodies erect, "[pull] the pelvis back and forth," and, with arms to their sides, bring their elbows from flexion to extension, turning their arms into raised and drawn hatchets grazing the outsides of their thighs as they strut on the tip of their toes.[97] Finally, there's the "the J-Sette walk." Gordon says "you'll see their hips the most—look like they finna pop out!" And, they do. In the J-sette walk, the J-Settes place their hands behind their head and lead their bodies with the pelvis, popping and panging their hips to adorn and propel each step forward. These struts are mechanically and sensorially complex. This is clear in their direction. Each of these struts push and pull the attentions of their audiences through owning the presence of a darned sweet woman.

In a "Strut Practice" YouTube video, majorette dancers (of the Southern University Dancing Dolls and the Alabama State Sensational Stingettes), La'Zhay, Alyx, and Maya, teach a class of majorette novices the signature struts performed by the Dolls and Stingettes. The coaches begin with somatic instruction: "Push down the middle and come straight up . . . and make sure you're cupping your butt." This is stated as the instructors demonstrate the arm's movement in the strut: with wrists flexed, but hands and fingers soft, alternating arms push down the middle of the back. When the hand reaches the small of the back—and upon cupping the butt—that hand leads the arm "straight up" and outward. As La'Zhay, Alyx, and Maya move through this strut's movements, their commentary on form dually become notes on stylings that inform and contextualize their choreographic instruction. "When you strut, you have the shoulders that's going—don't do too much. . . . It's more of a natural flow. . . . It should all be flowing like a smooth river," announces Maya. As Maya concludes, La'Zhay adds on: "It's about presence!"[98]

The presence to which La'Zhay refers says something about Lorde's and Hurston's ideas of embodiment, that there is a potential "truer word" on the Black femme power that spills out of the majorette dancer's performative strut.[99] In their instruction, they make clear that the execution of movements alone does not create or sustain the necessary drama of the movements' execution. They infer that the drama of their movements cannot be taken for granted. This strutting work is a historical drama. In form and content, this stunning, strutting scene continues to intersect with Hurston's investigation of Negro expression and the ongoing life of Black folk culture.

Hurston writes that Black folklore is not sutured in the past: "It is still in the making."[100] She contends that "nothing is too old or new, domestic or foreign, high or low" to be mechanized within Black lore. She argues that supposedly opposed entities are held together ("God and the Devil are paired") within and across Black cultural production. As Kevin Quashie writes, "An orientation of worldness is realized in the made-text," the made-text defined as "the aesthetics of the created thing: its shape and form, its poetics, its effects and affects rendered via language."[101] The strut is an element of majorette dance's made-text, and this made-text is continuously in the making. Majorette dance is suspended style, suspended form, suspended language draped across aesthetic formations made through embodied applications of a Black world in concert with the world at large. It is an application that begins to answer Glissant's queries around the language-culture-situation of subjects and objects. While the language of the Black femme body is easy to lose and bruise in translation, there is much to glean from its historical and mythological contingencies.

The majorette strut is not exactly a walk of dissent, and it is also not not a walk of dissent. Though majorette performance culture exists primarily within and abides by the suppositions of Black cultural spheres, majorette dancers are still susceptible to criticisms. As Asia N. Martin writes of her experience as a Sensational Stingette, these strutting dancers "are constantly over-analyzed, lied on, and ridiculed."[102] This is true for many artistic performances. Even truer for Black women who are, as feminist theorist Hortense J. Spillers suggests, marked.[103] The strut, then, might be marked as well. Or, the strut might be a mark, a moving and indicating target that misrecognizes a majorette strut as something more (or less) than a Black femme apparatus. Even in the context of a Black world, Black women are forced to move within the parameters of misogyny, sexism, and racism. In her work, Spillers names how Black women are perceived at rest, but we might ask what we are to make of viewing Black women in motion.

Dance scholar Jasmine Elizabeth Johnson takes up this question in her essay "Flesh Dance: Black Women from Behind." In this essay, she examines "embodied consent, creative labor, and black self-making" through what she names "flesh dance." Johnson defines flesh dance as "a choreographic/sonic coupling through which hip hop lyrics direct women to move in sexually mimetic ways." At its core, her argument uncovers the nuanced relations between sex, dance, and self-articulation. Further, it reaches toward possibilities beyond derogatory understandings of prurient movement.[104] More than prescribing a way to look at this movement, she invites us to pause with criticality when we gaze on Black women in motion. Of significance, her implementation of the word "flesh" is meant to signal Spillers's theorizing of Black women's agency and subjectivity.[105] For our purposes, interest lies in how this fleshy capacity is serviced and negotiated in the performance of majorette dancers.

The Fabulous Dancing Dolls and the Golden Girls are great test cases to consider this negotiation. Gracie Perkins, cofounder of the Fabulous Dancing Dolls, states that "you can tell a person's character by just looking at them . . . the way that they move." Other Forever Dolls delineate themselves from other HBCU dance lines, through describing a Doll as "a classy lady" who "always holds high standards for herself." They state that a Doll "possess[es] style and grace and confidence." [106] The rhetoric the Dolls use to describe themselves does not differ much from that of the Golden Girls; however, these team's movement couldn't be more different.

Across online forums and YouTube interviews, the Golden Girls describe themselves as regal, but others (mis)understand them as raunchy. My mother and father, alumni of Alabama State University, have jokingly stated that "all the Golden Girls need is a pole," and my older brother has shared with me that private Facebook groups dedicated to the SWAC often drag the Golden Girls for their supposed vulgarity. Even 2021–2022 captain of the Fabulous Dancing Dolls, Arielle Brookes, speaks of the (Dancing) Dolls in opposition to the (Golden) Girls. In identifying the Dolls styles against the Girls, Brookes states that a Doll's movement vocabulary "is not aggressive" and "gives you that sensual, but tasteful flare."[107] While Brooks goes on to state that she admires the style of the GGs, she is sure to make clear that a Doll's "tasteful flare" distinguishes the two troupes. This delineation is not precisely pejorative, but the commentary suggests that these dancers understand that their dance moves signify and reflect on their subjecthood. The pendulum swings both ways. In a post from 2013 on the online forum HBCU Sports, one commentator stated that they "get more excited about being able to be on the sideline to watch the J-Settes and the Golden Girls gyrate and [shake] their rumps."[108] In another post from 2021 on the same online forum, a commentator lauds the Golden Girls for "push[ing] the envelope" through their ingenious "risqué performance style" and suggests that the GGs influence other teams to dance edgier.[109]

While these dancers are not precisely participating in the flesh dance Johnson conceptualizes, their dance is a fleshy one, and they are aware of the implications and wages of their bodies in motion. More than this, I am interested in how the barometer for these dancers are understood within the scope of the performance tradition. Toward the conclusion of Spillers's "Mama's Baby, Papa's Maybe: An American Grammar Book," she writes that there is less interest "in joining the ranks of gendered femaleness than gaining the insurgent ground as female social subject" and that "claiming the monstrosity (of a female with the potential to 'name'), which culture imposes in blindness, 'Sapphire' might rewrite after all a radically different text for a female empowerment."[110] There is suggestion here that Black women's performances and beings exist within their own, separate lingua franca. Barbara Christian asserts that people of color are always, have always, theorized through language.[111] Body language must be taken up in such a claim. The anthropological work of Zora Neale Hurston helps us double down on Barbara Christian's assertion. The performances of the strutting majorette demonstrate that Black femme body (or, embodied) languages theorize. In light of this, let us return to the image of the majorette strut.

Panging and posing with a hip-swinging presence, the strut theorizes through performative embodiment. It provides space to consider the performative nature of race and gender. Spillers reminds us that Black women are already overdetermined through isolation by nominative properties such as "Peaches," "Brown Sugar," "Sapphire" (to name a few). What stands out about majorette dance within these designations is that its gestural vocabulary seems informed and inspired by these terms. Not to claim them as true, but to dance with them and potentially exploit their relation to nature versus culturally inspired techniques. Within the lexicon of HBCU majorette dance, "Brown Sugar" and "Sapphire" are performative. The mythological modes of Black female sexuality seem to be the dance's clay and the dancers mold performances with and around these mythic conceptions of Black womanhood. Said differently, majorette dance dances with these nominative properties, particularly a designation Spillers does not name, but one which often appears in essentialist discourses about Black women's hypersexuality especially in a southern context, the image of the Jezebel.

We have moved through these four terms—majorette, major, pageantry, and strut—and these categories will reappear in subsequent studies. What I outline above are post-Reconstruction forms of Black parody and reinscriptions of US militaristic forms. I argue that the majorette dance idiom, here described through its struts, extends and annotates long-standing projects of Black pageantry. The form illustrates fragments of the languages-cultures-situations that (in)form it. I begin this account of the HBCU majorette dancer and her dance as a varied strut across technical and militaristic, yet parodic, mechanizations of Black femme presence. The majorette dancer struts with the histories of Black femme misunderstanding and claims Black female subjectivity by remembering, rewriting, and remixing. Her demonstrative struts, bucks, panging, posing, and piercing glares are announcements of self-contained, publicly expressed Black femme power. They are affective labors best understood as applications of Black femme-inist presence.[112] This labor tests, extends, and pronounces her limits and possibilities. Her procession indicates that the prance of Zora Hurston's darned, sweet, knowing woman is HBCU majorette dance's unspoken inheritance. With every moment of her dynamic suggestion, the majorette dancer demonstrates that the dance indeed began before it was danced.

NOTES

1. In the premiere episode of the ESPN+ miniseries *Why Not Us: Southern Dance*, Camryn Harris, a 2021–2022 dancer of the Fabulous Dancing Dolls, defines a catch-on as "the sequences that we do in the stands to the band's songs. Airielle will start and then the rest of the team will follow." Its structure is recognized by the lead dancer performing a dance sequence (generally an eight- or sixteen-count dance sequence) that the dancers flanked behind the leader must follow. This term, *"catch-on,"* will be used and further detailed later in this chapter. The Fabulous Dancing Dolls are the premiere dance line of the Southern University Human Jukebox Marching Band. Southern University and Agricultural & Mechanical College is located in Baton Rouge, Louisiana. *Why Not Us: Southern Dance*, episode 1, "Dancing Dolls Are the Trend," August 11, 2022, ESPN+ video.

2. In mentioning "sissy indication," I attempt to identify comportments and posturing that manifest as something more "sissy" than specifically "feminine." In this present invocation, I speak of the broken (or limp) wrist of the sissy, which often indicates queerness: it colloquially exists to gesturally disclose a lack of maleness. For me, the "sissy" is something harder and more excessive—more obsessive, perhaps—and sharper than it is soft. Naming gestures "sissy" might provide clearer ways of speaking to the aesthetics that gather outside and around femininity but articulate performances that exists within the thresholds of (failed) masculinity, rather than any expression of "obvious" femininity. These performances

are contingent and tangential to femininity while having their own, separate characteristics and commitments. There are texts that account for sissy aesthetics; however, these works do not intend to name the sissy's performative and embodied doing in ways that I explore. I am not here thinking with work congruent to Jafari S. Allen's *There's a Disco Ball between Us: A Theory of Black Gay Life* (Durham, NC: Duke University Press, 2022). While that work is informative and a beautiful history and theory of Black gay life, I attempt to identify a (Black) sissyness that doesn't run parallel or work as a stand-in for (Black) gay lives and aesthetics. I rather think with works that clearly name the sissy as their analytical focus. These include, but are not limited to, the following: Marlon B. Ross, *Sissy Insurgencies: A Racial Anatomy of Unfit Manliness* (Durham, NC: Duke University Press, 2021); Vito Russo, *The Celluloid Closet: Homosexuality in the Movies* (New York: Harper and Row, 1981); Harry Thomas Jr., *Sissy!: The Effeminate Paradox in Postwar U.S. Literature and Culture* (Tuscaloosa: University of Alabama Press, 2019). I, too, include RuPaul's track "Sissy That Walk" (*Born Naked*, RuCo, 2014, MP3) as a prompt for my thinking, with particular interest in RuPaul's use of the term *sissy* as a verb.

3. Morgan Williams, "ASU Golden Girls vs SU Fabulous Dancing Dolls 2022 | Zero & Fifth Quarter | Review," October 18, 2022, YouTube video, 54:23.

4. I use the term *ritual* quite casually within this chapter's introduction; however, it is a term and concept I explore at length elsewhere in my work. This work leans heavily on the ritual studies work of Catherine Bell, Maya Deren, and Margaret Drewal. On the concept of ritual in embodied performance, see Maya Deren, *Divine Horsemen: The Living Gods of Haiti* (New Paltz, NY: McPherson, 1953); Catherine Bell, *Ritual: Perspectives and Dimensions* (New York: Oxford University Press, 1997); Catherine Bell, *Ritual Theory, Ritual Practice* (New York: Oxford University Press, 1992); Margaret Thompson Drewal, *Yoruba Ritual: Perform-ers, Play, Agency* (Bloomington: Indiana University Press, 1992). For an exploration of how ritual informs choreography and embodied practices, particularly in African and African diasporic contexts, see Margaret Thompson Drewal, "The State of Research on Performance in Africa," *African Studies Review* 34, no. 3 (December 1991): 1–64.

5. Jennie Livingston, dir., *Paris Is Burning* (New York: Off White Productions, 1990). On the performative and cultural significance of *Paris is Burning*, see bell hooks, "Is Paris Burn-ing?," in *Black Looks: Race and Representation* (Boston: South End, 1992), 145–56; Judith But-ler, "Gender Is Burning: Questions of Appropriation and Subversion," in *Bodies That Matter: On the Discursive Limits of "Sex"* (New York: Routledge, 1993), 121–40; Lucas Hilderbrand, *Paris Is Burning: A Queer Film Classic* (Vancouver: Arsenal Pulp, 2013); Marlon M. Bailey, *Butch Queens Up in Pumps: Gender, Performance, and Ballroom Culture in Detroit* (Ann Arbor: University of Michigan Press, 2013), 39–47; José Esteban Muñoz, *Disidentifications: Queers of Color and the Performance of Politics* (Minneapolis: University of Minnesota Press, 1999), 81–97. For a discussion on the representation of race, gender, and sexuality in the film, see Katherine Sender, "Queens for a Day. Queer Eye for the Straight Guy and the Neoliberal Project," *Critical Studies in Media Communication* 23, no. 2 (2006): 131–51. While I find these works useful in the analysis of the film *Paris is Burning*, I lean on personal interpretations of Extravaganza's use of gesture and rhetoric in her claims to "realness." In thinking through an autobiographical trans-femme context of "realness," see Janet Mock, *Redefining Realness: My Path to Womanhood, Identity, Love & So Much More* (New York: Atria Books, 2014).

6. *Why Not Us*, "Dancing Dolls."

7. While majorette dance has become a staple of many HBCU bands, including those belonging to the MEAC (Mid-Eastern Athletic Conference), I primarily focus my attention on dance troupes of bands belonging to the SWAC (Southwestern Athletic Conference). Headquartered in Birmingham, Alabama, the SWAC's membership comprises twelve schools: Alabama A&M University (Normal, Alabama), Alabama State University (Montgomery, Alabama), Alcorn State University (Lorman, Mississippi), Bethune-Cookman University (Daytona Beach, Florida), Florida A&M University (Tallahassee, Florida), Grambling State University (Grambling, Louisiana), Jackson State University (Jackson, Mississippi), Mississippi Valley State University (Itta Bena, Mississippi), Prairie View A&M University (Prairie View, Texas), Southern University (Baton Rouge, Louisiana), Texas Southern University (Houston, Texas), and University of Arkansas at Pine Bluff (Pine Bluff, Arkansas). Of note, Florida A&M University and Bethune-Cookman University became members of the SWAC beginning the 2021–2022 academic year. I choose to focus on majorette dance teams of the SWAC because online followings, social media, forums, and mentions suggest that these schools most heavily influence and inform majorette dance's performance styles. I, too, focus on these teams because promotional material across troupes belonging to the SWAC contest (against one another) the origin of majorette dance's stylings. These conversations and rivaling contestations do not exist within the MEAC.

8. For an audiovisual articulation of what it means to "get buck," refer to this video by the West St. Mary High School cheer team: West St. Mary High School (@wsmcheer), "wassup, get buckkkk," TikTok, December 13, 2022.

9. There is sparse mention of bucking, precisely, across the following texts; nevertheless, these works have proven useful in exploring bucking, particularly as it relates to histories of minstrelsy, vaudeville, and racial/sexual parody. Brooks, Harker, and Johnson's works are particularly helpful in thinking through minstrelsy and sexual parody. The others take up Black dance in compelling ways. Only the works of Self and Loyd-Sims speak directly to HBCU majorette dance and allude to bucking and its existence in that universe: Daphne A. Brooks, "Divas and Diasporic Consciousness: Song, Dance, and New Negro Womanhood in the Veil," in *Bodies in Dissent: Spectacular Performances of Race and Freedom, 1850-1910*, (Durham, NC: Duke University Press, 2006), 281–42; Thomas F. DeFrantz, "Introduction: From 'Negro Expression' to 'Black Performance,'" in *Black Performance Theory*, ed. Thomas F. DeFrantz and Anita Gonzalez (Durham, NC: Duke University Press, 2014), 1–17; Brenda Dixon Gottschild, *Waltzing in the Dark: African American Vaudeville and Race Politics in the Swing Era* (New York: Palgrave Macmillan, 2000); Brian Harker, "Louis Armstrong, Eccentric Dance, and the Evolution of Jazz on the Eve of Swing," *Journal of the American Musicological Society* 61, no. 1 (2008): 67–121; E. Patrick Johnson, *Appropriating Blackness: Performance and the Politics of Authenticity* (Durham, NC: Duke University Press, 2003); Lamont Loyd-Sims, "J-Setting in Public: Black Queer Desires and Worldmaking" (master's thesis, Georgia State University, 2014); Rico Self, "The Prancing J-Settes and Black Queer Feminist Worldmaking: 'Let's Set(te) the Scene,'" in *The Routledge Handbook of Ethnicity and Race in Communication*, ed. Bernadette Marie Calafell and Shinsuke Eguchi (New York: Routledge, 2024), 127–40. See also Brenda Dixon Gottschild, *The Black Dancing Body: A Geography from Coon to Cool* (New York: Palgrave Macmillan, 2003).

10. Beyoncé, "SWEET*HONEY*BUCKIIN' (Official Lyric Video)," featuring Shaboozey, released March 29, 2024, track 26 on *Cowboy Carter*, Parkwood Entertainment and Columbia Records, YouTube Music, "@Beyoncé @Parkwood Entertainment, Still Tippin x Buckin x Sorry – Jacobdior," TikTok, May 21, 2024; Ahsia Janaè (@ahsiajanae), "@Jacobdior you're nuts for this mashup," TikTok, May 26, 2024.

11. Crime Mob, "Knuck If You Buck," featuring Lil Scrappy, released May 25, 2004, track 2 on *Crime Mob*, Crunk Incorporated, Warner Bros., YouTube Music.

12. In Tavia Nyong'o's *Afro-Fabulations*, he "track[s] key moments of fabulation in contemporary black art and performance, honing in on moments in which black subversions of sexual and gender conformity prove excessive, disorderly, or simply unintelligible to an external gaze," (*Afro-Fabulations: The Queer Drama of Black Life* [New York: New York University Press, 2018], 4). While his work primarily surveys Afro-fabulation as a "queer hack," his theorizations are useful for my own, particular as I see "bucking" as an embodied form of mythmaking within Black southern cultures. I am moved and influenced by his speculation of the "'changing same' of black aesthetics and expressivity" as something that may have always been queer, adding to this my own suppositions of southernness as another form of queerness within (and outside of) Blackness (4).

13. "Stand routines," also known as "stands" are choreographed routines performed in front of the marching band in the stands (stadium, bleachers, chairs). These are generally eight-count or sixteen-count dance sequences "thrown," a term that signifies the captain's selected count being passed to, and caught by, her fellow dancers. In other dance vocabularies, these passed down movement repetitions from one dancer to the next are known as a contagion, or ripple. Stands are traditionally performed in this leader-follower, commander-platoon format.

14. Williams, "ASU Golden Girls."

15. "The Original Golden Girls Reflect on 50 Years as Pioneers of HBCU Dance Teams," Alcorn State University website, November 9, 2018.

16. Sage Howard, "We Need to Talk about the Appropriation of Majorette Dancing on TikTok," *HuffPost*, March 18, 2023.

17. "Howard University Marching Band Escorts VP Kamala Harris on Inauguration Day," Fox 5 Washington DC, January 20, 2021, YouTube video, 03:53.

18. Nakylah Carter, "The Rich and Beautiful History of HBCU Majorette Teams," *Good Morning America*, February 21, 2023.

19. Édouard Glissant, *Poetics of Relation*, trans. Betsy Wing (Ann Arbor: University of Michigan Press, 1997), 120.

20. Audre Lorde, *Sister Outsider: Essays and Speeches* (Berkeley, CA: Crossing, 2007), 37.

21. There are many ways to approach the stylings of majorette dance and to explore other ways in other notes. For example, we might rightly understand this movement vocabulary through the lens of the blues or funk; I play with other ulterior Black expressive approaches to the majorette dance idiom in sections not represented herein.

22. Barbara Christian, "The Race for Theory," *Cultural Critique*, no. 6 (1987), 52.

23. Christian, "Race for Theory," 56.

24. Important to note, in 1972, the form/genre of dancing was not called j-setting. In fact, although the Prancing Jaycettes (changed to "J-Settes" in 1982), were mentioned in the

article, they are not photographed. Further, the 1972 article's use of the term "dancing girls" (or "dance girls") is apt, as it is still a common, colloquial catchall for these women college dancers.

25. "Beauty—and the Beat: Black Colleges Feature Pretty Girls, Jazzy Bands at Football Halftime," *Ebony*, January 1972.

26. "Original Golden Girls Reflect."

27. Oral history interview with Gracie Perkins and Debra Womack, September 9, 2022, Southern University Dancing Dolls collection, East Baton Rouge Parish Library Special Collections, Baton Rouge, LA.

28. "Thee 'Prancing J-Settes,'" Jackson State University website, January 6, 2023.

29. Majorette dance has not settled on its name. Some refer to the tradition as majorette dance. Others might call it "HBCU dance," "HBCU majorette dance," or "j-setting." I choose the term "HBCU majorette dance" in my analysis but shorten the term to "majorette dance" across this chapter.

30. Roland Barthes, *Mythologies*, trans. Annette Lavers (New York: Hill and Wang, 2006), 128.

31. For a detailed account of the rise of Black beauty in the American pageant circuit, see Maxine Leeds Craig, *Ain't I a Beauty Queen? Black Women, Beauty, and the Politics of Race* (Oxford: Oxford University Press, 2002).

32. Craig, *Beauty Queen*, 3.

33. I lean heavily on Du Bois's writings to support this claim: W. E. B. Du Bois, *Black Reconstruction in America, 1860–1880* (New York: Harcourt, Brace, 1935); *W. E. B. Du Bois on Sociology and the Black Community*, ed. Dan S. Green and Edwin D. Driver (Chicago: University of Chicago Press, 1978); W. E. B. DuBois, "Returning Soldiers," *The Crisis* 18 (May 1919), 13. I am, too, greatly informed by the following texts: Laura F. Edwards, *Gendered Strife and Confusion: The Political Culture of Reconstruction* (Urbana: University of Illinois Press, 1997); Eric Foner, *Reconstruction: America's Unfinished Revolution, 1863-1877*, updated ed. (New York: Harper Perennial Modern Classics, 2014); Stephen Hahn, *A Nation under Our Feet: Black Political Struggles in the Rural South from Slavery to the Great Migration* (Cambridge, MA: Belknap Press of Harvard University Press, 2003); Helen Heran Jun, *Race for Citizenship: Black Orientalism and Asian Uplift from Pre-Emancipation to Neoliberal America* (New York: New York University Press, 2011); C. Vann Woodward, *The Political Legacy of the First Reconstruction* (New York: Oxford University Press, 1968).

34. Carter, "Rich and Beautiful History."

35. *Brewer's Dictionary of Modern Phrase and Fable*, ed. John Ayto and Ian Crofton (London: Chambers Harrap, 2011), s.v. "drum majorette."

36. *The Oxford Essential Dictionary of the U.S. Military* (Oxford: Oxford University Press, 2001), s.v. "drum major."

37. William Lewis, "Marching to the Beat of a Different Drum: Performance Traditions of Historically Black College and University Marching Bands," *North Carolina Folklore Journal* 50, no. 1–2 (2003): 21.

38. Lewis, "Marching to the Beat," 22.

39. Michael Hardt, "Affective Labor," *Boundary 2* 26, no. 2 (1999): 89–100.

40. Yvonne P. Chireau, *Black Magic: Religion and the African American Conjuring Tradition* (Berkeley: University of California Press, 2003), 4.

41. David D. Hall, *Lived Religion in America: Toward a History of Practice* (Princeton, NJ: Princeton University Press, 1997). Chireau, *Black Magic*, 4.

42. Zora Neale Hurston, *Mules and Men* (Philadelphia: J. B. Lippincott, 1935), 280. I am sure that within Christianity the term *conjure* might be contested; however, within Christian spheres calls unto and upon the Christian god for intervention is widely and ecumenically held. I also conceptualize my thoughts of African American religious histories alongside W. E. B. Du Bois's observations of religious "frenzy" in the US South and take up the notion of frenzy elsewhere. For more on Du Bois's musings on Blackness and religion in the United States, see W. E. B. Du Bois, "The Religion of the American Negro," in *Du Bois on Sociology*, 214–25. Kathryn Lofton's essay on the relationship between religious studies and religious history is also helpful in untangling the contingencies between the subject of religion and *religious* objects: Kathryn Lofton, "Religious History as Religious Studies," *Religion* 42, no. 3 (2012): 383–94.

43. For work on the subjects of secularization theory and secularism, see Gil Anidjar, "Secularism," *Critical Inquiry* 33, no. 1 (2006): 52–77; Talal Asad, *Formations of the Secular: Christianity, Islam, Modernity* (Stanford, CA: Stanford University Press, 2003); Tracy Fessenden, *Culture and Redemption: Religion, the Secular, and American Literature* (Princeton, NJ: Princeton University Press, 2007); and Sally Promey, introduction to *Sensational Religion*, ed. Sally Promey (New Haven, CT: Yale University Press, 2014). Promey's introduction provides a brief history of secularism's ties to the senses and materialism.

44. Zora Neale Hurston, *The Sanctified Church* (Berkeley: Turtle Island Foundation, 1981), 56.

45. Celeste Cummings and Amara Williams, *Speaking in Tongues and Dancing Diaspora: Black Women Writing and Performing* (New York: Routledge, 2015); Yvonne Daniel, *Dancing Wisdom: Embodied Knowledge in Haitian Vodou, Cuban Yoruba, and Bahian Candomblé* (Urbana: University of Illinois Press, 2017); Thomas F. DeFrantz, ed., *Dancing Many Drums: Excavations in African American Dance* (Philadelphia: Temple University Press, 2002); Sam Gill, *Dancing Culture Religion* (Lanham, MD: Lexington Books, 2012); Cécile Fromont, "Dance, Image, Myth, and Conversion in the Kingdom of Kongo, 1500–1800," *Journal of African History* 56, no. 2 (2015): 215–32.

46. Albert J. Raboteau, *Slave Religion: The "Invisible Institution" in the Antebellum South* (Oxford: Oxford University Press, 2004), 4.

47. P. Sterling Stuckey, "Christian Conversion and the Challenge of Dance," in DeFrantz, *Dancing Many Drums*, 41.

48. I think about the term *pageantry* in its most general sense, as an elaborate display, a ceremony, a show or spectacle. In detailing elements of Black band pageantry, I seek to demonstrate its styles and motivations.

49. Jacqui Malone, *Steppin' on the Blues: The Visible Rhythms of African American Dance* (Chicago, University of Illinois Press, 1996), 147.

50. Frederic Ramsey Jr., *Music from the South, Volume 1: Country Brass Bands*, (Folkways Records FA 2650, 1955, 1961), 3.

51. Ramsey, *Music from the South*, 3.

52. Ramsey, *Music from the South*, 3.

53. William Patrick Foster, *Band Pageantry: A Guide for the Marching Band* (Minnesota, Hal Leonard Music, 1968), v.

54. Birgit Meyer, "Introduction: From Imagined Communities to Aesthetic Formations: Religious Mediations, Sensational Forms, and Styles of Binding," in *Aesthetic Formations: Media, Religion, and the Senses*, ed. Birgit Meyer (New York: Palgrave Macmillan, 2009), 10.

55. Foster, *Band Pageantry*, vii.

56. Foster, *Band Pageantry*, 85.

57. Byron Dobson, "Cori Bostic Steps into History Saturday as FAMU Marching 100's First Female Drum Major," *Tallahassee Democrat*, September 1, 2018.

58. Foster, *Band Pageantry*, 85.

59. Foster, *Band Pageantry*, 85.

60. Blain Roberts, *Pageants, Parlors, and Pretty Women: Race and Beauty in the Twentieth-Century South* (Chapel Hill: University of North Carolina Press, 2014), 8.

61. Roberts, *Pageants, Parlors*, 8.

62. Roberts, *Pageants, Parlors*, 8.

63. Evelyn Higginbotham, *Righteous Discontent: The Women's Movement in the Black Baptist Church, 1880–1920* (Cambridge, MA: Harvard University Press, 1993), 192.

64. Elizabeth Alexander, *The Black Interior: Essays* (Saint Paul, Minnesota: Graywolf Press, 2004), x.

65. I borrow the distinction of "canonical sociology" and "canonical sociologist" from Roderick A. Ferguson. In his work *Aberrations in Black: Towards a Queer of Color Critique* (Minneapolis: University of Minnesota Press, 2004) he distinguishes canonical sociologists (i.e., "white") from African American sociologists, noting that sociologists of the canon apply themes of universality and its Western epistemology in their analyses of culture.

66. Ferguson, *Aberrations in Black*, 20.

67. At the start of her essay "Mama's Baby, Papa's Maybe," theorist Hortense J. Spillers names different nominal stand-ins for Black women. I further explore these terms and her essay later in this chapter, but invoke its pretenses here. Hortense J. Spillers, "Mama's Baby, Papa's Maybe: An American Grammar Book," *Diacritics* 17, no. 2 (1987): 64.

68. Tamura Lomax, *Jezebel Unhinged: Loosing the Black Female Body in Religion and Culture* (Durham, NC: Duke University Press, 2018), 2.

69. Lomax, *Jezebel Unhinged*, 21.

70. Carter, "Rich and Beautiful History."

71. *Oxford Dictionary of Literary Terms* (Oxford: Oxford University Press, 2015), s.v. "burlesque," by Chris Baldick.

72. Jayna Brown, *Babylon Girls: Black Women Performers and the Shaping of the Modern* (Durham, NC: Duke University Press, 2008), 105.

73. Brown, *Babylon Girls*, 105.

74. Roberts, *Pageants, Parlors*, 10.

75. For more information on the Black Pride movement and its attending aesthetics, see Hoyt W. Fuller, "Towards a Black Aesthetic," and Larry Neal, "The Black Arts Movement," in *Within the Circle: An Anthology of African American Literary Criticism from the Harlem Renaissance to the Present*, ed. Angelyn Mitchell (Durham, NC: Duke University Press, 1994), 199–206 and 184–98; Jeffrey O. G. Ogbar, *Black Power: Radical Politics and African American*

Identity (Baltimore: Johns Hopkins University Press, 2005); Amy Abugo Ongiri, *Spectacular Blackness: The Cultural Politics of the Black Power Movement and the Search for a Black Aesthetic* (Charlottesville: University of Virginia Press, 2009).

76. Livingston, *Paris Is Burning.*

77. In her searing critique of Livingston's *Paris is Burning,* "Is Paris Burning?," cultural critic and theorist bell hooks writes about the film's valorization of "not just any old brand of whiteness but rather the brutal imperial ruling-class capitalist patriarchal whiteness that presents itself—its way of life—as the only meaningful life there is" (149). The scene I discuss might exist within the parameters of that critique; however, my interests like in what Octavia St. Laurent names while discussing Paulina Porizkova's ability to emote. Laurent's words on Porizkova's modeling (and sitting) parallel my own when watching majorette dancers, at rest, in their stiller frames. I read majorette dancer's sitting with the same attention given to their movement. I find Laurent's comments and observations useful in comparing the affective labor of majorette dancer's quieter work.

78. Elspeth H. Brown, *Work! A Queer History of Modeling* (Durham, NC: Duke University Press, 2019), 70.

79. Sitting, colloquially known as "sit downs," are choreographed instances within the majorette dance idiom.

80. All dance genres evolve and change with time, and with time, new techniques develop. This can be seen in the ballet finding its form and style from court dances. However, majorette dance dances alongside contemporary dance and movement cultures. This is inherent to its form. This is expounded on later in the chapter.

81. Alecia Taylor and Brooklyn White, "Sass and Shimmer: The Dazzling History of Black Majorettes and Dance Lines," *Essence,* November 2, 2022.

82. Roberts, *Pageants, Parlors,* 8.

83. Foster, *Band Pageantry,* 7.

84. According to Airielle Brooks, 2021–2023 captain of the Fabulous Dancing Dolls of Southern University's Human Jukebox, there are three parts to majorette performance: the strut, the catch-on, and the field show. J'aime Griffith, former dancer for the Grambling State University Orchesis Dance Company, names these same three categories in her master's thesis focusing on HBCU dance lines. I, however, name these as "primary" categories because it could be argued that majorette dance has subcategories such as sitting. Sitting down and sitting pretty are explored in a separate note. Further, outside the confines of the HBCU marching band, categories are extended. J'aime Griffith, "Historically Black College and University Dance Lines: Redefining and Identifying Elements to Determine Aesthetic Value" ('master's thesis, University of Oklahoma, 2022).

85. Griffith, "Historically Black," 10.

86. *Why Not Us,* "Dancing Dolls."

87. I speak further about band's militaristic foundations and speculate the influences of the majorette dancer's strut in a later section of this chapter.

88. In the official history of the Prancing J-Settes, the organization writes that "it was completely unacceptable for any J-Sette to display mannerisms and stature of anything less than a model citizen" ("Thee 'Prancine J-Settes,'" Jackson State University website). Across HBCU dance troupe's' promotional and historical literature, the claim for regality, class, and

model behavior is often mentioned when speaking of majorette dancers within and outside of performances.

89. In her work *Shapeshifters: Black Girls and the Choreography of Citizenship* (Durham, NC: Duke University Press, 2015), anthropologist Aimee Meredith Cox expands our conceptions of choreography, especially as it relates to social ordering and spatial narratives. She defines the term expansively, writing that "choreography is embodied meaning making, physical storytelling, affective physicality, and an intellectual response to the question of how movement might narrate texts that are not otherwise eligible" (28). I use Cox's work much more intimately when taking up the dance of majorette dancers elsewhere; however, her text, too, informs the ways I evaluate the majorette strut.

90. Marcel Mauss, "Techniques of the Body," *Economy and Society* 2, no. 1 (1973): 70.

91. Mauss, "Techniques of the Body," 71–72.

92. Hurston, *Sanctified Church*, 50.

93. Alexander, *Black Interior*, x.

94. Hurston, *Sanctified Church*, 50.

95. Lorde, *Sister Outsider*, 37.

96. "The History of One of the Most Influential College Dance Teams in the World," digg, accessed April 28, 2019.

97. "The Dance Troupe Inspiring Beyoncé," Great Big Story, November 20, 2018, YouTube video, 03:20.

98. "Dance Strut Practice SU Dancing Dolls Forever Sensational Dance Clinic 2018," Tobi Famu, August 10, 2018, YouTube video, 11:17.

99. In mentioning a "truer word," I am thinking with the work of Hortense J. Spillers and Jasmine Johnson's extension of that "truer word" in her chapter in *Futures of Dance Studies*. Jasmine Elizabeth Johnson, "Flesh Dance: Black Women from Behind," in *Futures of Dance Studies*, ed. Susan Manning, Janice Ross, and Rebecca Schneider (Madison: University of Wisconsin Press, 2020); Spillers, "Mama's Baby."'

100. Hurston, *Sanctified Church*, 56.

101. Kevin Quashie, *Black Aliveness, or a Poetics of Being* (Durham, NC: Duke University Press, 2021), 57.

102. Asia N. Martin, *Legendary Loading . . .* (self-published, 2021), 26.

103. Spillers, "Mama's Baby."

104. Johnson, "Flesh Dance," 155.

105. Johnson, "Flesh Dance," 158.

106. *Why Not Us*, "Dancing Dolls." The Fabulous Dancing Dolls, like troupes belonging to other universities, are much like Black sororities. This saying that once a Doll completes a full term as a Southern University Fabulous Dancing Doll, she is considered a "Forever Doll." This is like what occurs when women cross over into sororities belonging to the Divine Nine Panhellenic Council. Those incarnates are meant to be lifetime members of their pledged-to organizations.

107. *Why Not Us: Southern Dance*, episode 5, "Fifth Quarter," September 8, 2022, ESPN+ video.

108. "SU Dancing Dolls, We're Ladies, We Don't Gyrate or Roll Around on the Ground!," HBCU Sports Forums, December 16, 2013.

109. "SOD And Golden Girls," HBCU Sports Forums, March 28, 2021.

110. Spillers, "Mama's Baby," 80.

111. Christian, "Race for Theory," 67.

112. I adopt this term from Sydney Fonteyn Lewis and from Omise'eke Natasha Tinsley's extension of Lewis's term. In both texts, these scholars declare and perform femme-inist critiques that make space for a sort of lipstick sexiness within their criticisms. Sydney Fonteyn Lewis, "'Everything I Know about Being a Black Femme I Learned from *Sula*': Or, Towards a Black Femme-inist Criticism," *Trans-scripts* 2 (2012); Omise'eke Natasha Tinsley, *Beyoncé in Formation: Remixing Black Feminism* (Austin: University of Texas Press, 2018).

Made in America

A (Preliminary) Genealogy of H Mart as Religious Icon

MIHEE KIM-KORT

A Korean Tradition Made in America. Since 1982.
—H Mart Slogan

Driving into the parking lot of H Mart in Ellicott City, Maryland, I am struck by the bright red H Mart sign with its "Groceries & More" tagline. It feels like I have discovered the holy grail of H Marts. The huge sign hangs over a large entrance with long lines of shopping carts organized into neat rows on the side and the typical sliding doors you see in every modern-day grocery store. It is nearly a stand-alone business but there is also a liquor store and dry cleaner to the right of the entrance. When I walk into this superstore H Mart with a cart, I glance down at the handle and observe the slogan: "A Korean Tradition Made in America. Since 1982." I recall the H Mart of my childhood, when it was still called 한아름 (Han Ah Reum) and barely the size of a 7–Eleven. Besides our church, it was the only distinctly Korean space. Although it was a good thirty-minute drive away from our house, it was the only place for my parents to get a forty-pound bag of medium rice, Napa cabbage for kimchi, and a box of goguma (Korean sweet potatoes). I remember happily walking up and down the few aisles over and over looking at all the shelves of snacks and grains, sauces and packages of miyuk (roasted seaweed) and gim (dried seaweed) while my mother carefully and thoughtfully shopped for the week. Like my childhood church it felt holy and special. Every trip was a pilgrimage.

Founded in 1982 in Woodside, Queens, New York City, H Mart is a Korean

American supermarket chain operated by the Hanahreum Group. Headquartered in Lyndhurst, New Jersey, the chain specializes in Asian foods and has locations throughout the United States and Canada, as well as two locations in London (United Kingdom). With eighty-four locations nationwide, it is the largest Asian American grocery store in the United States. The *H* in *H Mart* stands for 한아름 (Han Ah Reum), a Korean phrase meaning "one arm full." Its CEO, Il Yeon Kwon, is also the founder of the company with the rest of the company leadership his immediate family. According to the store's website, it "is the largest Asian supermarket chain in America and is the pioneer of Asian food in America. . . . [It] is America's premier Asian food destination and provides groceries and everyday essential needs as well as upscale products."[1] Today, the store has become a multicultural haven with everything from diverse employees to the products it carries on its shelves, to its food courts that include Korean, Chinese, and Japanese cuisines. But the story of H Mart is more than its corporate success in the United States. Rather, there is much longer history of its vivid place in the wider cultural landscape.

H Mart is an example of a grocery store that provides more than food—it is a safe and familiar space. *New York Times* writer Ligaya Mishan explores the evolution of H Mart in terms of the way the store has revolutionized how Asians in America "shop and eat."[2] H Mart is not only a store but an experience, as Mishan shows in her attention to detail like the care with which employees stack apples and pears that are individually wrapped in white mesh and all the signs in English alongside Korean. But she also includes interviews that hint at the ways H Mart has shaped not only the Korean diaspora in the United States but the wider US cultural landscape. Many describe H Mart and other similar ethnic food markets that were critical to their survival in surprising ways: "Deuki Hong, 31, the chef and founder of the Sunday Family Hospitality Group, in San Francisco, remembers the H Mart of his youth in New Jersey as 'just the Korean store'—a sanctuary for his parents, recent immigrants still not at ease in English. Everyone spoke Korean, and all that banchan was a relief."[3] Understanding H Mart as a sanctuary means not only seeing how it is a space for diasporic Koreans to engage with others in their own language and food but a space where they are able to possibly connect to something beyond their everyday lives—something that is described as sacred, and I would add, religious.

H Mart, and ethnic grocery stores like it, shape the collective identities of these diasporic communities. But they also participate in a larger project of national identity. I begin with the Mishan article to explore how H Mart is an example of perpetuating "America" as a religious project.[4] "The theme is abundance," explains Mishan, and there is no doubt about it as she provides a beautiful litany of every kind of Asian green in H Mart: "Broad perilla leaves with notched edges . . . yu choy, bok choy, ong choy, hon choy, aa choy, wawa choy, gai lan, sook got." This excess is especially poignant to immigrants as a sharp contrast to the experience of coming from war-torn, developing countries, or memories of it. For the various interviewees this plenitude acts as a sign and confirmation of being American. The overflowing shelves provide comfort, like for Ms. Lee: "I like going there because I feel good there," but feeling good comes from another characteristic of success: "In the context of hatred against my community, to see part of my culture being valued—it's exceptional."[5] In more ways than one, H Mart has become a microcosm of the (ethnic) American success story.

I look at H Mart in two ways: First, I take a materialist approach in reading H Mart as both physical site and textual site—the store itself, its aisles, its employees, its products and organization, its patrons and consumers, their interaction, as well as examine the company's genesis and origins, its history, its expansion as a business, its connection to local communities, its website as a particular cultural production. I argue that to read H Mart the store as a cultural production demonstrates the effects of a particular kind of racialization through commodification as embedded in the landscape of neoliberal capitalism. In the second part of the chapter, I aim to read H Mart specifically in its impact as a theological imaginary in other cultural productions to show how H Mart operates as an icon through a diasporic sentimentalism that solidifies Koreanity as a site of racialized religion. I look at the archives of popular culture including the memoir *Crying in H Mart*, cookbooks, travel books, and TV. I argue that H Mart as an object of study demonstrates how assimilability is a racialized characteristic of Koreanity, but even more, the way consumability is a marker of success that characterizes it as a religious category.

MYTHS OF EXCEPTIONALISM AND DIFFERENCE

H Mart describes itself as "a Korean tradition made in America." The slogan articulates the genesis of the company as both Korean and American with an emphasis on what is "made," and where, which is significant to understanding its exceptional presence in the United States. So, this is not simply a passive being made, although that is partially inferred here. To make something means to construct and create something, and H Mart tells a story about Korea and its traditions—broadly speaking, its culture, language, history, and food—that gestures toward aspects and processes of institutions that include rituals, roles, and perspectives that shape its participants. The story is about H Mart's unique emergence specifically in

America, which includes its originating and ongoing formation, which is pointedly in America. To make it also means to succeed and to accomplish something. This story gives us an explanation of how H Mart views and understands its success today, and it also confirms its participation in narratives of exceptionalism that are specific to America. H Mart is also a way that Koreans tell a story about themselves, to themselves, and to America. It is a way of saying: we made it, and we have made it. These kinds of stories map onto American myths of the self-made individual.

These words echo an American Christian exceptionalism that permeates much of the cultural landscape in the United States. This exceptionalism is lifted up as a characteristic that explains certain kinds of success—political and economic. Generally, this exceptionalism is often viewed as political in nature, but American Puritan roots make visible its religious origins. These same theopolitical imaginaries inspired President Ronald Reagan, who was a proponent and product of a specific American Christianity. In his election eve address, "A Vision for America," November 3, 1980, he echoed the words of Puritan leader John Winthrop's 1630 treatise with the promotion of the image of the United States as a shining "city upon a hill."[6] The link back to these Christian origins of America as a "city on the hill" would be the refrain of American self-identity. America is exceptional, as in successful, and it is exceptional in terms of being unique, and even more, transcendent. These values have remained a central component of American national identity for centuries. What I am to highlight is how these are not only political words but an expression of religious belief in the way they express the certainty of their purpose and the inevitability of their success. This religious belief shows us how American exceptionalism is a Christian exceptionalism.

The theologies that circulate through this Christian exceptionalism shape racializing discourses that promote a specific kind of model citizenship in terms of success. Once more, President Reagan in a 1984 speech explained the significance of the "success" specifically of Asian American Pacific Islanders—he praised "Asian and Pacific Americans for helping to preserve the American dream by living up to the bedrock values" of America.[7] But this is in conjunction with Asian Americans' position in relation to the broader US nation-state figured through numerous crises of national identity which occurred in periods of US war in Asia. Lisa Lowe explains how the Asian immigrant is figured as a "screen, a phantasmic site, on which the nation projects a series of condensed, complicated anxieties regarding external and internal threats to the mutable coherence of the national body."[8] One way to deal with the Asian in America was through a particular kind of assimilation through civilizing and domesticating procedures.[9] And so,

Reagan's words about Asian Americans do not elevate their status in the United States as examples of success necessarily but rather affirm the ongoing fantasy of American Christian exceptionalism as represented by the assimilated Asian.

Through the social and economic success of the company itself and its deployment of the language of progress, and its advancement of neoliberal capitalism with its ideals of diversity and inclusion, H Mart legitimizes and makes legible the presence of Koreans in the United States as both exotic and exceptional participants in wider American society. H Mart became an example of "a city on a hill," a model of Christian exceptionalism—of achievement, of success, of the ability to produce and reproduce itself—-of what makes America America. The story Koreans tell through H Mart is a claim on America, and we see the ways in which Koreanity is a phenomenon that naturally and logically belongs in America because it too shapes, impacts, and makes America.

NEOLIBERAL CAPITALISM, RELIGION, AND COMMODIFYING RACE

The model minority myth, or, specifically, the fantasy of Asian/Korean success, is made legible by a Christian exceptionalism with its particular enactment in neoliberal capital structures.[10] The aim of these neoliberal capitalist structures was deregulation, emphasizing individualist ideals around fairness, meritocracy, and globalization and financialization as important features of economic systems. And yet, institutional oversight increasingly became a necessity in the midst of liberalization and privatization as these markets became less "free" and at the mercy of certain political and cultural forces.[11] Grace Kyungwon Hong confirms this by underscoring how other forces impacted these structures: neoliberal capitalist structures, initially viewed as a shift away from systems of inequality, persisted as repackaged colonial and imperial projects, and in particular, were used in conjunction with other institutions to further the power and influence of countries like the United States across the world.[12] Transnational immigration to the United States from the 1980s onward can be seen as a feature of this process, or what she calls "capital's global phase."[13] The persistent contradictions between state and capital are managed by late twentieth-century systems, which have their "own universal mode: paradoxically, a universalized fetishization of difference."[14] The model minority myth is an extension of American exceptionalism through the fetishization of the Asian figure in America. In the neoliberal capitalist system—that is, the marketplace—this fetishization would result in and require the commodification of race.[15]

In examining H Mart, I build on Kathryn Lofton's argument: "Religions have always been reflective of economic ideas."[16] I elevate model minority myth(s),

which are linked to American exceptionalism because they are tied to Protestant theologies of expansion, power, and success. The commodification of race
in these neoliberal structures is a marker of success, one imposed by institutions,
but as Ellen D. Wu shows us in her work, the model minority is also taken up by
Asian Americans.[17] It is translated and affirmed in the context of economies—
the exchange of commodities and the circulation of wealth, the establishment of
corporations as viable members of society, and the role and impact of other insti-
tutionalized forms of value-driven interactions/relationships. Koreans in the United States are an example of the immigrant success story not just because of their
lives overcoming the struggles and multiple barriers in the United States but because the myths of the model minority narrate material and economic success as
a marker of the racialized Asian in the United States. However, this model minority myth is also rooted in Koreans' reception and incorporation of American
Protestant Christianity into Korean culture, or what I will describe here as their
"consumption" of Christianity.

I employ Koreanity as an analytic, a deliberately strange neologism that was
a slip of the tongue, an accidental mishmash of *Korean* and *Christianity* that
increasingly became a resonant way to engage a phenomenon that was constructed
by and constructs the citizen-as-subject seeking legibility and legitimacy: a site
of racialized religion. Koreanity inflects the racializing assemblages associated
with networks of American Protestantism that are made manifest in projects of
US American militarism and the perpetual aftermath of war—all underscored by
structures of an American Orientalism. I aim to show how H Mart is an extension
of the Korean figure both representationally in terms of the idea of the diasporic
Korean in the United States as well as literally, the Korean diaspora where H Mart
is a site of domestication and exemplary multiculturalism in the United States.
And so, this chapter examines H Mart as a cultural production of an exceptional
success story, and in particular, the relationship between religion and capitalism in
the racialization of Asians, but specifically Koreans in America.

PART 1: THE PRODUCTION OF KOREANITY

When one enters the store the entryway is filled with huge bins of watermel-
ons and neat stacks of boxes of quick and easy foods like instant ramen, the
bulk version of a variety of these kinds including jjajjangmyun, shin ramen, jjam-
pong, and anything that can be squeezed into boxes of six, twelve, or twenty-
four. On the other side there are some posters of promotional items in the store
and the discount prices for these items. On the other side there are simply stacks
of gim (dried seaweed), in individual packages but in bulk—eight or ten, maybe
twelve, to each one. There are so many different flavors and brands. The feeling

it engenders is both a feeling of scarcity and abundance—the discounted prices cause me to feel pressure to buy them immediately, and the bulk packaging makes me feel like I'm getting an even better deal. It strikes me that I don't remember seeing this kind of packaging when I was a child. The stark contrast between the individual packaging of my childhood and the option to get instant noodles or gim in bulk signals an indicator of the growth not only of H Mart but of a market for Korean foods and cuisine.

On the other side of the store, where customers are funneled toward the exit, the space is reminiscent of my childhood H Mart. After paying for my purchases, I push the grocery cart through the sliding doors of the only exit. It is a similar setup to the entrance, although a bit smaller: on the left side is a wall full of bulletin boards covered in community advertisements—piano lessons, translation services, fliers for concerts and church events, and most of these fliers are in the Korean language, but some are in English. On the right side there are numerous shelves with little cubbies, and each one is full of CDs, postcards, or brochures of local church communities. Some of them have Christian tracts. The CDs are recorded worship services or sermons from individual churches. On the floor near these shelves there are stacks of newspapers in the Korean language but also some in the Chinese language. On closer inspection of the religious communities' fliers and brochures, all in the Korean language, I notice they are colorful, they span numerous denominations, and they are barely distinguishable from one another. They all promote their choirs, "biblical" or traditional preaching, youth groups and Sunday school, and emphasize the urgency of salvation.

It is no coincidence that the experience of shopping at H Mart is bookended on each side by an overt demonstration of neoliberal capitalism—on the one side, there are some of the cultural staples found in any grocery store in a particular form, bulk and instant—that is, foods in abundance and foods that can be prepared quickly. These are meant to signal convenience, as well as accessibility, and this moment gestures toward the kind of consumption the shopper will partake in throughout the store. Everything is available and available in surplus, and this opening, this initiatory moment, is a kind of invocation, a particular kind of welcome. On the other side, a variety of services, including religious communities, geared toward the community encouraging a particular kind of acculturation and participation are marketed as consumer products, too. It is easy to pick up a brochure of a church or a (free!) CD of a sermon on the way out or pick up a postcard about a special gospel choir event. Whether one does or does not pick up one of these advertisements, the space works in a meaningful way, as a reminder of the presence of an American Christianity at the very least, and more broadly how religious sensibilities are indelibly enmeshed with H Mart as a business corporation. These two vestibular spaces offer a particular liturgy of consumerism enacted in and through H Mart, and it is a liturgy with elements from religion, capitalism, and race. In this section, I will proceed by textual ethnography of H Mart as a market—its physical site (here, I am focused on 3 H Marts in Maryland), its history, its website, its appearance in news media and other local publications in examining its place in the larger cultural landscape.

The Corporatization of Koreanness

In order to explain the corporatization of Koreanity in and through H Mart, I build on Lofton's theorization of religion and consumerism, which leads us to look at "systems of social organization that claim to supersede political borders, such as commodities and corporations, as well as the units of social experience (family and community) often imagined to be universal in form. In these structures of human sociality we find new kinds of orthodoxy."[18] To corporatize Koreanity means making a particular kind of religoracial subject legible in order to capitalize on the social organization of the Korean diaspora in the United States.[19] To capitalize on the Korean diaspora requires more than a market strategy based on Koreans who need Korean ingredients. Ethnic or specialty markets like H Mart are an example of the necessity for immigrant and diasporic communities to participate in capitalist systems of production in order to thrive in the United States. However, H Mart is also an example of how these systems of social organization reveal different and emerging forms of human sociality. Lofton further explains: "Neoliberalism might therefore be understood as a form of religious occupation of the economy: a way of seeing the self in the world as a calculatingly sovereign person enfolded in systems of power, class, and experience through the selection of particular goods and services. The product is a material way to access something ineffable."[20] The sociality that materializes in and through H Mart is a religious sociality—its space, its products, and the people who both work and patronize it—and it creates a communal affect through opportunities for purchase and consumption. These practices of purchase and consumption are devotional practices cultivated by and for the assimilated subject who legitimizes and is legitimated by spaces like H Mart.

H Mart's origin story is familiar and fits into US neoliberal narratives, and yet its unique enterprise, as well as the way it has become not only a grocery store but a successful retailer, is one representation of Koreanity as the store further legitimizes its place in the larger US cultural landscape. It had to begin somewhere, and like many grocery stores it started out as a mom-and-pop type market. The H Mart chain began in 1982 in Woodside, Queens, as

a small corner grocery store. This original store still exists but does not operate in the same manner as other H Marts and maintains the original Han Ah
Reum name. According to its website, from 1982 to 1991, the company added
ten stores, mostly in the northeastern United States. In 1997, the company
opened its first store in Falls Church, Virginia, in the Washington-Baltimore
metropolitan area. On October 19, 1998, the chain opened its current head-
quarters in Lyndhurst in Bergen County, New Jersey, the US county with the
highest Korean population percentage. As of 2021, there were H Mart stores
in New York, New Jersey, Arizona, California, Colorado, Georgia, Hawaii, Illinois, Maryland, Massachusetts, Michigan, North Carolina, Oregon, Pennsylvania, Texas, Virginia, and Washington. Stores were also open in Canada and
the United Kingdom.

H Mart's genealogy highlights its rise and expansion. Its progressive genealogy narrates its success, not only as a capitalistic venture but as participating in the kinds of US narratives that underscore a specific kind of social
and economic achievement, a "making it"—that is, starting from scratch or
from zero (one corner grocery store) to attain both a high level of profit and
visibility. H Mart not only opened in major urban centers with large Korean
populations, which is to be expected because of a large Korean population that
would naturally patronize it, but opened in the Midwest and other regions
away from the coasts and urban centers. By doing so it became a "center,"
a centralized space for people to find and connect to the Korean diaspora.
H Mart also eventually opened "super stores," an example of the kind of
American exceptionalism associated with American success. A super store
indicates the highest level of store in terms of size but "super" as a superlative
also suggests "superior quality." What is especially distinctive is the way these
self-descriptions are not just a business motto or mission statement but a statement of faith by H Mart. Belief is invoked here in the statement "We believe [in] the excellence of our products." The inclusion of "belief" on top of
this exceptionalist self-representation indicates not only aim or intention but
something religious. These unique signals of (theological, cultural, religious)
belief enact a particular work in terms of communicating the type of corporation embodied by H Mart—and it implicates not only its employees but its
consumers.

Their narratives are also constructed in other ways, as seen on the "About
Us" section—on H Mart's website. Under this tab there are three main pages
that give a glimpse of the company's ethos: The "Founder's Greeting" page
reads in a more personal tone: "For over 30 years, H Mart has worked its
best to provide quality Korean food and service to communities throughout

the U.S. . . . We encourage our fellow Koreans to have profound pride and dignity in the magnificent culture of our motherland, South Korea." Language that includes words like "best," "quality," "excellence," and "magnificent" not only expresses this family's pursuit of a specific form of success but also gives us the familiar American ideals articulated as hard work and dedication, and other individualist ideals of achievement. The emphasis on a lengthy "service to communities throughout the U.S." reminds potential customers that the company's credibility is based on longevity and sustainability, a constant and consistent presence—these are all legible to the US consumer. Similarly, H Mart offers its "mission," which has four short lines: "Our mission is to offer the superior products, if that means we have to get our fish from the Fulton Fish Market, we do it. If it means we have to negotiate directly with farmers, it's done. If it means we have to go out of our way, and bend over backwards for the best price, it's just not a problem. So when the time comes to make that 'magical' meal . . . we think your ingredients had better be, better than the best." Once more, the company invokes language that is familiar, found in other grocery store mission statements. Stores like Wegmans and Safeway also lift up their service and aim toward exceptionalism: "the best," the best products, the best prices, the best ingredients. H Mart highlights it in terms of loyalty and accommodation of the customers. In invoking similar language to Wegmans and Safeway, they demonstrate an ability to compete with "big name" grocery stores. H Mart is not simply a specialized grocery store or corner bodega (often racialized as an ethnic/immigrant store) but like Wegmans and Safeway it is marketed for the everyday American everywhere.

Expansion is not only an indication of successful reproduction but reproducibility. H Mart's growth follows a trajectory of expansion as other American grocery stores through processes of standardization. Historian Tracey Deutsch explains how these supermarkets "became a model for how all retailers, not just grocers, to sell larger amounts of goods at lower prices."[21] But H Mart's initial success extended beyond selling products at bulk or at affordable prices. It is reflected in H Mart's mission: "H Mart is America's premier Asian food destination and provides groceries and everyday essential needs as well as upscale products."[22] H Mart seeks to provide it all, and this has become a driving force in its expansion across the United States, which is documented not only on its website through graphics and time lines but through write-ups in news media and other local, residential, and regional publications. City officials embraced one new store in an *East Bay Times* write-up: "It's great to see Hmart here," San Jose city councilman Chappie Jones said. "It's another option for residents here. This will be great for residents of San Jose and this council district." The options that are already present in the region include 99 Ranch, as the article explains in great detail: "A primary rival for Hmart is 99 Ranch, which has 42 stores, including 36 in California, 16 in the Bay Area and 18 in Southern California. 99 Ranch also has stores in Nevada, Texas and Washington, and it's planning to expand into New Jersey and Oregon."[23] H Mart has sought to not only establish itself as a rival to other specialty and ethnic stores but also to be competitive with US name-brand markets. It brands itself in numerous ways in order to be the singular option that appeals to any and every American.

The Domestication of Koreanness

Supermarkets have been a part of the domestic cultural landscape in the United States especially beginning in the twentieth century. A Google Maps search of H Mart in the DC-Maryland-Virginia area brings up numerous options, with Frederick, Maryland, offering the most northwest option and an H Mart in Manassas, Virginia, about thirty miles southwest of DC The prolific existence of H Mart seems unremarkable though as another quick search of "Asian grocery" in the area fills the page with even more red markers tagging other popular stores like 99 Ranch and smaller, lesser-known ones named Po Tung Oriental, Palawan, and Hung Phat.[24] Most of these stores, especially H Mart, are stand-alone stores, but many are part of strip malls that include multiple other convenience stores, restaurants, and other retail stores. And yet, the emergence of a variety of Asian grocery stores suggests something more than the unsurprising expansion of a niche industry commensurate with a growing Asian immigrant population. Asian grocery stores, but H Mart specifically as one of the most successful ethnic supermarkets, demonstrate a particular kind of assimilation and its role in a neoliberal capitalist ecosystem in the way it is embedded in the larger cultural landscape, specifically, of suburban America. In this section I aim to show how H Mart is an example of the domestication of Koreanity—that is, the kind of assimilation that happens through the intersection of American Protestantism and consumerism as it emerges in a particular relationship with the larger culture through deploying a commercial appeal. This domestication is grounded in civilizing processes—that is, to make civil in terms of behavior and interaction, but also in terms of relating to citizenship, and making citizens in the US body politic.

One of the major components in these domesticating processes is the role of family. It is no coincidence that a familial structure is built into these types of corporations, although this is not distinctive to H Mart. Nevertheless, the original founder of H Mart and CEO, Il Yeon Kwon, occupies a significant role in the company structure as along with his former wife. Mishan explains that "Mr. Kwon, 66, has two children with Elizabeth Kwon, 59, who grew up two blocks from the Woodside shop (where her mother still lives) and oversees store design. (Mr. Kwon has since remarried; he and his wife, Jinny Kwon, have three daughters.) From the beginning, it was important to Elizabeth Kwon that the stores were clean, modern and easy to navigate, to defy the stereotype of Asian groceries as grimy and run-down."[25] H Mart is an expression of familial ideals; even divorce and marriage is subsumed in this space to enact certain priorities and not only a kind of aesthetic but a demonstration that it is distinctly American (as opposed to Korean or more broadly, Asian). And yet, H Mart's appeal and success is grounded in its ethnic character. Indeed, Kwon was listed in a *Forbes* article in 2009 as part of a "grouping of prominent Korean-Americans in business in the U.S." and representative of "the leaders of this emerging ethnic sector."[26] Each pithy description demonstrates the kind of progressive narrative associated with immigrant and racial/ethnic success—what it means and looks like to make it. This success and value requires the enlistment of his whole family, as Mishan further describes: His son, Brian Kwon, "never intended to devote his life to the store. But not long after he went abroad to take a job in Seoul—seeking to improve his Korean—his father asked him to come home and look over the company's books, to make sure everything was running smoothly," and his daughter, Stacey Kwon, is a president of the company.[27] For the Kwon children, their active roles in the company are also rooted in a filial piety, a requirement of offspring to care for their parents and grandparents and maintain an enduring connection.

Filial piety has roots in Confucianism; according to Korean cultural resources, it is an important characteristic structuring relationship, in particular, the kinship systems and relationships between parents and children. In Korea, emphasis is placed on children's filial duties toward their parents, making filial piety more of a unilateral concept. This is extended to grandchildren's filial piety and respect for their grandparents and is the basis for ancestor worship rituals.[28] Confucian principles shape these social obligations by connecting them to virtues like righteousness and faithfulness. These concepts especially find purchase for Koreans who hold to them in the US diaspora, as they are contiguous with American Protestant ideals and values of family, especially those centering the institutions of the heteronormative family, and respect for one's parents with commandants and teachings like "Honor thy father and mother." And so, not only does filial piety operate in the structure of the Korean family, in this case especially the leadership of H Mart, it provides a larger framework for the (in)corporation of Koreanity in an entity and organization like H Mart. Additionally, it gives shape to the structures of the company by rooting the overlapping ideals of dedication, commitment, and obligation in social relationships.

This filial piety includes the larger community in which an H Mart is situated, whether a neighborhood, city, or county. H Mart's website includes a whole section under its "About Us" tab dedicated to its philanthropy and outreach and support of nonprofit organizations under "Community." At the top of the page it shares another slogan: "For the love of our community": "Hmart is committed to giving back to our communities. We have a longstanding commitment to support non-profit organizations, various scholarship funds and youth development programs. We also support big and small organizations throughout the country with continuing efforts to reach out to local communities with a substantial number of grants that are directed to local communities across the country. Hmart cares for and takes great pride in giving back to our neighbors, friends, and local communities."[29] At first glance this brief statement is generic and straightforward: it includes in the opening a commitment to "give back" at the beginning of the paragraph and reiterates it once more at the end. The paragraph includes a broad explanation of the kinds of organizations it supports, emphasizing scholarships and programs for youth and not limiting itself regionally but reaching out all "across the country," even as their focus is local. The language is familiar and echoes other commitments as found on the websites of US supermarkets. These statements and descriptions are a way to make visible their place in the wider American cultural landscape. At the same time, H Mart offers a distinct articulation of their commitment to community through the language of love. No other store uses the word *love* as a way to describe their endeavor to support nonprofit organizations, agencies, schools, neighborhoods, and communities. It is an example of how H Mart brands itself in a religious way: H Mart is more than a store; it is a space in which to enact a specific kind of sociality and relationality where its commitments are not simply philanthropic but religious. This love is a motivating force, a responsibility and duty enacted outward toward the larger community.

The kind of multiculturalism that is performed in H Mart is an expression of their religious values—a belief that they are enacting the same American Protestant formulaic beliefs of hard work and inclusion that make a capitalist venture successful in the end. Its ongoing structure and organization become necessary for the confirmation of its authenticity as an American grocery store. This multiculturalism is found in H Mart's foods and products, but it is also demonstrated in the makeup of its employees, as well as how the company endeavors to present itself. H Mart's website has a video under a tab labeled "People," where one can "hear our people talk about the experiences they have had at H Mart."[30] A two-minute video is frozen on an initial image of a white male employee, but once the video begins with a short musical background and the image of the H Mart logo, the video shows a non-Korean female employee who says, "It's really an amazing market," before flashing to another white male employee who agrees: "There's always something new to discover at H Mart," quickly transitioning to another non-Korean male employee: "I always feel good to be here at H Mart." H Mart is not only a desirable and ideal place of work for potential employees, it is a positive space, a place of discovery and fulfillment. The video continues with "Paul E. Moore/Sales Associate," (who is incidentally the person captured on the video when initially visiting the web page) saying: "Working with the company, you get to work with a lot of different kinds of people—normal Americans as well as people from all over Asia." Both he and another white male employee, Will Wood, a store manager, repeatedly emphasize encounters with numerous people from all over the world (albeit, mostly "Asia") as one of the benefits of working for H Mart. But it is also a major source of pride: as Wood explains, there are "a variety of people from different backgrounds, it's a dynamic environment, it makes me proud to work here." H Mart is a place to find connection, but a particular kind of connection, one that is global and international, one that gives you access to the strange, exotic cultures of "Asia" but safely within the bounds of America; as Moore explains, even "normal Americans" both work for and patronize the company.

At the very end of the video, Mario Carchi/Store Manager says: "I immigrated from Ecuador. All employees are welcome regardless of nationality" and "We are waiting for you." Most of the employees interviewed use "we" to explain H Mart's viability as a place of work, and it is especially noticeable when Wood and Carchi use this plural pronoun. With a variety of ethnic and racial representations, "we" is not embodied in only Korean employees/patrons or soley white ones, but everyone. On another page, an advertisement with job descriptions for produce associates include the following:

> We are H Mart, the largest Asian supermarket chain in America. Starting in 1982 with a single store in Woodside, Queens, H Mart has grown to include more than 71 stores across the United States. H Mart is America's premier Asian food destination and provides groceries and everyday essential needs as well as upscale products. H Mart offers a full line of Asian foods as well as a broad range of Western groceries to complement its full scale offering to that

of a traditional supermarket. H Mart is also known for its innovative new food halls which are an extension of over 37 years of providing eateries in its stores.[31]

Over and over, H Mart highlights its history and genealogy, its progress and success, its ability to innovate, and its diversity and multiculturalism to justify its existence as a viable American company. Moore describes the "positive experience with management," and Wood explains the many opportunities at H Mart to discover "always a new skill to learn or apply." A nonwhite, non-Korean female employee, Anita Davis, reiterates her first statement: "I recommend people to work at H Mart." It is an evangelizing moment, an invitation not only to work but to participate in a positive and productive community, and a welcome into its domesticating projects of legibility and assimilation.

Selling Koreanity

In this section I aim to provide a textual ethnography of H Mart to explore the mutual imbrication between religion and capitalism in the racialization of Koreans. I argue that H Mart contributes to the production of Koreanity through corporatizing and domesticating procedures, but that it is also a product of Koreanity, showing how religion and race are inflected in a phenomenon like H Mart. To return to the exit space of the Ellicott City H Mart where there are the little cubbies of church paraphernalia, each shelf is also methodically and meticulously organized in its own way, the sight of which is like a benediction at the end of a capitalistic liturgy that includes perusing bright fruits and vegetables, standing in a whole aisle of just-dried seaweed, shivering through the frozen section full of ready-made dumplings and frozen fishcake, and eating a jjigae in the food court: a reminder that H Mart participates in the production of a Koreanity through assimilating the store into the larger American cultural landscape and by specifically shaping the citizen-as-consumer.

PART 2: THE CONSUMPTION OF KOREANITY

These days Korean food culture is its own genre—it is disseminated throughout the world through a variety of cultural forms. Its ubiquity, I argue, is not only connected to the production of Koreanity in a particular way; it also demonstrates how a phenomenon like H Mart as an aspect of Koreanity becomes a part of the American cultural landscape. Its increasing accessibility through popular culture signals a complex assemblage of race, neoliberal capitalism, and religion. In this section, I aim to look at the significance of H Mart occupying the role of the singular, and how its metonymic position also signals its iconicity. I argue for a reading of H Mart specifically as a religious icon and its role as a theological imaginary in other cultural productions to show how H Mart produces Koreanity and is itself a production of Koreanity. I look at the archives of popular culture in examining the memoir *Crying in H Mart,* cookbooks and travel books to explore how H Mart demonstrates that assimilability is a major characteristic of the production of Koreanity but that it is specifically consumability that inflects Koreanity as a religioracial category.

Diasporic Sentimentalism

H Mart is compelling in the way it evokes particular feelings, especially for those who identify with or reside in the Korean diaspora. I build on Rachel B. Gross's work on nostalgia as a religious practice, and how "nostalgia as wishful affection or sentimental longing for an irrevocable past functions as religion for American Jews."[32] Gross's chapter specifically on the Jewish deli menu looks at the interaction between various actors across new food movements, Ashkenazi revivalists, and restaurateurs, as well as families with their stories and histories with Jewish delis and markets, to look at how nostalgia shaped their relationship to certain foods and recipes in the landscape of kosher systems, global capitalist markets, and sustainability movements. She explains that "the revivalists present their Ashkenazi culinary nostalgia as both uniform and accessible to a broad audience even as it can be molded to fit the particulars of their own experiences and family histories as well as that of their patrons, forming the emotional bonds that are the basis of American Jewish religion."[33] This aim at both authenticity and accessibility is resonant with what I see happening in/at/through H Mart and how it is engaged in cultural examples. However, Jewish delis and markets are distinct from H Mart, and so rather than nostalgia, which is more of a feeling and longing for something past (in time), I aim to use something I call diasporic sentimentalism, which I describe as a feeling and longing for something distant (in space), or the transnational circulations of affect to describe how H Mart acts as a religious icon in the memoir *Crying in H Mart.*

H Mart has materialized more visibly through a recent "cultural moment" in the memoir *Crying in H Mart* (2021) written by the musician behind Japanese Breakfast, Michelle Zauner.[34] The memoir came out of a the *New Yorker* personal essay "Crying in H Mart" published in August 2018, an extended meditation on grief at the loss of a mother and their complicated mother-daughter relationship throughout her life. Zauner was born in Seoul, the daughter of Chongmi, a native of the city, and Joel, a white American. When she was a year old, the family relocated to Eugene, Oregon, where her mother parented with an exacting nature. Zauner's mother was a woman in pursuit of perfection in everything, and of course this prodding extended to her only child. The story of her mother's death comes halfway through the memoir, and the rest of the book is her own grappling with her identity and the importance of food to guide and ground her. Zauner is not only a talented musician and artist, but her ability to craft a narrative, a story from her life that has touched millions (by early June 2022, she has been on the *New York Times* bestsellers list for forty straight weeks and her book has been translated into dozens of languages) is nothing short of . . . iconic. But it is also the distinct way that Zauner situates H Mart in her work that gives us an entry point into understanding how an entity/object like a Korean supermarket could function as religious icon.

Today, broadly speaking, an icon might be anything, including a celebrity, a symbol, or a piece of religious art that holds sacred meaning. In Orthodox Christian traditions (Eastern and Byzantine) icons have historically and culturally functioned as portals through which the sacred is experienced by religious adherents—they are expressions of the divine and a form of communication by the divine. While their sacramental importance took root in the Eastern Church, a strong opposition arose in the Western Church that argued icons were objects of worship and encouraged idolatry. The continuous through line is how an icon is a symbol of devotion, an object of reverence, a visible expression of the sacred, and a mode of communication of the ineffable—the icon occupies a mediatory role between a person and something beyond, and it can produce a sensational affect.

First, H Mart as icon in Zauner's story activates the feeling of loss. It is a space that provides the right conditions to remind her of what is gone—a place overflowing with the sights and smells of her mother, her childhood. But even in that absence there is discovery, too, of something present, if distant, when she explains: "I find myself again, searching for the first chapter of the story I want to tell about my mother." (10). Through H Mart, she understands that loss even as she recovers bits of the relationship with her mother, and herself. Around every corner in H Mart there are surprising moments when she is caught up as she reflects: "Catch me at H Mart when some kid runs up double-fisting plastic sleeves of ppeongtwigi 뻥튀기 and I'll just lose it" (4). H Mart seems to activate an unraveling of unrelenting grief that lingers right beneath the surface of her life. She explains that she can talk about the raw details of caring for her mom during her last days "with a straight face," and yet, a seemingly mundane moment undoes her: "I'll cry when I see a Korean grandmother eating seafood noodles in the food court, discarding shrimp heads and mussel shells onto the lid of her daughter's tin rice bowl" (4). She's haunted by the small gestures of filial duty as H Mart mediates these experiences in which she engages this profound loss.

However, it is not simply loss but its twin that affects Zauner, and an aspect of the diasporic sentimentalism that characterizes H Mart as an icon—longing. But it is not only longing for her mother but also longing for a country to which she found connection because of and through her mother. Korea as a place is located in her mother, too, as she recounts stories about their time in Korea. And so she discovers this longing through the most ordinary objects: giant vats of peeled garlic "because it's the only place that truly understands how much garlic you'll need for the kind of food your people eat." (3). Like a mother, H Mart sees her, knows her, as well as the generic "you," signaling diasporic Koreans like her, gathering all of them together in this place bound together by specters of a life on the other side of the world. Zauner expresses longing specifically for connection through those experiences that not only remind her of her mother and family but also connect her to Korea as a way to ground her identity: "The food court is the perfect place to people-watch while sucking down salty, fatty jjajangmyeon. I think about my family who lived in Korea, before most of them died, and how Korean-Chinese was always the first thing we'd eat when my mom and I arrived in Seoul after a fourteen-hour flight from America" (8). Eating noodles is a ritual of longing as she not only remembers her family but lives out the connection to Korea.

But H Mart also acts as a kind of portal, a throughway, a mode of transport. Although she does not profess a Christian faith, she spends most of the time fleshing out a more religious description of H Mart, especially as a site of religious experience when she describes it as a destination and the journey to it like a pilgrimage throughout the rest of the book: "You'll know that you're headed the right way because there will be signs to mark your path. As you go farther into your pilgrimage, the lettering on the awnings slowly begins to turn into symbols that you may or may not be able to read" (6). The lettering is the Korean language, and a signal of both its foreignness and familiarity, even as we sense the reverence in her description of the place. H Mart is the place that also activates a longing for her mother, and for Korea, and here is an example of the diasporic sentimentalism that characterizes her story. It is not only longing for her mother but also longing for the place to which she found connection because of and through her mother. The feeling of this place is first in her mother, and through her relationship to her mother as she recounts the stories of their annual trips to Korea, but Korea as a place is located in her mother, too.

H Mart acts as a bridge which Zauner reflects on toward the end of the book in the story about her imo (her mother's sister) who died shortly after her mother. An aunt is like a second mother, so she narrates how deeply this double loss affected her:

So, when I go to H Mart, I'm not just on the hunt for cuttlefish and three bunches of scallions for a buck; I'm searching for memories. I'm collecting the evidence that the Korean half of my identity didn't die when they did. H Mart is the bridge that guides me away from the memories that haunt me, of chemo head and skeletal bodies and logging milligrams of hydrocodone. It reminds me of who they were before, beautiful and full of life, wiggling Chang Gu honey-cracker rings on all ten of their fingers, showing me how to suck a Korean grape from its skin and spit out the seeds. (10, my emphasis)

It was H Mart as a bridge that allowed her to enter into the larger story of her identity and a different understanding of her genealogy. Zauner collects evidence that she is still alive, and H Mart is a portal to that life as she narrates the grief that consumes her even as she consumes the remnants of her mother, of Korea found in cuttlefish and scallions and packages of crunchy sweet snacks. It not only allows her to access something sacred but is an expression of something sacred in the unique way it draws her and others like her. She emphasizes the contrast to other popular and trendy grocery stores: "What we're looking for isn't available at a Trader Joe's. H Mart is where your people gather under one odorous roof, full of faith that they'll find something they can't find anywhere else" (10). So she sojourns with other pilgrims to H Mart "full of faith" even if she cannot always describe it exactly, she will find what she needs in and through this place.

Family and kinship are major through lines in this work, especially in H Mart as a space to practice a specific kind of consumption as an expression of filial piety. Here, consumption occurs at two levels: First, in terms of patronage, the purchasing of goods that are specifically Korean, whether beauty products, rice cookers, or ingredients for kimchi jjigae, which I explored in the previous section. Here I focus on consumption in terms of the role of food and the act of eating and the role that H Mart plays in avenues for consumption. Zauner reflects on how important eating is for connection: "I wonder how many people at H Mart miss their families. How many are thinking of them as they bring their trays back from the different stalls. If they're eating to feel connected, to celebrate these people through food. Which ones weren't able to fly back home this year, or for the past ten years? Which ones are like me, missing the people who are gone from their lives forever?" (8). Eating activates both the feeling of connection and the longing for connection specifically in terms of kinship. But here, consumption also becomes a duty and obligation of, and expression of, filial piety. It is present in the religious lives of Korean diasporic cultures in order to solidify family, kinship structures, and community and to invoke certain ritualist practices associated with ancestor worship. In this case, consuming Korean food at H Mart is ancestor worship, an act of filial piety—it activates both the longing and belonging of a diasporic sentimentalism.

The Sacred and Exotic

At the same time, H Mart can also play a more whimsical role in the sacred and exotic as the store is experienced in ordinary ways that emerge in travel books. There is once more a sense of the otherworldly as we see in the *Food Lover's Guide to Portland*, where the author explains:

> Ten miles south of Portland in Tigard is the enormous Korean H Mart with its fluorescent-lit, clean, well-stocked aisles of Asian food, drink, and more. The first thing you encounter at H Mart is the food court, with everything from frozen yogurt and smoothies to rice puffs, noodles, and sweet red bean waffles. In the deli you'll find huge dishes filled with loads of pickled and salted vegetables and seafood, including small, salted clams and salted calamari. Go to the meat department for a large selection of thinly sliced beef and pork, and peruse the non-perishable aisles for Asian beer, condiments, dried noodles, and teas.[35]

This description of H Mart is similar to the descriptions of H Mart in previous examples—an explanation of the cleanliness and orderliness of the space, how each shelf and aisle is "well-stocked," a brief list of the kinds of food that would be appealing, as well as highlighting the food court. These descriptions are formulaic in their reifications of H Mart as a singular entity, solidifying it as a figure not only in popular culture but in the larger cultural landscape. But that this is included in a travel guide to Portland indicates that it is specifically a noteworthy destination, and it makes the city of Portland itself occupy some category of colorful and curious. At the same time, the description once more is full of exotic items even alongside familiar items, so that the tourist can find a mix of comfort amid the discomforting or uncomfortable foreign items. H Mart is a site of the sacred and the exotic.

H Mart is ubiquitous, and it is meaningfully so as a persistent fixture in popular culture. In a similar way, cookbooks employ similar descriptions of H Mart. For example, it appears in *The Kimchi Chronicles*, an American food program that aired on PBS in 2011 that is part travelogue, part food narrative, and part documentary of self-discovery where host Marja Vongerichten, a Korean American adoptee, explores Korean food and culture and shares her unique life story throughout the series. The show, and the host, do not necessarily feature H Mart in prominent or overt ways but casually invoke it throughout the show and in the blog within its recipe stories and interviews. Vongerichten has also published a book under the same name, *The Kimchi Chronicles: Korean Cooking for An American Kitchen*, and mentions H Mart here:

> Like pizza for New Yorkers, jajangmyeon is an imported dish (the black bean paste is a Chinese ingredient) that's become part of the Korean identity—it's eaten everywhere, especially late at night and especially as takeout. When I first returned to Korea as a grown-up, the taste brought back a flood of memories. Now I make it at home or eat it in the food court at H Mart, a chain of Korean groceries with a huge store in New Jersey. A word of caution though: Don't get jajangmyeon on your clothes as it won't come out.[36]

The point is the food: jajangmyeon is to Korea as pizza is to the United States— an imported dish from another country now belongs there. But what makes jajangmyeon accessible to the United States is H Mart, which is dropped in there, like a marker of authenticity to show that H Mart makes it palatable and provides access to this food culture. H Mart legitimizes a particular kind of connection and experience as Vongerichten recounts her time in Korea and how eating jajangmyeon reminds her of this part of her history and identity. That she ends the description with something mundane makes both the food and H Mart feel ordinary, and as American as anything else that might get on your clothes. Indeed, the casual ease of naming something like H Mart signals a specific kind of assimilation—it is another way of "making it."

The Kimchi Chronicles was sponsored by the Visit Korea Committee, Korean Food Foundation, Ministry of Culture, Sports and Tourism and Ministry for Food, Agriculture, Forestry and Fisheries geared toward an international audience, and particularly a US viewership. It is telling that there are numerous "actors" involved in this production, not only those celebrities who appear in the show but the numerous institutions behind the scenes: the production company (which is based in France), the various national Korean sponsors, and PBS, an American public broadcasting nonprofit organization that is a noncommercial, free-to-air television network based in Arlington, Virginia, known for providing educational programming. H Mart also looms a bit larger in the background. Vongerichten includes it in the short list of resources for Korean ingredients and equipment in the very back: "www.hmart.com is a great Korean grocery store with locations that include those I visit nearly every week in New York and New Jersey. Their website is very helpful for finding great ingredients."[37] In the back of the book there is a list of sponsors ranging from Samsung to Korean national agencies and foundations, but near the bottom of the list is H Mart. That H Mart is the only grocery or market included in the list suggests its status as not only the best store but, in some ways, the only store.

Conclusion: The Consumption of H Mart

H Mart as a physical site certainly has a material impact as we read in these examples, in Zauner's memoir and the travel guides and cookbooks. Her engagement of H Mart is both personal and relational, and although the space itself is not a religious one, it is a "beautiful, holy place," (3) where Zauner shares both litanies and liturgies of belonging and engages in rituals of consumption. H Mart as religious icon is a portal that is situated right on the border of the everyday and exotic. It operates through a diasporic sentimentalism, that longing for what is distant, and allows for what is simultaneously present and absent to operate in that liminal space of both-and. It offers a way to something not only fun, cute, or interesting but otherworldly, mysterious, and strange. But all these examples together show us the complexity of H Mart as "a Korean tradition made in America" emphasizing the dual nature of an icon that is made legible through the sacred. It gives us an example of the kind of unfixedness that comes with processes of commodification, of domestication, of assimilation as a product of (religious) racialization. I argue all of this is an extension of the kind of American Orientalism (that according to Lowe endeavors to mitigate the double threat and encroachment of global rivalries and perpetuate a racialized labor force) operational in the formation of Koreanity.[38] H Mart is a figure that is interpellated by the US nation-state, and recognized through its own production, commodification, and consumption.

To make oneself consumable is a way of being assimilable. H Mart shows us how consumption is a particular form of assimilation—that is, the palatability of Koreanity by being a place to consume Koreanity. H Mart operates as more than a literary device or even as a microcosm of the Korean diaspora, but as a religious icon, a spiritual commodity, exchangeable and fungible, a theological imaginary that constructs Koreanity in the United States through the deployment of a diasporic sentimentalism: as exotic, as sacred, and specifically, consumable.

NOTES

1. "About Us," H Mart website, accessed March 1, 2021.

2. Ligaya Mishan, "The Lure of H Mart, Where the Shelves Can Seem as Wide as Asia," *New York Times* (website), May 11, 2021.

3. My emphasis. Mishan, "Lure of H Mart."

4. What I mean to signal with the label "American" is the way in which it compels a

particular kind of formation extending Lisa Lowe's explanation in the opening pages of the "nation" as "juridically legislated, territorially situated, and culturally embodied." In this chapter, I look at "America" as a religious project—I argue that the myths of success, abundance, and exceptionalism find a through line to the theological imaginaries of blessing and prosperity located in Christianity. Lisa Lowe, *Immigrant Acts: On Asian American Cultural Politics* (Durham, NC: Duke University Press, 1996), 1–36.

5. Mishan, "Lure of H Mart."

6. Ronald Reagan, "Election Eve Address 'A Vision for America,'" November 11, 1980, Ronald Reagan Presidential Library and Museum website, National Archives, accessed March 1, 2022.

7. Ronald Reagan, "Remarks at a Meeting with Asian and Pacific-American Leaders," February 23, 1984, Reagan Presidential Library website, accessed March 1, 2022.

8. Lowe, *Immigrant Acts*, 11. American orientalism displaced US expansionist interests in Asia onto racialized figurations of Asian workers within the national space. From World War II onward, Asia has emerged as an expressly complicated double front of threat and encroachment for the United States: on the one hand, Asian states have become prominent as external rivals in overseas imperial war and in the global economy, and on the other, Asian immigrants are still a necessary racialized labor force within the domestic national economy.

9. I work with Bruce Lincoln's notion of myths as narratives in ideology form and how they legitimize social orders and provide framework for understanding cultural narratives, but I also aim to emphasize the significance of its literary forms here as not only narratives of origins but fantasy and how in this regard myth shapes imaginaries and identities. See Bruce Lincoln, *Theorizing Myth: Narrative, Ideology, and Scholarship* (Chicago: University of Chicago Press, 1999).

10. There is so much scholarship on this particular trope of the Asian American figure and experience.

11. David M. Kotz explains:

We use the concept of neoliberalism, or neoliberal capitalism, more broadly to refer to a particular institutional form of capitalism along with the dominant ideas associated with that form of capitalism. The concept of neoliberal, or free-market, capitalism does not mean that the state plays no role in the economy. Market relations and market exchange require a state, or state-like institution, to define and protect private property and to enforce the contracts that are an essential feature of market exchange. Every large-scale society requires a state, or a state-like institution, to preserve order. The maintenance of a strong military is fully consistent with the neoliberal view of the proper role of the state. The meaning of "'free-market'" in this context is that the state role in regulating economic activity is limited, apart from the preceding essential state functions, leaving market relations and market forces as the main regulators of economic activity—but of course operating within a framework provided by the state." (David M. Kotz, The Rise and Fall of Neoliberal Capitalism [Cambridge, MA: Harvard University Press, 2015], 9)

12. "The increasing militarization of the world, and the development policies dictated by the hegemony of U.S.-controlled financial institutions and the violence brought about by capitalist development." Hong explains further the impact of the "social relations of capitalism within the history of U.S. liberal democracy" and how global "economic restructuring turned postindustrial nations like the United States into service economies, dependent on cheap, easily exploitable labor." Grace Kyungwon Hong, *The Ruptures of American Capital* (Minneapolis: University of Minnesota Press, 2006), 15.

13. Hong, *Ruptures of American Capital*, 14.

14. Hong, *Ruptures of American Capital*, 15.

15. The commodification of race is in part a product of an American exceptionalism, which is itself an extension of American Protestantism, and I work here to link it specifically to more recent scholarship around religion, consumerism, and the marketplace. Jonathan Tran's *Asian Americans and the Spirit of Racial Capitalism* (New York: Oxford University Press, 2022) gives us one way to think about the impact of political economies on racial(ized) identity and the reminder that capitalism is key not only to our understanding of the initiating cause of racial inequality but also to its perpetuation. His work gives a critique of identitarian approaches to theologizing, which results in/is an effect, too, of the commodification of race—the case studies give us examples of alternatives that look beyond modern racial logics. But I especially rely on the critical religious studies approach offered by Kathryn Lofton, Bethany Moreton, and others in Jan Stievermann, ed., *Religion and the Marketplace in the United States* (Oxford: Oxford University Press, 2015), where we see religious beliefs and practices overlap with market practices in concrete intersections, for example, in the ways Protestant theologies and communities are shaped by consumer, neoliberal, and global capitalist systems. But these currents flow both ways as Moreton explains in her case study on Wal-Mart: "For the emerging Wal-Mart constituency, faith in God and faith in the market grew in tandem." (*To Serve God and Wal-Mart: The Making of Christian Free Enterprise* [Cambridge, MA: Harvard University Press, 2009], 5). The framework of religion with neoliberal capitalism is useful here as I seek to examine how consumerism and consumption constructs racialized identity.

16. Kathryn Lofton, *Consuming Religion* (Chicago: University of Chicago Press, 2017), 23.

17. Ellen D. Wu, *The Color of Success: Asian Americans and the Origins of the Model Minority* (Princeton, NJ: Princeton University Press, 2014).

18. Lofton, *Consuming Religion*, 24.

19. I am indebted to the scholarship that looks at race and religion as a way to talk about identity, but particularly inspired by Judith Weisenfeld's work on "religio-racial," specifically in the unusual movements that rejected the racial identities of Negro, Afro-American, or colored in favor of alternative identities such as Moorish American, Ethiopian Hebrew, Asiatic, or simply human, "race-less angels" and children of the one true God thereby shifting the American religious landscape as these groups worked to relocate themselves within the larger social fabric of the United States. My work looks at the "religio-racial" subject of Koreanity as the visibly "foreign" participant who perpetuates the complex projects of assimilation and legibility. Judith Weisenfeld, *New World A-Coming: Black Religion and Racial Identity During the Great Migration* (New York: New York University Press, 2016).

20. Lofton, *Consuming Religion*, 24

21. Tracey Deutsch, *Building a Housewife's Paradise: Gender, Politics, and American*

Grocery Stores in the Twentieth Century (Chapel Hill: University of North Carolina Press, 2010), 2.

22. "About Us," H Mart website.

23. George Avalos, "New Asian Market Opens, Plans San Jose Expansion," *East Bay Times*, April 6, 2017.

24. Although geographically specific to Los Angeles, a large part of James Zarsadiaz's recent work highlights "the ways in which Asian immigrants fashioned spaces of belonging in the East San Gabriel Valley through the incorporation" in the 1980s and 1990s, especially looking at religious and retail spaces like grocery stores, especially 99 Ranch. He argues that these spaces were not spaces of resistance or "cultural retaliation" but that these "landscapes were gestures toward assimilation." James Zarsadiaz, *Resisting Change in Suburbia: Asian Immigrants and Frontier Nostalgia in L.A.* (Berkeley: University of California Press, 2022), 82.

25. Mishan, "Lure of H Mart."

26. "Bankers, Grocers and Lots of Kims," *Forbes* (website), January 2, 2009.

27. Julia Moskin, "The Unlikely Rise of H Mart as a Cultural Hub," *New York Times* (website), May 11, 2021.

28. Choi Gil Sung (崔吉城), "Filial Piety," Encyclopedia of Korean Folk Culture, National Folk Museum of Korea.

29. "Community," H Mart website, accessed March 1, 2021.

30. "Our People," H Mart website, accessed March 1, 2021.

31. "Job Posting: H Mart," Dayforce HCM (website), accessed March 1, 2021. An advertisement for produce associate.

32. Rachel B. Gross, *Beyond the Synagogue: Jewish Nostalgia as Religious Practice* (New York: New York University Press, 2021), 5.

33. Gross, *Beyond the Synagogue*, 5.

34. Michelle Zauner, *Crying in H Mart* (New York: Vintage, 2021).

35. Liz Crain, *Food Lovers' Guide to Portland* (Portland, OR: Hawthorne Books, 2014), 45–46.

36. Marja Vongerichten, *The Kimchi Chronicles: Korean Cooking for An American Kitchen* (Emmaus, PA: Rodale Books, 2011), 315.

37. Vongerichten, *Kimchi Chronicles*, 495.

38. Lowe, *Immigrant Acts*, 5.

Subtle Energy, Extracted Energy

Ley Lines and Oil in North America

JUDITH ELLEN BRUNTON

In a 2018 YouTube video "Relationship between the Planetary Grid, Technology of the Ancient Civilization & the Modern Energy," Michelle Gibson explains: "After I became aware of the existence of the North American Star Tetrahedron, and as I started to become aware of the symmetrical geometrically shaped features of the landscape when I was living in central Oklahoma, I started to see how the layout of the grid and ancient infrastructure were being utilized by the energy industry unbeknownst to the general population."[1] In the video, Gibson brings the audience along as they discover that a nearby town, Woodward, Oklahoma, "fell on the alignment with Houston, Dallas, Woodward, Denver, and Edmonton, Canada, in Alberta." What these places have in common, aside from being mapped together on the Star Tetrahedron she has discovered, is that they are prominent spaces for resource extraction, its refinement, and its transport. Gibson argues that this energy infrastructure is placed on mounds, earthworks, and other "ancient infrastructure" by energy companies, explaining "there is most definitely a connection between the planetary grid, ancient technology, and our modern energy industry." Ley lines, energy vortexes, the planetary grid, the crystalline grid, spirit roads; these designations and many others are articulations of theories about the planet and the divine that ground global connections in specific places. The specificity of the land and its use in the North American West insist on spiritual energy being theorized alongside the locally prominent energy industry and the work of resource extraction. The geological information that is used to assess the land and extract oil is reframed as evidence of a spiritual bounty. Or, in some instances, oil and its infrastructure is theorized as disrupting the flow of ley lines and compromising the spiritual energy of the place.

Michelle Gibson's YouTube video about the planetary grid of ley lines and the energy industry is meant to serve an esoteric and conspiratorial community—her many videos offer suspicions on subjects ranging from historic fires to wormholes—but the theorizing in this video echoes a kind of thinking that circulates more broadly. Growing up in Alberta's oil culture, and eventually doing fieldwork there, I would sometimes hear similar claims in conversation: that an important ley line runs through the province and that this energy line was a contributing factor in the province's oil wealth. While not frequently articulated, this kind of knowledge has a cousin in a more popular assertion: that oil is evidence of Alberta's identity as an "energy center," a quality that destines and equips the province for energy dominance despite energy transitions. This assertion travels as the secular speech of economic development enthusiasts and businesses, while the speech of ley line thinkers is notable as metaphysical or new age. However, in theorizing the logics of earth energies and their agency, both display a North American vernacular knowledge that does not distinguish between a spiritual energy and a thermodynamic one. This chapter examines how new age theorizing entangles spiritual and earth energies with the energy of oil extraction, illuminating a knowledge-making about land and extraction as broadly metaphysical.

This chapter also builds on the contributions of those who have argued that metaphysical religion, unseen power, self-help, and magic practices outside institutional settings are—as Catherine L. Albanese says—"key to making sense of the nation's religiosity."[2] However, while metaphysical religion and its kin often center the mind as the ultimate source of power, I join others in emphasizing the dialectic between the "meta" the mind is seen as accessing with the "physical" of the natural world and its local specificities.[3] If the metaphysical is a "cosmological theory of correspondence between worlds," then the medium of settler relationships to land and water in North America and the relationship of extraction shapes that correspondence.[4] Historical settler efforts to imagine this land as a partner to correspond with, and their contemporary legacies, are shaped by histories of prospecting and resource use on this land. Studying these resource imaginaries generally allow for an understanding of what Alicia Puglionesi describes as the "process that fuses materials and narratives, that turns land into property, matter into energy, and desire into a desperate faith" within a white settler normativity.[5]

Thinking about resource extraction as a way people theorize and are in relation to land also contributes to our understanding of how land is spiritual in North America. Vernacular religious expressions that align oil extraction with ley lines (and similar concepts) push against the possibility of collapsing categories of nature religion into "green" religion. Ley lines run through sacred mountains and fracking wells, they crisscross crystal clear lakes and pumpjacks, and—alongside the pipelines that transport oil—traipse across the United States–Canada border. Herein lies the stakes of this investigation. By examining theories about how ley lines, energy, and land relate to oil, I illuminate how resource extraction is always being theorized within a cosmology in North America: theorizing about ley lines and how to hunt them are one tip of a cosmologic iceberg regarding land and how to be in relation with it. The combination of the specifics of American land and American metaphysical thinking results in ley line theories, which include knowledge about energy and power awaiting individuals to claim them. However, the language of ley lines and global energy grids also abstract these theories from their historical and geographic specificities. This move to abstract and universalize something as specific as the land and air and water that a community depends on reaches beyond the North American context. Studying the American and Canadian case as I do here opens up the possibility of questioning how resource extraction is embedded in spiritual and cosmologic frames in different places around the world. How is oil invited into a cosmic story? And what broader ideas about power and who should have it does this cosmic story suggest? In North America what we learn about power by looking at the metaphysical world of resource extraction can impact how we see problematic relationships to the natural world and their environmental effects and how we hope to address ongoing colonial antagonisms concerning Indigenous people and nations in North America. In what follows I map what I see as the concepts and histories needed to follow how the metaphysics of extraction and energy production make broader arguments about how power is understood to be produced and wielded.

LEY LINES, VORTEXES, DOWSING

The first time I remember hearing of energetic intersecting lines in the Calgary context was in a story about a cat. The cat, I was told, was transitioning well from its time as my companion in my terrible first apartment to its new lush life in a loving home with a local counselor and Reiki practitioner. Since I had left town, the cat had thrived, even taking up its own energy healing responsibilities in the household, sitting on the laps of particularly vulnerable clients and laying at important points around the house to neutralize the potent power of ley lines. It was explained to me that, like some other special places around the world, Calgary is at the intersection of powerful energy lines, which makes it both spiritually potent and bountiful when it comes to energy resources like oil and gas. All I can remember thinking at the time—as I pictured the giant crystal blue skies, Rocky Mountains, and the tides of people coming to try for some luck in the oil industry—was: of course, that sounds right. Since then, I have noticed this kind of speech periodically and noted how it overlaps with less overtly metaphysical or spiritual descriptions of this oil town. Calgary's official slogan is "Be part of the energy," and local business people and community organizations describe the space as an energy center, a landscape laying in wait for people to come and realize its energy potential, first through agriculture, then through oil, and now, they insist, through new energy technologies. Energy is a ubiquitous but powerful gloss in this place, at once meaning specific kinds of energy and philosophizing about energy generally.

Like the term *energy* more generally in Calgary, the energy of a ley line, of an energy vortex, or of an earth grid, has explanatory power without having to be specific about which metaphysical tradition or theory such an evocation is referencing. This imprecision seems aligned with the ideas of wider metaphysical theorizing regarding humans as a microcosm within a macrocosm.[6] Within metaphysical traditions the thinking seems to be that when you are trying to use mere human language to describe universal forces, it is forgivable to gesture more than classify with various terms. That said, there are some common concepts that are used when people are theorizing about interesting energy lines. Ley lines, when called such, have their origins in the writing and theorizing of British archaeologist and photographer Alfred Watkins (1855–1935), who, through his study of images and maps and his long walks, observed that many ancient local landmarks could be seen as laying along straight lines.[7] For Watkins, these discoveries indicated the existence of an ancient knowledge about the land that was hidden but could be discovered by the right seeker. The practitioner's guide *The Ley Hunter's Companion: Aligned Ancient Sites; A New Study with Field Guide and Maps* described how in the 1921 moment when Watkins discovered these alignments, he experienced a "flood of ancestral memory."[8] *The Ley Hunter's Companion* begins practically, saying that "leys are alignments of sites which, ley hunters believe, were surveyed and marked in prehistory" before it expands, using its logics to theorize more generally.[9] A section on "Earth Force" reads:

> It can be seen that most branches of Earth Mysteries research finally read out to the fundamental question: is there some as yet undesignated form of natural energy at certain prehistoric sites? The corollary to this is: are ley lines connected with this, as channels of the energy or as a marking system indicating where the

energy flows? If the answer is positive to any of these questions, then it means that at some point in prehistory there was a practical, if instinctive, knowledge of a form of natural science related to the planet, the surrounding cosmic influences and, perhaps, the human mind itself.[10]

For Devereux and the practitioners he writes for, the possibility of this prehistoric practical knowledge of the earth, the cosmos, and the human mind is what motivates their inquiry and interest. It's this hope, and the questioning that accompanies it, that traveled into contemporary metaphysical thinking most from Watkins and the members of his "Old Straight Track Club" who read his books and walked the leys with him; this uncovered knowledge that there is, as Sarah M. Pike articulates it, "power crisscrossing the earth."[11]

This idea of crisscrossed energy has been embraced widely in new age and metaphysical religion, either endeavoring to remain consistent with Alfred Watkins's maps or following different geometries and grids. There are many different grid theories, geometric designs, and associated narratives about what these structures indicate. Practitioner Hugh Newman, in his book *Earth Grids: The Secret Patterns of Gaia's Sacred Sites* (2008), offers a good example, theorizing with geographic information, fault lines, magnetism, electrical force, archaeological information, stories, and other sources to map grids of energy across the earth and then analyze the shapes made where these grids overlap on a map.[12] Newman credits a planetary grid developed by American Bethe Hagens and William Becker for his mapping, as do many others when describing energy grids online. Hagens, an anthropologist by training, has written extensively on the subject of energy grids, geometry, and geomancy from 1984 when she and Becker published "The Planetary Grid: A New Synthesis" in *Pursuit: Journal for the Society for the Investigation of the Unexplained*, putting forth what they called the Unified Vector Geometry grid.[13] Like Watkins and the British ley hunters, Hagens saw cascading meaning within global culture and the physical world, each new line illuminating more knowledge and affinities than the last. In the journal *Anthropology of Consciousness* she writes, "World mythology and religion are replete with evidence of an ancient, eclectic, integrated geometric art/science (geomancy) in which certain principles of shape, numeracy and connection unified the experience of body, mind and essence through metaphors of Earth and the elements, All Beings, and Sky."[14] Hagens goes on to say that "romance with geometric consciousness is how I experience geomancy."[15]

Hagens is not alone in experiencing meaning, rapture, or romance within geomancy and energy grid theorizing. The concept of ley lines and global energy grids have been adopted into popular new age practice, either through

sources like Alfred Watkins, the ley hunters, and Bethe Hagens' Unified Vector Geometry (UVG), or through more general adoption. Susannah Crockford's *Ripples of the Universe* chronicles a community of people who live within
this spiritual culture in Sedona, Arizona. In Crockford's ethnography, as in the
guides made by ley hunters and UVG cartographers, Sedona is understood as
an energy vortex by many, a place where the energetic grids of the earth overlap to release a potent spiritual power. This mapping of an energy vortex is
aligned with people in Sedona's overarching theories about energy. As Crockford explains, "Energy is the central organizing concept of cosmologies of spirituality in Sedona. Everything is energy; it composes the substance of everything in the universe. Energy vibrates at specific frequencies and this creates
the appearance of mass."[16] For the spiritual community in Sedona, everything
is energy, but energy also manifests in place and in natural settings in particular ways. The town is surrounded by rock formations that Sedonans believe
are a result of this energy—that "the vortexes are swirling energy spirals cal-
cifying certain rock formations and other locations in Sedona, imbuing these
physical entities with agency."[17] Crockford writes that her interlocutors can feel
these energy vortexes and that Sedona also draws millions of annual tourists
who seek this experience, sometimes through vortex tours.[18] For Sedonans
and spiritual tourists, the energy is what draws them to Sedona; ultimately a
conviction—held sincerely, playfully, or both—that the earth is mapped with
secret energy and power along invisible lines.

Without a vortex tour—away from the pilgrimage infrastructure of Sedona—
people in North America have historically found, and continue to find, ways
of identifying energy lines themselves. Dowsing is a prominent practice in
this regard, giving people the technology to incentivize themselves to correspondence with the energy of the world or other elements. The practice of
dowsing typically refers to the divining of subterranean water or minerals using a stick or pendulum—a method that was popular before other technologies for discovering where these materials existed. It isn't common now to
hear talk of dowsing outside new age contexts, but dowsing had popular appeal for hundreds of years with everyday people and scientists engaging with it
for their own purposes. In an example from the German context, Warren Dym
chronicles the history of the Freiberg Mining Academy, which was founded in
1765 with the intention of systematizing mining and replacing miner beliefs
and practices with enlightenment sciences but ultimately experimented with
dowsing as a method of finding mineral veins. The Academy, convinced of
dowsing's effectiveness but uneasy with its lack of scientific rigor, wrote a code
of conduct that worked to differentiate between "superstitious and legitimate

practice." Part of this code of conduct theologized that because "God the Almighty is to thank for the blessed gift that the dowsing rod dips for him and is used toward the exposure of crevices, mineral veins, branches, and other such things that are hidden to human eyes under the earth" then the dowser must "in no way misuse it to the harm of his neighbor, and much less perform superstitious things with it." In this historical context, the possible divinity of the powers dowsing interprets wasn't in conflict with the developing sciences of mining. Instead it affirmed those sciences and insisted on similar protocols of handling.[19]

Dowsing practices in North America are legacies of this European history, another example of which can be found in the reflections of French physiologist and Nobel Prize winner Charles Richet (1850–1935), a physiologist enthusiastic about the metaphysical world and about dowsing. In his 1923 book *Thirty Years of Psychical Research; Being a Treatise on Metapsychics* Richet points to the divining rod, or dowsing rod, or pendulum as an ancient technology used for finding minerals or water.[20] Speaking through some case studies and experiments Richet argues that "the movements of the rod are due to the unconscious muscular contractions of the individual holding it. It is therefore averred that subterranean waters and metals deep in the earth or hidden in boxes exert an action on our subconsciousness, and that mysterious action is an unknown physical force, for it is neither humidity, heat, nor electivity."[21] Through Richet's confirmation of the functionality of dowsing, he also articulates two wider theories: that earth things like minerals or water send out a message, and that the human body can receive those messages if sensitive enough. He says: "If natural forces (underground water and metals) exercise an unknown action upon the subconscious mind, there must be unknown vibrations that awaken cryptesthetic sensibility; and we are brought back to the metaphysic that deals with the unknown vibrations of things."[22]

While these historical examples suggest a time when dowsing was a more legible method of engaging with the world and its energies, the contemporary moment includes passionate believers and practitioners of dowsing. The Canadian Society of Questers collaborate to "encourage and promote our natural abilities to locate water, mineral deposits and other information" through what they describe as dowsing, questing/seeking, radiesthesia, and psi and psychic abilities. In describing dowsing, the questers' understandings align with Richet and with people who believe people can be taught to become sensitive to earth elements and forces. Once a practitioner is experienced, the website lists uses for dowsing that are "only limited to the imaginations": "Locate underground water, oil, or minerals . . . find lost articles . . . local archaeological sites . . . locate geopathic zones, ley lines, and radiations . . . locate the flow of energy through a building," among others.[23] The American Society of Dowsers also has training goals and advertised similar uses for dowsing for their members. In *The Ley Hunter's Companion*, Devereux noted the American Society of Dowsers' zeal, explaining, "American dowsers are no less active in these Earth Mysteries than their British counterparts."[24] With their logo, an image of a pendulum hovering over the globe to divine its unseen elements, the American Society of Dowsers point to how the diving done through dowsing is paired with ideas of ley lines, global energy grids, and vortexes.

METAPHYSICAL AMERICA

These energy grid theories and the dowsing that maps them are situated in a wider context in which metaphysics is not peripheral but central to North American religion. Catherine L. Albanese documents this centrality in *A Republic of Mind and Spirit*, writing to correct totalizing narratives that articulate American religion as either oriented solely by evangelicalism or a "state-church denominational religion."[25] Instead, she argues, "Metaphysics is a normal, recurring, and pervasive feature of the American spiritual landscape."[26] One of its central qualities is its addition to these logics of energy I have been describing: "Metaphysicians," Albanese writes, "find a stream of energy flowing from above to below—so powerful and constitutive of their reality that they discover themselves to be, in some sense, made of the same 'stuff.'"[27] The term *metaphysics* in the context of ley lines and energy grids applies both because of its affinities with energy and also because it casts a wide net to include in its topography all kinds of associated ideas, traditions, and obsessions that condition the landscape onto which a ley line would appear: "'cunning' and magical practice in colonial America, spiritualism in the mid-nineteenth century, and occultism in 1875 and after that among former spiritualists, theosophists, and an urban literary and artistic avant-garde on both sides of the Atlantic. Wide enough, too, to give a comfortable home to a small army of meditators, visionaries, would-be mystics, and do-it-yourself religious philosophers who have used abstract language to signal their extra—and post-Christian concerns in spiritualism, Christian Science, New Thought, the New Age, and, now, new spirituality."[28]

All these different traditions and engagements with metaphysics create the conditions that made energy lines crisscrossing the country seem plausible or likely. With their metaphysical kin, ley lines and energy vortexes fit into American cultural cosmologies regarding invisible forces, a kind of "vernacular American poetics" regarding "ineffable enormous power," as Susan Lepselter calls them in *The Resonance of Unseen Things*.[29] In chronicling this unseen resonance, Lepselter engages with people who experience the prominence of UFO stories, threats of UFO abductions, or experiences of abductions. These people, like people who theorize about ley lines and energy vortexes, endeavor to know a vast unknown world through a series of relationships and connections that they discover or construct, a mode Lepselter describes as apophenia: "The experience of perceiving connections between random or unrelated objects."[30]

For Lepselter's interlocutors and for the energy theorists I have been describing, this cognitive approach is not a lapse in judgment; instead, they "begin seeing those things that have become invisible. They foreground the naturalized patterns that normally go without saying."[31] Finding resonance, looking for connections and living within the meaning these affinities make, is both a reaction to the specificities of American culture (and the American West in particular) and an act of political creation. In both the American West and the Canadian West, the experience of settler colonialism and resource extraction, prospecting, the mythos of frontier, bountiful and terrible land, along with other historical and contemporary conditions stimulate and create room for connection making, pattern identifying, and resonance. Lepselter's description of the West articulates the space as ideal conditions for UFO theorizing, which are also ideal for energy theorizing: "The inextricability of the uncanny and the ordinary expressed a particular blend of desire and nostalgia—a mix of otherworldly displacement and the deep specificity of a heavily entextualized, lived-in place in the American West. The ways these discourses came together suggested other kinds of anxiety about colonization and the earth, secrecy and theft, nature and loss, and the vulnerable boundaries of the human body."[32] These conditions are the ones that invite oil into a cosmic story, insisting that settlers and others situate not only oil in their metaphysics but its discovery and extraction too. Religion in America is metaphysical, but it resonates with connections to earth and elements that go beyond the mind. Metaphysical practitioners and theorists' vulnerable bodies live in relation to the land but also to the vast energy (fuel) infrastructure that shapes the space. For some, these are body-mind-land relations often "go without saying," but for others these meanings need to be mapped.

RESONANCES OF OIL IN THE ENERGY GRID

Indeed, metaphysical people *are* incorporating oil into their theorizing of energy grids. In a place like Calgary, as I have described, the prominence of the local energy industry and the work of resource (particularly oil) extraction means that spiritual energy gets collapsed into these other energies. The presence of saturated subsurface reserves of oil in Alberta and the wealth that comes from it give the impression of hidden bounty. The relation to land in these places, oriented by the practice of discovery, yielding, and extraction, also positions seekers as capable spiritual energy miners. For some, the prevalence of oil in Alberta is part of a wider natural bounty of the space that includes naturally occurring spiritual energies. Wholistix wellness shop in Red Deer, Alberta, dedicates a page on their website to what they call "vortex energy," and describe Alberta as "the place where powerful subtle-energy is circulating all around throughout this land. In addition to being beautiful and most bountiful, Alberta, particularly the central region of Alberta, is swirling with vibrant and exciting energy, mystery and magic. . . . A powerful energy vortex!" Here, the material bounty suggests a spiritual bounty waiting to be discovered.

For some metaphysical energy theorists, material oil deposits are also considered part of a dataset that contributes to mapping energetic lines. Planetary grid developer Bethe Hagens has described different indicators for where grids intersect. For example, presence of food, minerals, or "other energies needed by lifeforms" suggests intersection. For Hagens, the grid points allows her to see both "subduction zones" where there is no grid overlap and give an intuitive "feeling that they suck energy—perhaps even emotional energy." While other areas are energetic "expansion zones," suggesting grid intersection. Hagens points to a couple examples of these expansion zones, at important points of the geometric grid she calls dodecahedron: "Point 8 in Alberta and Point 2 near Chernobyl."[33]

Similarly, Hugh Newman uses Alberta's energy to support the rightful placement of energetic lines in his own mapping. Next to an image with many lines intersecting across the United States and congregating in Alberta he writes, "Grid-points 8 and 18: Point 8 is near Buffalo Lake, Alberta, Canada. Large gas and oil reserves, major wheat farming, also with a 5000-year-old 'medicine circle' near Majorville."[34] Meanwhile, Michelle Gibson, whose YouTube video "Relationship between the Planetary Grid, Technology of the Ancient Civilization & the Modern Energy" opened this paper, also sees mineral bounty and oil extraction as confirmation of energetic lines. The tone of Gibson's video differs from the other examples in that her discovery suggests to her that oil companies are aware of these energy lines and ancient infrastructure and intend to access the spiritual power along with the mineral fuel and potentially limit others' access to the spiritual energetic bounty. How energy is theorized here characterizes it temporally as something ancient and universal. The energy sought by oil and gas companies shares an essence with the energy that spiritual ley line theorists seek, such that the use and misuse of that energy is an issue.

While some metaphysical theorists see oil and mineral bounty as evidence of ley lines and energy grids, others theorize oil and its infrastructure as disrupting the flow of ley lines and compromising the spiritual energy of place. One Michigan-based blogger points to Alberta oil coming into the United States through pipelines in such a way. In a post titled "Lines upon the Landscape: Spiritual and Energetic Ramifications of Oil Pipelines and Fracking" the author explains how, while doing her Celtic May Day Beltane ritual in her sacred circle, she had suddenly felt "very, very wrong. Wrong in the deep, gut sense." The author explains that "behind the circle was a ley line (in an energetic sense)" that "created an abundance of positive energy upon the land. This ley line ran a good ½ mile or more. But on Beltane over a year ago, the energies of the line had substantially diminished." She goes on the chronicle her discovery:

> This change had been going on slowly for some time, but this new development was immediate and intense. I knew that a company called Enbridge was putting in an oil pipeline and a compressor station; the pipeline ran less than half a mile from my land and the compressor station was about 3 miles north of my home. I knew that this was the worst kind of oil with a horrific environmental toll—the tar sands oil from Alberta, Canada. But what I didn't know was that that pipeline was turned on that exact day—Beltane of 2014. . . . I investigated the energetics further, and I found that where the now-active pipeline crossed the ley line, the line's energy just stopped, cut off, and that the pipeline was corrupting and weakening the line tremendously.

The author is alarmed by this experience and questions what oil pipelines will do to the other energetic pathways running across the earth. She says, "Like the lines our ancestors once set, these profane oil and gas energy lines are the legacy we leave our ancestors. What energetic pattern do these lines create? What will this new energy line system to do our lands long-term?" She concludes by advising that readers to adjust their fuel/energy used to be more sustainable and, also, to begin doing spiritual energy work to heal the world's energy. People flood the comment section with suggestions and questions about how to heal the energetic lines and share stories about encroachment of extraction into landscapes they know. One commenter, Jennifer, writes, "I knew something was wrong, I could feel it. The energy from my childhood lake is weak. . . . Time for me to investigate further."[35] This theorizing characterizes oil energy as different from the spiritual energies of ley lines, such that its profane power can corrupt the ancient power of the other earth energetics of that land.

In addition to these two dynamics—oil as evidence for energetic bounty and oil infrastructure corrupting energy lines—there is one more dynamic that positions ley lines and oil in relationship: energy lines and spiritual energy generally as data for finding and extracting oil through dowsing. This was a prominent phenomenon historically—as the example of the dowsing miners of Freiberg suggests—when it was difficult to determine where it would be most expedient to start digging or drilling. The Alberta government highlights this practice on its website "Alberta's Energy Heritage Resources" on the page titled "Petroleum Geology." During a time when oil emerging on the land itself was the only way to speculate about oil's subterranean presence, the website text explains that "there were a number of other theories—scientific, numerological, mythological and even religious—that claimed to be able to predict the presence of oil."[36] The author seems deeply uncomfortable with this, however, and immediate says this had "spotty" results before seeming to concede that "there have been claims that dowsing or divining, using a forked rod to detect underground reservoirs, was used with some success through the 1920s, but only for locating the presence of oil, not for determining its quantity or depth."[37]

Skepticism about the success of dowsing for oil doesn't seem to have reduced the cultural impact of the practice in Alberta, nor did it in the wider North American context. Alicia Puglionesi describes the spiritual awakening that came along with the initial days of oil extraction in the early 1800s in Petrolia, Pennsylvania, where "the discovery of oil only heightened the feeling that another world was close at hand, just below the surface of things. The earth," she writes, "was teeming with invisible forces, if one only tapped in."[38] These were the conditions under which Puglionesi describes oil dowsing as rising to prominence. The expertise of so-called "oil wizard[s]" were deferred to; a "motley class of diviners, penetrating the earth with occult energies and elaborate visions, claimed to sense the crevices and caverns where oil lurked."[39] Dowsing, in this context, was the "most popular method of wizardry. . . . Dowsers held a forked stick from a hazel or peach tree and walked until the stick dipped and lurched, pointing like a compass needle to oil."[40]

Like the concerned web text writer on the Alberta government website, people in the nineteenth and twentieth centuries moved between skepticism and respect for this practice as yet undefined science. Puglionesi describes a journalist named William Wright who, remarking on a tour of Petrolia, "was not a believer" but who "despite his skepticism . . . 'had to acknowledge the existence of the phenomenon for which he could not account,' explaining it as 'magnetic influence, or some other cause.'"[41] The prominent twentieth-century dowser Evelyn Penrose reflected on this uncertainty in a 1932 article on dowsing for *Blackwood's Magazine* writing from her experience as the provincial government of British Columbia's "official water-diviner." After describing her position's beginning as being greeted with both excitement and skepticism she explains that the innate gift of the ability to dowse is "generally to be found amongst the peasant and uneducated classes, and this is probably why divining has always been reckoned amongst the unaccountable phenomena."[42] Penrose, however, understands dowsing to be accountable and undertakes this in her work for the government: "It is one of the main reasons why I was so pleased to accept this post," she says, "as I knew I should have unlimited opportunities of putting my theories to a varied and severe test and of making further discoveries."[43] For some theorists and skeptics, the earth energies were part of a set of natural laws that were undiscovered, and dowsing and spiritual practices of discovery were accessing these laws without knowledge of their function.

This is where dowsing continues to exist in the contemporary context: spiritually potent, effective for practitioners, and undescribed by scientific forms of knowledge-making. The particular practice of oil dowsing continues to be a subject of interest for contemporary dowsers like those in the Canadian Society of Questors and the American Dowsing Society. Castle Books publishes a guide, *The Art of Dowsing*, which teaches how to find oil, among other things. "When we are dowsing for water or oil," it reads, "we do not know exactly where we will find it. But the universal mind knows, as it knows everything."[44] Guidance is also offered on how to dowse for oil through the societies. An Albertan website Mirrorwaters directs readers to the Greater Boston Chapter of Dowers' website to learn from "Master dowser Joe Smith," who had uploaded a document on the subject. Here he explains how to dowse for oil using a pendulum and a map, emphasizing the importance of asking very specific questions of the pendulum or rod because there is so much oil underground. "Some people," he says "can get down level with the map and actually see energy lines coming from the map. I'm not that good. I trust my pendulum above all else."[45]

The tone of Joe's guide and the open invitation of the various dowsing and questing societies suggest that anyone can learn to read energy lines or dowse. The world is filled with sacred energy, intersections of energy lines reveal opportunities to correspond with the macrocosm throughout the globe, and ley hunters travel about seeking them. Access to the sacred, to belonging, in these theories is open to everyone everywhere. The implicit argument of this energy theorizing is that it doesn't matter who you are or where you are, the energy can be yours.

POWERLINES

This democratizing gesture is present across the diversity of ley line theorists; their knowledge is esoteric but not secret, and many—from Michelle Gibson in her YouTube video to Evelyn Penrose dowsing for oil in British Columbia— would consider equal opportunity for finding power and resources import- ant. These treasures belong to the person who can find them. This reasoning shows another entanglement between oil and the hidden spiritual powers of energy lines in North America: the believed righteousness of discovery and use. The idea that North American bounty, spiritual or material, is available to anyone who can find it is a quality of the region's violent history of forcing Indigenous people from their land and communities and evicting their lan- guages and knowledge of place. The metaphysical tradition of energy grids, despite its universalizing language and invitation for people to take up their theories and technologies for seeing and harnessing energy, is situated in this wider settler-colonial understanding of land and time. This context of a wider interest in discovery as acquisition is a quality of the neoliberal conditions of North American life, insisting at every turn that a person's relations—to family, to community, to the land—matter less than aspiration and profit.

In relation to oil extraction, ley lines, energy grids, energy vortexes, and dowsing practices are theorized, to return to Lepselter, in "the deep specific- ity of a heavily entextualized, lived-in place in the American West."[46] Here, In- digenous people, the land and waters they have lived with, and imaginaries of ancient peoples (who, in the theorizing of some ley hunters, may or may not be related to the living Indigenous people in the present) are all potent sym- bols and narratives for the wider quest. Indigenous people and their knowl- edge are used by these metaphysical theorists to tell a story about the world that has nothing to do with their own stories and experiences. Crockford as- serts this reality in regard to the "sacred space" of Sedona. Crockford writes, "The physical and sacred space is reinscribed with a new religious history, re- writing and co-opting Indigenous history and practice, and claiming what has been stolen and settled as rightful inheritance."[47] One can read this happening in real time in *The Ley Hunter's Companion* when the author offers his readers a report from America: "T. Edward Ross II, president of the American Society of Dowsers, has stated that members of his society have undertaken 'dowsing forays' to the ancient mounds, Indian ritual areas, and other sacred sites of paleo-Indian and pre-Columbian America. Much of this work, says Ross, has confirmed the correlation of leys, blind springs, and sacred sites, reinforcing British findings."[48] This dynamic—using the lives, land, histories, and spirituality of different Indigenous communities to "reinforce British findings"—is replicated in the histories of resource extraction. Puglionesi notes how "promoters of the early oil industry also anchored their new power in the Indigenous past," in multiple ways, but "most explicitly, Spiritualist mediums claimed to channel Indian spirits from the afterlife, who told them where to drill profitable wells."[49]

The thinking of individuals who theorize about ley lines and earth energies enchants the North American landscape with spiritual ideas about the connection between people, land, and energy that are always in conversation with natural and supernatural resources. In reading how these theorists understand and situate oil and its extraction we have a glimpse into how spiritual and thermodynamic energy are being theorized in conversation with each other in this kind of knowledge-making. These thinkers take metaphysical analysis, experimentation, and mapping as central to understanding a reality that encompasses natural laws and spiritual laws that have not yet been entirely defined, leaving room for the thinker to build a personal relationship to this knowledge and, as a result, this energy. In the wider North American public, this intellectual and spiritual project is not at the forefront of how people think and talk about energy. However, while wider metaphysics of energy are not outwardly discussed, they are still present, positioning people, land, energy, and spirit in relation. Ley line theorists articulate a theory of energy in a way that reveals the unvoiced presence of other theories of energy. What might be shared between ley line theorizing and wider energy theories? The world is a net of powerlines—energy infrastructures like pipelines, roads, and electric wires—and it is governed by lines of other kinds of power that intersect with this infrastructure: political, spiritual, and cultural. Ley line thinkers illustrate how all maps of these intersecting powers are also always theories about the world.

NOTES

1. Michelle Gibson, "Relationship between the Planetary Grid, Technology of the Ancient Civilzation & the Modern Energy," July 16, 2018, YouTube video, 09:26.

2. Catherine L. Albanese, *A Republic of Mind and Spirit: A Cultural History of American Metaphysical Religion* (New Haven, CT: Yale University Press, 2007), 4.

3. Catherine L. Albanese, "Introduction: Awash in a Sea of Metaphysics," *Journal of the American Academy of Religion* 75, no. 3 (2007): 582–88.

4. Albanese, *Republic of Mind and Spirit*, 14.

5. Alicia Puglionesi, *In Whose Ruins: Power, Possession, and the Landscapes of American Empire* (New York: Scribner, 2022), 8.

6. Albanese, *Republic of Mind and Spirit*, 36.

7. *Oxford Dictionary of National Biography*, s.v. "Watkins, Alfred (1855–1935)," by R. G. Fellowes, accessed March 6, 2023."

8. Paul Devereux, *The Ley Hunter's Companion: Aligned Ancient Sites; A New Study with Field Guide and Maps* (London: Thames and Hudson, 1979), 9.

9. Devereux, *Ley Hunter's Companion*, 7.

10. Devereux, *Ley Hunter's Companion*, 68.

11. Sarah M. Pike, *New Age and Neopagan Religions in America* (New York: Columbia University Press, 2004).

12. Hugh Newman, *Earth Grids: The Secret Patterns of Gaia's Sacred Sites* (Glastonbury, UK: Wooden Books, 2008).

13. William Becker and Bethe Hagens, "The Planetary Grid: A New Synthesis," Vortex Maps (website), 2021.

14. Bethe Hagens, "The Divine Feminine in Geometric Consciousness," *Anthropology of Consciousness* 17, no. 1 (2006): 1.

15. Hagens, "Divine Feminine," 7.

16. Susannah Crockford, *Ripples of the Universe: Spirituality in Sedona, Arizona* (Chicago: University of Chicago Press, 2021).

17. Crockford, *Ripples of the Universe*, 35.

18. Crockford, *Ripples of the Universe*, 35, 8.

19. Warren Dym, "Scholars and Miners: Dowsing and the Freiberg Mining Academy," *Technology and Culture* 49, no. 4 (2008): 842–43.

20. Charles Robert Richet, *Thirty Years of Psychical Research: Being a Treatise on Metapsychics* (New York: MacMillan, 1923), 228.

21. Richet, *Thirty Years*, 235.

22. Richet, *Thirty Years*, 233

23. "Dowsing FAQ" and "About Us," Canadian Society of Questers website, 2023.

24. Devereux, *Ley Hunter's Companion*, 68.

25. Albanese, *Republic of Mind and Spirit*, 2.

26. Albanese, *Republic of Mind and Spirit*, 16.

27. Albanese, *Republic of Mind and Spirit*, 6.

28. Albanese, "Introduction," 583.

29. Susan Lepselter, *The Resonance of Unseen Things: Poetics, Power, Captivity, and UFOs in the American Uncanny* (Ann Arbor: University of Michigan Press, 2016), 1.

30. Lepselter, *Resonance of Unseen Things*, 3.

31. Lepselter, *Resonance of Unseen Things*, 4.

32. Lepselter, *Resonance of Unseen Things*, 11.

33. Bethe Hagens, "Planetary Grid Update," 1987, Vortex Maps (website), 2021.

34. Newman, *Earth Grids*.

35. Dana O'Driscoll, "Lines upon the Landscape: Spiritual and Energetic Ramifications of Oil Pipelines and Fracking," *Druid's Garden* (blog), June 15, 2022.

36. "Petroleum Geology," Alberta's Energy Resources Heritage, government of Alberta website, 2023.

37. "Petroleum Geology."

38. Puglionesi, *In Whose Ruins*, 103.

39. Puglionesi, *In Whose Ruins*, 104.

40. Puglionesi, *In Whose Ruins*, 105.

41. Puglionesi, *In Whose Ruins*, 105.

42. Evelyn Penrose, "Dowsing," *Blackwoods's Magazine* 232 (1932): 346.

43. Penrose, "Dowsing," 346.

44. Richard Webster, *The Art of Dowsing: The Art of Discovering Water, Treasure, Gold, Oil, Artifacts* (Edison, NJ: Castle Books, 2001), 82.

45. "Joe Smith's Dowsing Stories Corner," Greater Boston Chapter of Questers website, 2005.

46. Lepselter, *Resonance of Unseen Things*, 11.

47. Crockford, *Ripples of the Universe*, 35.

48. Devereux, *Ley Hunter's Companion*, 68.

49. Puglionesi, *In Whose Ruins*, 11.

A Disciplined Wilderness

Nostalgia at Midcentury Evangelical Summer Camp

Sarah Hedgecock

Jacky Everett, a teenager in Richmond, Virginia, knew exactly when she first became "serious about Christ": November 1972, when she attended a weekend retreat at her local Young Life camp. She spent the next eight months "reading and learning about God" before going to a weeklong summer camp with the same organization in the summer of 1973. In a letter to Tom Raley, one of Young Life's regional directors, she wrote, "The knowledge and understanding that I discovered about my relationship with God last week far surpasses what I had learned in those eight months."[1] For Everett, summer camp had succeeded in its mission: to create evangelical youth by isolating them in a nostalgic, all-Christian environment—and causing them to be nostalgic for that environment themselves.

The nostalgia baked into a camping environment that gestured toward the myth of manifest destiny and the transformation of allegedly unpeopled wilderness into a Christian America; nostalgia for this imagined Christian America would, theoretically, make former campers want to recreate it in their lives outside of camp. Nostalgia is affectively central to white American evangelicalism, undergirding other affective modes like fear and sentimentality, which are themselves grounded in temporality. But more than affect, it is an affective *practice*, and thus the exploration of nostalgia at evangelical summer camp offers opportunities to consider what other affective practices do in other religious environments.

Summer camps for American children and adolescents had their inception in the late nineteenth century with an aim to, in the words of historian Leslie Paris, "physically and morally invigorate" largely urban campers in their time off from school.[2] This moral reinvigoration was not necessarily reliant on an explicitly religious approach, although many early summer camps were started by organizations such as the YMCA. For the first several decades of the movement, most summer camps attracted middle-class Protestant boys and explicitly forbade Jewish campers from attending. Despite not explicitly aiming to bring about conversions like their successors did, these early summer camps engaged in an ambient Protestantism that inevitably impacted ideas about what camp was and what it was for. As the movement grew, camps diversified, often exclusively: camps were opened specifically for girls, or Jewish campers, or the children of immigrants, or members of particular organizations. Thus, although summer camps as a category may have diversified, the camps themselves often engaged some particular clientele, forming "villages" of campers who shared something in common in a way that did not naturally occur in most campers' diverse urban environments—to both their benefit and their detriment.[3] This trend continued through the rise of the already-segregated suburbs and, with them, the increasing percentage of suburban summer camp participants; it was largely from this suburban contingent that Young Life and Pioneer Girls, the two networks of evangelical summer camps explored here, drew their camping populations.

Regardless of their particular markets, however, summer camps all had in common the promotion of a "carefree childhood," a middle-class ideal (regardless of campers' actual economic positionality) that began to be cemented around the same time the summer camp movement began.[4] This was especially true in the post–World War II era, with the increasing prevalence of intensive child-rearing. Summer camp presented an opportunity to use a nostalgic idea of childhood to create good middle-class citizens. Evangelical summer camps took this idea and added it a nationalistic, proselytizing religious character, aiming to create not only citizens but Christians, and even evangelists.

Although the broader (ambiently Christian) summer camp movement began in the 1880s, evangelical summer camps of the type examined here only hit the scene in the 1940s and 1950s. Although camps were variously started by denominations and nondenominational parachurch organizations, the former tended to have a large amount of independence, placing them in what Rebecca A. Koerselman has called a "unique space between parachurch organizations and denominational structures."[5] Regardless of their links with particular denominations, then—and the specific camps examined here had none—evangelical summer camps functioned something like a separate category of parachurch organization, helping bind together evangelicalism as a pandenominational identity and orienting it toward a focus on children and youth through a critical nostalgia oriented around both children themselves and the wilderness environment in which they were placed for stretches of the summer.

The mid-twentieth-century United States saw an explosion of youth-centric evangelical programming, including the rise of Christian summer camp. Evangelicalism is definitionally complex. There sometimes seem to be as many definitions of evangelicalism as there are scholars who study it but, as Molly Worthen has noted, as an analytical term, "we are stuck with it."[6] I use "evangelicalism" to describe the relational form of Protestant Christianity that Daniel Silliman has described as "anyone who likes Billy Graham."[7] That is to say, evangelicalism is about feelings and relationships, not only between the believer and Jesus or the believer and the Bible (although those are the core relationships in question), but also believers and each other, and believers and potential future believers. Because of its emphasis on the individual, centers of gravity tended not to be denominations (considered divisive) but parachurch organizations that worked across denominations and nondenominational churches.[8] Called neo-evangelicalism by Graham and others, the new movement, which began around the end of World War II, emphasized the individual-relationship approach to Jesus and scripture, drawing on an affective emphasis from evangelical prehistory and a renewed focus on evangelism. Though this new evangelicalism has frequently been portrayed as a clean break with a previous reclusive fundamentalism, it is more accurate to consider it in terms of a reorientation.[9]

The youth parachurch programs that bound evangelicalism together treated children and especially teenagers as a population unto themselves, with their own needs and desires—and with the unique potential to carry the new American evangelical movement into its next era.[10] To do this, they employed nostalgia as an affective practice toward creating an envisioned better future. I date this evangelical nostalgic practice to the same postwar era to which I date modern American evangelicalism itself, when movement leaders began to organize around the restoration of a (theoretical) harmonious former Christian America.[11] The nostalgia had a number of focuses, including nostalgia for the innocence and potential of childhood, nostalgia for some imagined simpler time, and nostalgia for the early church. Evangelical summer camps harnessed all of these into a critical nostalgia aimed at forming the next generation of American Christianity.

Critical nostalgia, as coined by Shannon Lee Dawdy, entails using objects and practices from an idealized past as a roadmap for the future.[12] What is being restored is not a copy-and-paste version of that past; rather, it is its perceived virtues, which are only accessible by emulating aspects of the past in which those virtues originate. Like narratives about childhood, critical nostalgia is always future-minded. Evangelical summer camp in the mid-twentieth century, two parachurch-affiliated networks of which I explore here, employed critical nostalgia for two different stories: the biblical tradition of the wilderness and the evangelical narrative of some past Christian America. Lauren R. Kerby has attributed stories like these to "white evangelicals' hunger for a national myth of origin in which they play a starring role."[13] Summer camp provided myths not only of origin but of national redemption. As wilderness fantasy, camp provided an opportunity to enact stories about Christian struggle and redemption in a controlled environment. Meanwhile, it also provided an all-Christian community by reviving an idealized all-Christian past to create a model of evangelized Christian community for campers to bring back into the "real world." Further, in doing so, these camps constructed for campers the idea of "the world" itself, defined against the idealized summer camp environment. Although the phrase "in the world, but not of the world" had not yet become iconic evangelical shorthand, summer camps in this period exemplified the aphorism.

This is not the first place where references to the outdoors and to Christian America have converged in evangelical nostalgic practice. Christian summer camps, especially in the mid-twentieth century, threw back to referents including camp meetings and tent revivals. They also enacted, and trained campers to enact, a form of modern-day manifest destiny, bringing Christianity into (a fantasy of) untamed nature in order to then bring it to a fallen world. Using materials from Young Life and Pioneer Girls summer camps during the Cold War era, this paper explores how summer camps employed these heritages to form the next generation of the movement.

A WORLD APART

Scholars of summer camp tend to characterize camp in one of two ways: as a site of nostalgia for some kind of pure humanity, and as a blank slate on which to build a new and better way of life.[14] Evangelical summer camps took a little of both, envisioning a week at camp as a kind of Eden—the innocent, pure blank slate (devoid of Indigenous or any other human presence) at the beginning of the white American evangelical historical imaginary, elements of which could then be brought back into campers' normal lives once they were properly taught through a pedagogy of nostalgia. The camps explored here followed similar models:

campers would arrive from around the camp's geographic region at the beginning of the week and be placed in a rustic, bunk bed–filled cabin based on their age and gender. This cabin would be the group with whom campers would spend the bulk of their time, including not only meals and outdoor activities like canoeing and hiking but also chores and evening Bible study. While Bible study was incorporated throughout the day and week, typically a camper would be scheduled to spend time alone each morning praying and contemplating a Bible verse in nature and in the evening discussing an often-different passage with her cabinmates. The week at camp typically culminated in an all-camp bonfire and altar call to cap off the week.

For this research, I examined materials from two large evangelical youth organizations, Pioneer Girls and Young Life, both of which ran networks of summer camps (and still do today). The bulk of these materials were written by adults: staff training materials, guides for counselors, promotional pamphlets advertising the results of camp to potential donors or the excitement of camp to children and teenagers, although I do use materials written by campers themselves, like Jacky Everett, where I can. This research thus focuses primarily on the goals and pedagogy of evangelical summer camp rather than its lived experience. Even the children who do appear in the archive are largely mediated: their letters were considered exemplary or otherwise important enough for adult recipients to keep, or to publish in a newsletter. This mediation further speaks to the ultimate goals of camp by forcing the question of why these particular child-authored materials survive and what purpose they may have served.

I primarily look at camps from the 1950s through 1970s, when the evangelical summer camp movement was in full swing, although both organizations opened their first summer camps in the mid-1940s and the archives I examine contain materials through the early 1980s. In addition to marking one high point of evangelical youth culture, this period also covers the three middle decades of the Cold War and social justice movements in the United States including the Civil Rights Movement, the American Indian Movement, and the rise of second-wave feminism. In the camping materials examined here, none of these international and national developments are addressed directly; rather, the adults promoting the camps and writing pedagogical materials seem to have preferred a more oblique approach, portraying the summer camp environment as distinct from the world in which these events were occurring. What materials I could find from campers themselves followed suit. In this way, Christian summer camp was portrayed not quite as a walled garden but certainly as a kind of Eden: an ideal environment that was both already past and would inevitably become past once the week at camp was over.

During the Cold War, the air was thick with concern about imminent nuclear war. In this context, summer camps were in a position to pivot and train campers in wilderness skills they may need after the end of the world. However, in reality, summer camps both secular and religious more frequently presented the outdoors and the camping experience in terms of a lost past that, if regained, could redeem the present. One thirteen-year-old conveyed this in the pages of a 1966 Pioneer Girls publication, writing in a poem, "If only the world could rest here / We'd have our problems solved in a year."[15] The version of Eden presented at these evangelical summer camps was a nationalistic one, inspired by the myth of manifest destiny. White American westward expansion was a major part of popular culture throughout the period explored here, particularly children's culture; *Davy Crockett* ran on ABC from 1954 to 1955, and *Little House on the Prairie* premiered in 1974. This was likely compounded by Young Life and Pioneer Girls' origins in Texas and the Midwest, respectively, both centers of gravity for the white American mythology of the taming (and Christianizing) of untouched wilderness.

This nostalgia for the purity of nature was part of a long American tradition, much of it religious even if not always part of the evangelicalism that is my focus here. The creation myth of white people in America, after all, begins with the Puritans' "errand into the wilderness"—one of a few such narratives that were especially popular as the United States found its new place in the Cold War world order.[16] The American wilderness myth continued through Ralph Waldo Emerson, Henry David Thoreau, and the transcendentalists' spiritual attachment to unspoiled nature; manifest destiny and the white settling of the American frontier (the other narrative popular during this period); and the religious imperatives behind the creation of the national parks system.[17] Indeed, even putting aside the evangelical character of the summer camps discussed here, reverence for a certain version of the outdoors that downplay or ignore the land's long habitation by Indigenous communities have long been part of American civil religion. As such, by the Cold War era it was important to pass on beliefs and practices around the ideal of unspoiled American nature to the children who would carry those traditions into the future, in contrast to the industrialized Soviet threat. The central figures in these American wilderness narratives were (largely) white and (often) male, bent on setting out into an imagined unpeopled natural environment to simultaneously conquer it and use it to access spiritual truths about the American continent. Both are themes worth bearing in mind when considering the use of wilderness in all summer camps, and especially those evangelical camps whose end goal was conquering America for Christ.

Literary scholar Emily A. Murphy has proposed that, prior to the Cold War, Americans broadly understood their national identity through a lens of innocence, comparing the nation to a child in ways both implicit and explicit.[18] But after two world wars, Murphy argues, the country (or at least the country's educated elite) registered that loss of innocence in a transformation of identity, with literature of the era tending more toward adolescent protagonists struggling toward adulthood. A large component of that identity transformation was a nostalgia for the vanishing figure of the rural child in the face of a modern industrialized society. Considered in this light, the rapid rise of summer camp as an important part of American childhood makes sense, as adults figuratively sent their children into the lost past in order to create Americans who could redeem the future. For evangelicals, this past was not only wholesome but specifically Christian, whether a past Christian America (often imagined as part of the frontier, rid of any existing Indigenous presence) or the wilderness of the biblical past engaged by everyone from Abraham to Jesus Christ.

The summer camp materials I examine here rarely use the term *wilderness* explicitly, instead turning to less loaded terms such as *nature* and *the outdoors*. It is nevertheless the term I use here precisely *because* it is loaded with the theology and history that the evangelical summer camp enterprise leaned on to create its nostalgic pedagogical environment. Nostalgia for a once and future Christian society was at the heart of the project, but wilderness has long been a part of American Christian narratives. The story of manifest destiny–tinged white Christian wilderness mythology goes back to Methodist circuit riders spreading the gospel in isolated white frontier communities and, most significant to the evangelical story, camp revivals. These multiday outdoor church meetings became popular in the early nineteenth century and were a particular marker of the early evangelical movement.[19] Despite the fact that camp meetings and summer camp represent two apparently different strands of evangelical experience, the weeklong structure of most such camps was, in fact, inspired by the camp revival tradition.[20] This genealogy is worth bearing in mind especially in the context of evangelical nostalgia and its relationship to both wilderness and the idea of a Christian America.

The two youth parachurch organizations I focus on here had slightly different approaches, but their aims and in particular their camping environments were largely the same. Young Life was incorporated in Texas in 1941.[21] The organization began as an after-school Christian club for teenagers, geared toward both those who attended church and the as yet unreached, as Young Life leadership characterized those who did not practice Christianity. Even before any camping became involved, Young Life was described as a "series of tent meetings for young people," hearkening back to a great age of American Christian revival.[22] The organization bought its first summer camp property, near Colorado Springs, in 1946, with a second nearby camp following just three years later.[23] Today, Young Life runs around thirty-two camps across the United States, though camps also exist in Scotland, Nicaragua, the Dominican Republic, Armenia, and Canada, home to the Malibu Club, which Young Life has run as a summer camp since 1953.[24]

Pioneer Girls, founded as Girls Guild in Wheaton, Illinois, in 1939 by students at Wheaton College and using the Pioneer Girls name by 1941, was a kind of evangelical Girl Scouts catering to girls from elementary all the way through high school. While the organization did encourage missionary work abroad in the Wheaton tradition, it was more focused in its day-to-day work on local youth outreach. It was a no-boys-allowed affair until the 1980s, when the organization began experimenting with a small number of coed groups. The renamed Pioneer Clubs is now fully coed, although within that model many single-gender clubs do exist. Like Young Life, Pioneer Girls also expanded into camping early on. The organization held its first summer camp in Aurora, Illinois, in 1940.[25] By 1973 it ran twenty-three camps across the United States and Canada, concentrated in the Midwest and Northeast but present in all four time zones; that number is down to just six camps today.[26] From the beginning, every camp under the Pioneer Girls/Clubs umbrella has been called Camp Cherith, after a refreshing stream found in 1 Kings.[27]

Both organizations were pointedly nondenominational, on the theory that general evangelizing among youth (and using themes that would appeal to them) was more important than sticking to the rules of any one denomination. This also describes evangelicalism as a whole at this time, making these youth organizations a significant proving ground for the new evangelicalism.[28] Though for much of its history Pioneer Girls groups met primarily in Baptist churches, many other denominations were also represented, and the organization emphasized "Christ in every phase of a girl's life" over membership in any specific church.[29] Young Life, too, took pains to position itself outside of any one denomination. Indeed, in 1960, almost twenty years after its founding, it faced a major crisis when the Presbytery of Northeast Texas (part of the United Presbyterian Church in the United States of America, a large mainline denomination) condemned the organization for siphoning off its youth from denominationally specific activities.[30] Ultimately, however, it was by positioning themselves alongside other nondenominational evangelical organizations, rather than within any one church, that both parachurch youth organizations were able to pursue their missions of evangelizing both Christian and not-yet-Christian youth.

When developing their summer camps, both organizations tended to buy properties that had already been built, whether as secular camps, retreat centers, or some other place to live in nature. Thus, rather than civilizing the wilderness whole-cloth in the most straightforward manner of the manifest destiny narrative, these camps instead Christianized that mythic foundation, helped along by early sites being located in the actual American West, and oriented it around impressionable children and adolescents.[31] The population of each summer camp session was drawn from members and friends of members in existing Young Life or Pioneer Girls groups in the camp's geographic region, bringing together campers who may have already known each other with those with whom potentially lasting friendships could be formed across club lines.[32] These relationships could be intense, and one Pioneer Girls handbook refers to each cabin group as a camper's "cabin family."[33] Such intensity, however, was not unusual for summer camps, and in fact was part of the foundation of the summer camp project. The difference was that rather than merely forming good citizens to improve the world, evangelical camps aimed to form good *Christians* to *transform* the world.

A NEW (OLD) COMMUNITY

One way summer camp has been described is as a kind of tabula rasa; in the words of historian Björn Lundberg, it "offered an abstract space . . . that could be filled with meaning to counterbalance urban modernity."[34] Camp not only represented a pastoral past but also served as a "place beyond civilization or culture," theoretically creating an opportunity for campers to build an ideal society from the ground up. In the case of evangelical summer camps, this idealized society was pointedly Christian, a short-term wilderness utopia. Christianity was, in fact, essential to this utopian project: as individuals are reborn in Christ, so society could be reborn at summer camp.

Adults working for both Young Life and the Pioneer Girls (and, for that matter, elsewhere) were ready to note the bad influences of the world on malleable children and teenagers. One Young Life counselor orientation handbook articulates a bleak view of the camper population, noting that "the teenager is the product of two inheritances; one being the state of inability and sin inherited from Adam, and the other being the sum total of the influences that bear upon his life."[35] Those influences, articulated here and in sundry other materials about the Christian youth of America in this period, include conformity-driven peers, "slick" magazines and obscene literature, materialistic social values, and potentially domineering or else too-lenient parents. Read in this light, camp's removal from civilization's negative influences offered a chance to jump-start campers' lives as Christians without the complicating factors that might arise even in an after-school youth group.

Generally summer camps, and not just Christian ones, relied on the idea that campers could be best set up for success if they started in a nebulously premodern environment; such a propitious beginning could apparently prime them for it within the week. For evangelical camps, this success was specifically understood as religious: creating a new society also entailed creating a new person, and Christianizing the child and the wilderness could ultimately, through campers' nostalgia for the Christian world of camp, lead to Christianizing the actual world. This often meant the suburban American world from which campers were pulled: stories abound of campers returning with a desire to convert other students at their schools or members of their own families.[36]

The premodern ideal across camps both religious and not goes part of the way to showing that summer camp has long been both a vehicle for and an object of white American nostalgia. It is the former—the tendency to valorize camp as a return to the freedom of pastoralism—that drove most of the summer camp project, but especially for evangelicals, the latter also played its role. Leslie Paris has written of the early twentieth-century summer camp movement, "Camp advocates aimed to return children to rural environments, in the context not of productive labor but of productive leisure."[37] This "return" functioned as a manifestation of critical nostalgia. This form of nostalgia—much like the raising of children—has been described by Ray Cashman as "future-oriented": despite its reference to the past, it aims to critique the present and to build whatever the practitioner sees is a better future.[38] In terms of summer camp, this past is the carefree, preindustrial time that hearkens back to the Romantics and transcendentalists and is negatively contrasted with the urban, scheduled, mechanized postindustrial era. If they could inculcate a love of disappearing wilderness in the next generation, early summer camp creators believed, then that next generation would then have the knowledge to create a better future.

The idea of the wilderness disappearing was the key to the nostalgia at the heart of the summer camp enterprise. Camp inculcated a nostalgia for a past that neither campers nor their parents or counselors had actually experienced. Indeed, especially during the Cold War era examined here, with even Alaska and Hawaii having reached statehood or close to it, manifest destiny as it applied to the American continent (as space) wasn't an option anymore, so camps employed nostalgia for it toward the new project of manifest destiny as it applied to the world (as mind-set). For evangelicals, this manifest destiny mind-set was especially salient. Kerby has argued that, for white evangelicals, "the past provides a blueprint for how things ought to be: Christians running a Christian nation."[39] Thus, a narrative of civilizing (and Christianizing) the American continent by sending pioneers out into the wilderness was easily applied to the present: bringing children into the wilderness to affectively re-enact the imagined Christianizing activities of their forebears. This, then, cre-ated another kind of nostalgia: the children's own nostalgia for summer camp, where they enjoyed an idyllic, rustic Christian America—a Christian America they may themselves, in another critical-nostalgic turn, have then been moti-vated to create in the "real world." Evangelical summer camps not only were built on nostalgia, then, but also created a pedagogy of nostalgia to inculcate this value within the next generation.

In addition to the nostalgia for a vague past that is part of the general sum-mer camp project, evangelical summer camps practiced other nostalgias in-formed by evangelical Christianity. One of these is nostalgia for a biblical past and desire to become close to the feeling of the early church. Evangelicals have long enacted this biblical-critical nostalgia in their rejection of so-called smells, bells, and other accretions of church history; their (allegedly) straightforward reading of scripture; and their widely reported feelings of embattlement. Even during the Cold War's fight against godless Communism, that fight was some-times envisioned as a modern-day version of early Christians being oppressed by pagan Rome. One 1968 Pioneer Girls Bible study guide contains a table, under a "Paul's World" heading, characterizing the religious situation as "Pa-gan majority; Christianity—new dynamic force," which contrasted with "Our World" characteristics such as "Committed Christians a minority; Christianity often stagnant" and "World outside the West largely pagan."[40]

This biblical nostalgia has been enacted as critical nostalgia in the prev-alence of contemporary music at worship services and the rise of home churches in the present.[41] I argue that it is, and has been in the past, also prac-ticed in the world of church camp. The entirely Christian society of the evan-gelical summer camp had the potential to create the kind of evangelical com-munity that was impossible to achieve in once-a-week services, or even in a midcentury evangelical environment increasingly saturated with new para-church organizations. Summer camp's employment of a wilderness fantasy, in particular, evokes two distinct strands of evangelical nostalgia: the biblical wilderness as a place for the believer to be challenged and eventually achieve a closer relationship with God, and the early American wilderness at the heart of the Christianizing mission of manifest destiny (narratives that are, of course, not unrelated). In both narratives, wilderness presents an opportunity to take on the Great Commission, and engagement with that allegedly unpeopled wilderness ends in the salvation of the believer and, sometimes, the world.

A third strand of nostalgia also plays a role in the project of evangelical summer camp: adults' nostalgia for childhood itself. As other scholars have noted, children represent a key tension for adults: they are both the product of a fallen past and the embodied hope for a better future.[42] They are, as Anne Higonnet has noted, *inevitably* objects of nostalgia: they bring to mind adults' own lives as children, which they tend to conceive as perfectly innocent compared to where they are in life now.[43] These characteristics, utopian future plus object of nostalgia, make childhood an ideal site for adults to practice critical nostalgia—and summer camp, with its image as a controlled yet somehow also untamed wilderness, an ideal location to do it.

Children and teenagers also occupy a special place within American evangelicalism. Their status as future redeemers of the world notably led, in the Cold War era and after, to a focus on them within the movement, driven by a fear of what might happen were they to grow up wrong.[44] This very fear of a potential lost future, however, concomitantly fed into a nostalgia for the purity of childhood, free from the worries of the future. These strands of nostalgia all combined at summer camp, with adults nostalgic for childhood using nostalgia to teach children and teenagers how to be nostalgic themselves, all to build toward a more Christian future.

Not all of the children and teenagers in this archive are real. Some may have been fictionalized versions of real campers, while others appear to have been invented whole-cloth by adults working to promote their summer camps to either patrons or potential future campers. Nevertheless, even these imaginary campers are of interest, particularly in how they show both adults' goals for summer camp and the nostalgia of those adults for the kind of childhood shown in the stories they write. The exercise of writing about or as (potentially fictional) children allowed the adult authors to engage with the sentimental strand of American evangelical affect, a hallmark of which is characterizing all Christians as children, no matter how old.[45] By inventing or even inhabiting the voice of a child, the adult authors of these pieces may also have been engaging in yet another form of critical nostalgia, reaching toward a childlike faith they desired for themselves.

Hardest to pin down are the stories of anonymous campers that adults used in fundraising letters. These letters often include short paragraphs describing the impact of camp on different students who converted at camp or returned with a zeal for evangelism, even "corner[ing] everybody at school" to get them to come to Wednesday-night youth group.[46] Because these campers go unidentified, it is unclear whether these stories are true, inspired by true stories, or entirely made up. I propose that these anonymous and potentially invented stories gave a clear lesson in faith and the importance of camp that real life almost never can. These stories present idealized children and adolescents, and girls in particular, in order to raise money for programs intended to impact real ones.

More revealing, though, are the letters, particularly common in the Pioneer Girls organization, purported to be written by campers themselves. These letters, published beginning in the October 1952 edition of the organization's *Hitchin' Post* newsletter, encouraged girls to sign up for Camp Cherith through a fictional girl's reminiscences of her own time at camp the previous summer. Beyond the clear promotional character of these letters—one starts off singing the praises of the great food at Camp Cherith—there are other reasons to be suspicious of their provenance.[47] For one, the *Hitchin' Post* also published stories written by campers themselves in its annual writing contest. In these stories, girls are identified by first and last name and city of residence, whereas the authors of the promotional letters are given only first names. Furthermore, whereas winners of the contest tended to focus their stories on one particular event, the promotional letters tend to devote a paragraph each to all of the best aspects of camp to get readers excited. One such letter, accompanied by an introductory paragraph explaining that it was mysteriously left in the corner of a cabin instead of being mailed, describes the author and her friends making crafts, playing music, swimming, and playing softball, as well as praying in the quiet of nature—"just me and the Bible and all that time"—and giving "her life to the Lord to do anything He wants with it." [48] Even the drawbacks are laughed off in these promotional letters, like one alleged camper who "really didn't mind K.P. [kitchen patrol] *very* much."[49]

Despite being fabricated, these letters convey what adults hoped their charges would get out of the summer camp experience, especially considering that they were published in the Pioneer Girls' participant-facing newsletter. Authors may have thought that potential campers would be more credulous of the letters' rosy portrayals of Camp Cherith if they came from a fellow camper rather than an authority with a vested interest in their enrollment. These letters allowed adults to create an idealized peer or friend for the actual girls in their audience—perhaps a friend they would even get the chance to meet next year at camp. Because children represent the future, as Anna Strhan has noted, "their involvement or non-involvement in religion can therefore provoke anxiety."[50] Adults assuage this anxiety by working to keep children within a religion with instruction and, in the evangelical context, positive religious relationships. While evangelicalism is built on the practitioner's personal relationship with God and Jesus, Strhan observes that evangelical adults also work to ensure children form positive interpersonal relationships within the church. By writing in the form of a potential church-world friend, and about other (fictional) friends, adults could model what that kind of relational religion should look like.

A DISCIPLINED WILDERNESS

A theme of summer camps generally around this time is that they leaned into the idea of wilderness while at the same time enforcing discipline among young campers with strategies like schedules and chore rotations. However, the freedoms of wilderness and the constrictions of discipline were not as opposed as they may seem, and each side of the coin tended to inform the other. In the case of the evangelical summer camps I discuss here, the wilderness was engaged in theological terms to enforce prayer practices and to teach campers to *want* to maintain discipline in this regard.

Incorporating wilderness into prayer discipline, at least according to some reports, seems to have had the intended effect. Everett, the Young Life camper who wrote the letter to Tom Raley mentioned at the beginning of this chapter, noted that the "different atmosphere" of camp, and in particular the twenty quiet minutes campers spent each day in prayer, made her want to be more disciplined in her religious practices.[51] Stories like this were valuable to the organization: one Young Life mailer from this period tells the story of "Lucille," who told her youth group leader that she had been "doing a lot of praying" since her week at camp. The narrative was part of a bigger fundraising push for Star Ranch, at the time the organization's marquee camp.[52] Clearly an evangelical summer camp's unique ability to create religious discipline in young people was valuable to the larger evangelical movement, even within circles already dedicated to evangelizing the youth of America.

Wilderness at camp, after all, was itself disciplined. Like the national parks mentioned earlier, summer camps worked to control and commodify the outdoors toward a goal of introducing children to a more wholesome world from before the rise of cities and industry.[53] The wilderness created at camp, however, could not be too controlled, lest character-building opportunities associated with the frontier era slip by. The American summer camp movement aimed not to recreate the past wholesale but to employ critical nostalgia toward recreating the right parts of the past. Although the earliest summer camps did look more like camping in the

woods, by the Cold War era camp architecture had become increasingly specialized, with dedicated areas for things like swimming, playing, crafting, and worship. Despite the focused construction of these environments, however, the aesthetic ideal of wilderness was foregrounded, allowing organizers to present the
experience as rugged and pastoral while also controlling just how wild the wilderness of camp could actually be. While one stated goal of Pioneer Girls camp,
for instance, was "to be able to get along without the comforts of modern living,"
campers nevertheless slept in real beds in sturdy cabins, ate warm meals in a din-
ing hall, and engaged in scheduled activities bookended by individual morning
devotions and evening group Bible discussions.[54]

At evangelical summer camps, then, the wilderness created was intended
to be the best possible place to form Christian subjects, and through this environment organizers aimed to create discipline in the campers themselves.
A large portion of this entailed framing the outdoors as an ideal environment
for hearing the voice of God. Sometimes the results manifested in dramatic
fashion: Marion Perrigo, an elementary school–aged Pioneer Girl from New
Jersey, won the organization's annual summer camp writing contest in 1952
with a story that mirrored biblical tales of wandering in the wilderness. Her
group got lost in the night, with four flashlights doing little to penetrate the
darkness. Feeling "pathetically small and helpless," Perrigo writes, the group
sat down to rest, pray, and read the Bible. "Suddenly," she continues, "a great
peace filled our hearts," and as so often happens in the Bible, God "directed
our footsteps to the road that led to camp."[55]

But more often, finding God in the primeval(-ish) wilderness happened
more quietly. Both networks of summer camps, in addition to daily Bible studies and nightly theological discussions, instituted times for campers to pray
alone in the outdoors. At the various Camps Cherith, campers received morning watch booklets, small devotionals to use outdoors at set times every morning. In explaining how the practice should work, a booklet from 1973 instructs
campers to find "a quiet place . . . to talk with God / the God who made the
trees that shade you . . . / the pine needles and sand to walk on . . . "[56] Meanwhile, a 1978 edition makes clear the relationship between the camper praying
alone in the controlled wilderness of camp and the Bible story of Jesus going
alone to pray in the wilderness.[57] Camp Cherith sent campers home with new
morning watch booklets to continue their practice individually every morning,
and eventually began publishing the daily devotionals in the organization's
monthly.[58]

The other forms of discipline practiced at these camps, the ones common to American summer camps more generally, were also, unsurprisingly,

presented as religious practice. Usually this meant counselors and campers talking about room inspections and kitchen patrol in the same breath as Bible study and testimony, but one (fictional, promotional) story in particular stands out for its portrayal of what organizers hoped camp could be for participants. In the story, written by a counselor at a Camp Cherith and published in the Pioneer Girls' *Hitchin' Post* newsletter in 1957, the heroine resents having to do chores at camp until she realizes that those chores are God working through her. She then decides to help out more at home when camp is over so that her unsaved mother can have more time to learn about Jesus.[59] This was not just wishful thinking: the very real Everett notes in her letter, too, that she felt a "special joy . . . in serving Christ by cleaning the prop room, washing windows and mopping floors."[60] By thinking about chores—and gendered chores at that—as religious practice, Everett could contribute to the goal of a once and future Christian America.

All of this discipline had a pedagogical purpose: creating better Christians or, for those who arrived at camp unconverted, creating new ones. Materials for Young Life counselors emphasize the disciplined, rational character of the Christian life, noting that "emotion is not a method to find God, but a response."[61] Accordingly, counselors not much older than their charges were instructed to be firm and emotionally stable, which sometimes led to angst on the part of the counselors. All of this affective control, however, was aimed not at suppression of emotion but instead at creating the right kind of emotion to create a lasting born-again experience. Despite instructing counselors not to lead or let their campers lead with emotion, Young Life counseling materials also note that "no decision was ever made by the head alone, the heart must be touched."[62] The disciplined wilderness of camp, then, was intended not just to develop disciplined religious practices but also to create religious affective discipline that would allow campers to, in the manner of their wider evangelical community, feel Jesus in their hearts.

Camps used wilderness as a tool and metaphor in areas beyond explicitly building prayer discipline. Camp Cherith materials, in particular, tend to reinforce the parallels between the environment at camp and biblical times. Girls were encouraged to imagine themselves as biblical heroes, as in an advertisement for Camp Cherith that pointed out: "When we look into our Bible, we find that one of the greatest and wealthiest Hebrews who ever lived made his home in tents—Abraham."[63] Although the part of Abraham's story that is arguably most wilderness-oriented focuses on a woman—Hagar—girls were largely encouraged to imagine themselves in the roles of biblical men, who were perhaps more commonly understood as representing the independence and self-sufficiency that the Pioneer Girls promoted to its charges. In this case, they were encouraged to imagine themselves in the place and time of Abraham, whose location in the untouched wilderness is implied to have played a large part in his role as the Bible's patriarch par excellence. If campers could experience this kind of wilderness past, then they, too, could be positioned to push their own religious tradition to ever greater heights.

GENDER AT CAMP AND IN TIME

Much like the Pioneer Girls organization specifically, evangelical summer camps broadly instructed female participants in something more complicated than the submissive gender roles that might be expected from the era that produced *The Feminine Mystique*. In an advertisement for Camp Cherith in a Pioneer Girls guidebook from 1950, the organization claims for girlhood a group of characteristics that has been historically more commonly associated with boyhood or yet-to-be-gendered childhood: "The desire to be out-of-doors," the ad reads, "to be able to get along without the comforts of modern living, and to learn new things about nature seems to be born into every normal American girl."[64] The use of "normal" here is especially interesting, implying that perhaps a gendered preoccupation with home-oriented activities was *not* normal and may need to be rectified.

Part of the project of childhood and (especially) adolescence is to learn to be a gendered subject. For evangelicals both in the Cold War era discussed here and in the present, those gender roles have widely been understood as religious practices. Gender here is God-given, and therefore properly being a boy or girl, and future man or woman, is part of being a good Christian.[65] For both (and they did insist on that binary), gender was temporal as well as physical and social. Here my focus is on girls, though the camps also promoted an evangelically inflected masculinity. The role of girls and the role of women in this model were not the same: the normal traits of girls described above were not the normal traits of women, and children and teenagers attended summer camp largely during the transition period from one to the other. Sometimes the pedagogy of gender was subtle, as in the statements about what being a normal girl means, and sometimes it was explicit: in an undated strategy report from Young Life titled "Objectives of the Adolescent Period," the second objective is "establishing heterosexual interests," and goals within that objective included transitioning teenagers from "interest in members of the same sex" (presumably platonically, but the author does not specify) to "interest in members of the opposite sex."[66] One place to do that was, perhaps surprisingly, in single-sex environments.

Christian summer camp was, to varying degrees, a homosocial environment.

Some, like the Camps Cherith from the 1940s through the early 1980s, were entirely single sex; others, like all of the Young Life camps as well as Cherith after boys' and coed programs were introduced, were coed but separated boys and girls into different cabins with whom they spent not only night hours but, in fact, most of their time. In addition to reflecting social norms, this move provided a straightforward environment where campers could be taught gendered religious expectations. By excluding the opposite sex from many of a cabin's activities and, in particular, their deeper discussions, adult organizers both allowed campers the freedom to experiment and ask questions around their gendered experiences and preserved their sexual innocence, a metonym for more general aspirational innocence rooted in nostalgia for childhood.[67]

This is evident in one 1973 morning watch devotional for Pioneer Girls campers around middle-school age, called "You and the Early Church."[68] This document is rather explicit in its focus on what makes a good Christian girl and, subsequently, woman, in the context of how that related to her (understood) gender opposite. In a lesson entitled "GUYS! Yea!! GUYS! Ugh!!," camp's homosocial environment is addressed at the outset. "Why think about guys at camp?" it asks, as though boys should be the last thing from campers' minds in the parallel universe of summer camp. Rather than dwelling on the needlessness of thinking about boys at camp, however, the anonymous author of the lesson quickly pivots to memories of her own junior-high experience, when she thought about boys all the time—but what she was not considering was "what God wanted me to think about guys." Here, the devotional's author employs a critical nostalgia that has been the focus of this chapter, this time using memories of her own childhood to create a better version of it for her girl readers.

The lesson focuses on a passage from Genesis describing the courtship of the patriarch Isaac and his eventual wife Rebekah, asking girls to think specifically about "what it was about the girl that caused her to be chosen for a bride" and whether the reader herself had the same qualities.[69] When Rebekah first appears halfway through the passage, she is described first as beautiful and a virgin, then as kind and helpful, and finally as modest. These are characteristics that appear throughout the evangelical conversation around complementarian gender roles, but what is striking is that, apart from kindness and helpfulness, the virtues demonstrated in the passage are not the same virtues (adventurousness, independence) that are otherwise highlighted at camp. That is not to say that these virtues are opposites. Rather, they all serve to situate a girl in time, with some virtues more important in girlhood and others more important in womanhood.

This devotional lesson thereby serves, perhaps unintentionally, to highlight those differences, pointing to the idea that evangelical girls are not merely evangelical women in miniature but a different category of practitioner with different needs and characteristics. Girlhood has long been conceptualized by adults as a distinct life stage that, though especially prone to corruption, is also a time of freedom and adventurousness before the constraints of womanhood set in.[70] Girl and woman are both gendered here, but in different ways and sometimes in contrast to one another. Late childhood and adolescence, then, represent a transition period from one kind of femininity to the other, and camp as a safe place to make it happen. As with American summer camp itself, evangelical environments distinctly inflected what exactly these femininities were and thus how the transition period worked.

As it wraps up, the lesson briefly pivots away from considering its reader as a future wife. Concluding that the Bible passage shows that God wants love between girls and boys/women and men, the author clarifies: "Brother/sister kind [of love] for us and husband/wife kind for married people."[71] Here, after encouraging girls to consider what they need to do to become good future wives, the devotional places them right back in the present. The kind of love Isaac and Rebekah had is for husbands and wives, but we, the youth, need only consider boys as brothers in a Christlike sense. (As has long been common to evangelical purity culture, no time is spent on getting from the one to the other.) Here is the evangelical understanding of the temporality of girlhood, in the twentieth century and beyond: girls as both future wives and righteous church members, and also girls as eternally inhabiting an innocent, sexless childhood. That innocence is preserved in the pastoral virgin land of summer camp, but girls must be prepared for the boys beyond.

CREATING CHRISTIANS

A centerpiece of life at camp was the conversion experience. Instructions for counselors at Young Life camps during the 1960s and 1970s encouraged them to lead their campers "to the point of decision," not pressuring them to come to Jesus but definitely pushing them in that direction.[72] The process involved three basic steps: talking with a camper extensively one-on-one and ensuring they understood "the truth of the Gospel"; explaining "how to invite the Lord into your heart"; and having the camper pray, which they should do on their own with extensive explanation from the counselor, including another three-point checklist. Some counselors reported feeling pressured to say the exact right things, to the point of feeling like they were role-playing.[73] Still, the organization continued to give very specific instructions to counselors attempting to lead their charges to conversion.

Materials from both networks of summer camps show a preoccupation with conversion. Both winners of the 1951 Camp Cherith writing contest told stories of summer camp conversion, one of a friend's and one of her own; both responded to a prompt about their "most treasured experience at Camp Cherith."[74] Fundraising letters, too, always seemed to make note of campers who dedicated their lives to Christ over the previous camping season.[75] Missionaries running American-style Christian summer camps abroad reported on their own successes—and sometimes the opposite: in 1957, a missionary in (West) Germany, reporting on her camp in the Pioneer Girls newsletter, included a photo of a camper who "went home without Christ" and asked for prayers for the "free thinker."[76]

At set times every night across both networks of camps, campers were invited to discuss Bible lessons with their cabin or in a bigger group around a campfire; these rituals were designed to include campers learning these lessons for the first time. Counseling materials from both Young Life and Pioneer Girls show that both organizations arranged for Bible study activities to build over the course of the week, reaching a crescendo on the last night of camp. At Young Life camp, counselors were encouraged to allow campers to "give a word for the Lord" on the last night, offering a platform for campers to convert each other, peer to peer.[77] Camp Cherith also encouraged campers to convert peers by using the last night to encourage them to think about "whom you'll share Jesus with" and to share that person's first name. Counselors were instructed to write down those first names next to the camper's name in order to "refer to that list and keep praying for them."[78]

Building a conversion strategy around a short summer camp experience speaks to the perceived ease of having frequent conversations around the topic in what was understood as an isolated, totally Christian society in the wilderness. "Nowhere is the bond of Christian love stronger than at camp," wrote one Camp Cherith participant in 1952.[79] Summer camp was frequently counterposed to "the world" in this way, which both participants and organizers portrayed as full of bad influences. Removing children to a Christian wilderness environment could potentially jump-start their lives as Christians. This, combined with the fact that camp was often just a week or two long, engendered an intensity that was not found in a modern, pluralistic world. In a letter Tom Raley wrote back to Jacky Everett, Raley observes, "It just seemed like from your letter everything that we want to have happen in the life of a kid, and every thing that we want them to see in the different parts of the program, God seemed to really say to you in the course of that week."[80] While organizers hoped to maintain create long-term Christians and evangelists, they saw camp as an important, maybe even necessary, catalyst for that transformation, and the short but intense amount of time it occupied in campers' lives was part of that strategy.

Although camp was idealized as "a week to forget the confines of society," its end was rarely far from organizers' minds.[81] Guides for counselors cautioned them to ensure right away that their new converts have a Christian adult to guide them once they came back to the real world and to collect cards with each camper's information so that progress could be shared between counselors and the camper's "home field."[82] Those leaving Camp Cherith brought home morning watch devotionals to continue their Bible reading practices at home, even if doing so was acknowledged to be more difficult when the camper wasn't surrounded by nature.[83]

Christians newly minted in this intensely Christian environment could then bring lessons from camp back into what one Young Life organizer called the "valley." At least, this is what the organizing adults hoped for. This is made explicit in a number of different venues: one Young Life fundraising letter points to a new camp convert who then worked to convert everyone at her school.[84] A different letter, this one published in the Pioneer Girls newsletter in 1953, puts the same sentiment in the words of a (possibly fictional) camper: "I wish we had camp all the year 'round. But sometimes I guess it's good to stand for the Lord when there when there aren't just Christians around."[85] This letter, published to plant the idea in readers' minds, emphasized both that campers should yearn for the kind of nostalgic all-Christian wilderness environment found at camp and also that there was virtue in bringing that affective practice into the other fifty-one weeks of the year.

The practice of nostalgia did not end with the conclusion of camp. After all, in the words of camper Betsy in a postcamp letter, "It takes *months* for everything to sink in."[86] Campers were encouraged to think back on their time at camp throughout the school year, which served both to anchor their religious experience in a past all-Christian society and to get them excited to attend camp again and perpetuate the program. Although the wrap-up to camp was often forward-looking—emphasizing bringing the lessons of camp back into the world—that attitude took an inevitably critical-nostalgic cast. In her letter to Raley, Everett wrote, "If I really want to grow in Christ I musn't dwell on the time I spent there" but look forward instead.[87] But while *dwelling* on time at camp may not have been recommended, referring back to it and longing for it were part of the process, and one in which Everett herself clearly engaged.

Thanks to the sheer amount of archival material, this longing is especially clear in the Pioneer Girls organization. In a typical year, at least two of every four quarterly newsletters to young participants referred to Camp Cherith, and many of these mentions explicitly encourage girls to remember their time there and get excited for next year. Even one of Cherith's official camp songs—which was sung *at* camp, not after—prepared girls to be nostalgic for camp: "Memories of camp we'll cherish / Everywhere we roam," campers sang, "Looking toward that glad reunion / In our heavenly Home."[88]

Inculcating a nostalgia for camp was an integral part of adult organizers' goals to create the next generation of evangelical Christianity. First, campers learned the joys of an all-Christian society of the type found in various pasts (American, biblical), which would build their enthusiasm for bringing back such a society into the present. Then, once that nostalgia was established, campers were taught to be nostalgic for camp itself, which would both feed into the greater nostalgia and maintain their excitement into the next year's enrollment period, thus maintaining the centrality of summer camp to American evangelical children and teenagers' experience throughout the year. Nostalgia was not just a feeling, it was a practice that linked appropriate emotion to appropriate action. As an affective practice, it has been a major driver for the transmission of American evangelicalism from one generation to another. In other traditions, too, affective practice is key to understanding such transmission: to be religious is, in many ways, to feel religious, nostalgically or otherwise.

NOTES

1. Jacky Everett to Tom Raley, August 4, 1973, box 1, 2016-019, Barbara Priddy papers, Evangelism and Missions Archives, Wheaton College, Wheaton, IL.

2. Leslie Paris, *Children's Nature: The Rise of the American Summer Camp*, American History and Culture Series (New York: New York University Press, 2010).

3. Paris, *Children's Nature*.

4. Abigail Ayres Van Slyck, *A Manufactured Wilderness: Summer Camps and the Shaping of American Youth, 1890-1960*, e-book ed., Architecture, Landscape, and American Culture Series (Minneapolis: University of Minnesota Press, 2006).

5. Rebecca A. Koerselman, "'Invading Vacationland for Christ': The Construction of Evangelical Identity through Summer Camps in the Postwar Era" (Ph.D. diss., Michigan State University, 2013), 10.

6. Molly Worthen, *Apostles of Reason: The Crisis of Authority in American Evangelicalism* (New York: Oxford University Press, 2014), 4.

7. Daniel Silliman, "An Evangelical Is Anyone Who Likes Billy Graham: Defining Evangelicalism with Carl Henry and Networks of Trust," *Church History* 90, no. 3 (2021).

8. Daniel Vaca, *Evangelicals Incorporated: Books and the Business of Religion in America* (Cambridge, MA: Harvard University Press, 2019).

9. For an overview of this historiography, see Matthew Avery Sutton, "New Trends in the Historiography of American Fundamentalism," *Journal of American Studies* 51, no. 1 (2017):

235–41.

10. Vaca, *Evangelicals Incorporated.*

11. For an in-depth look at why this period is so significant for American evangelicalism, see Darren Dochuk, *From Bible Belt to Sunbelt: Plain-Folk Religion, Grassroots Politics, and the Rise of Evangelical Conservatism* (New York: W. W. Norton, 2011); Lisa McGirr, *Suburban Warriors: The Origins of the New American Right* (Princeton, NJ: Princeton University Press, 2001); Vaca, *Evangelicals Incorporated.*

12. Shannon Lee Dawdy, *Patina: A Profane Archaeology* (Chicago: University of Chicago Press, 2016). Dawdy's work builds on Svetlana Boym's foundational distinction between restorative and reflective nostalgia. Svetlana Boym, *The Future of Nostalgia* (New York: Basic Books, 2001).

13. Lauren R. Kerby, *Saving History: How White Evangelicals Tour the Nation's Capital and Redeem a Christian America* (Chapel Hill: The University of North Carolina Press, 2020), 4.

14. For the former, see Sandra Fox, *The Jews of Summer: Summer Camp and Jewish Culture in Postwar America*, Stanford Studies in Jewish History and Culture (Stanford, CA: Stanford University Press, 2023); Leslie Paris, "The Adventures of Peanut and Bo: Summer Camps and Early Twentieth-Century American Girlhood," in *The Girls' History and Culture Reader: The Twentieth Century*, ed. Miriam Forman-Brunell and Leslie Paris (Urbana: University of Illinois Press, 2011), 84–108. For the latter, see Mandi Baker, *Becoming and Being a Camp Counsellor: Discourse, Power Relations and Emotions* (Cham, Switzerland: Palgrave Macmillan, 2020); Björn Lundberg, "Localized Internationalism: Camping across Borders in the Early Swedish Boy Scout Movement," *Journal of the History of Childhood and Youth* 15, no. 1 (2022): 75–92.

15. Cathy, "I Am Cathy: I Am 13," *Compass*, Spring 1966, box 2, folder 23, CN 264, Pioneer Ministries Records, Evangelism and Missions Archives, Wheaton College, Wheaton, IL.

16. Emily A. Murphy, *Growing up with America: Youth, Myth, and National Identity, 1945 to Present* (Athens: University of Georgia Press, 2020).

17. Evan Berry, *Devoted to Nature: The Religious Roots of American Environmentalism* (Oakland, CA: University of California Press, 2015); Kerry Mitchell, *Spirituality and the State: Managing Nature and Experience in America's National Parks*, North American Religions (New York: New York University Press, 2016).

18. Murphy, *Growing up with America.*

19. Jon Butler, *Awash in a Sea of Faith: Christianizing the American People*, Studies in Cultural History (Cambridge, MA: Harvard University Press, 1990); Russell E. Richey, *Methodism in the American Forest* (Oxford: Oxford University Press, 2015).

20. Jacob Sorenson, *Sacred Playgrounds: Christian Summer Camp in Theological Perspective* (Eugene, OR: Cascade Books, 2021).

21. Émile Cailliet, *Young Life*, 1st ed. (New York: Harper and Row, 1963).

22. Cailliet, *Young Life*, 17.

23. Cailliet, *Young Life*; Jeff Chesemore, "Eighty Years of Camping," *Relationships*, Spring 2022, full digital edition, Young Life website. Notably, this was decades before the founding of Focus on the Family, which is usually characterized as the epicenter of an evangelical takeover of the city.

24. "Find Our Camps," Young Life website, accessed February 22, 2023; Julia Duin, "Inside the Christian Camp That Used to Be Oregon's Infamous Cult Ranch," News, *Religion Un-*

plugged (blog), June 13, 2019.

25. Pioneer Girls, *Cherith Chips*, 1st ed. (Wheaton, Illinois: Pioneer Girls Inc., 1943).

26. "35th Anniversary" (Pioneer Girls Inc., 1974), box 1, folder 11, Pioneer Ministries Records; Pioneer Clubs, "Find a Camp," Pioneer Clubs website, accessed December 5, 2022.

27. "The History of Pioneer Clubs," Pioneer Clubs website, accessed December 5, 2022; "The Camp Cherith Name," Pioneer Clubs website, accessed December 5, 2022.

28. Vaca, *Evangelicals Incorporated*.

29. Timothy Larsen, "Pioneer Girls: Mid-Twentieth-Century American Evangelicalism's Girl Scouts," *Asbury Journal* 63, no. 2 (2008): 59–79; Pioneer Girls, "Christ in Every Phase of a Girl's Life" (Pioneer Girls Inc., ca. 1964), box 1, folder 9, Pioneer Ministries Records. This does not mean that Pioneer Girls or other organizations like it did not converge on a particular theology, as numerous scholars of evangelicalism have suggested of the movement as a whole.

30. "Roy R. Riviere to Board and Advisory Committee," March 25, 1960, box 70, folder 4, CN 020, Herbert J. Taylor papers, Evangelism and Missions Archives, Wheaton College, Wheaton, IL.

31. To run further with the manifest destiny metaphor, the move of appropriating existing environments initially settled by other people is closer to what actually happened than the narrative would imply.

32. "Barbara Priddy to Marlene," November 8, 1969, box 1, Barbara Priddy papers; "Joyce," "Camp Cherith Echoes . . . 1952," *Hitchin' Post*, October 1952, box 2, folder 19, Pioneer Ministries Records.

33. Kathleen Graham, ed., *Stepping Stones*, 2nd ed. (Wheaton, IL: Pioneer Girls Inc., 1977).

34. Lundberg, "Localized Internationalism."

35. "Young Life Leadership: Orientation in Camp Counseling" (Young Life, n.d.), box 1, folder 50, Barbara Priddy papers; Hope Warwick and Kathy Graham, "A Profile of Today's Girl" (Pioneer Girls Inc., June 1971), box 8, folder 27, Pioneer Ministries Records.

36. "Letter from Orien Johnson," fundraising letter, n.d., box 70, folder 19, Herbert J. Taylor papers; Alison F. Short, "How Janet Gave Away Her Hands," *Hitchin' Post*, December 1957, box 2, folder 21, Pioneer Ministries Records.

37. Paris, *Children's Nature*, 88.

38. Ray Cashman, "Critical Nostalgia and Material Culture in Northern Ireland," *Journal of American Folklore* 119, no. 472 (2006): 148.

39. Kerby, *Saving History*, 6.

40. "Explorer Leadership Conference 1968" (Pioneer Girls Inc., 1968), box 1, folder 13, Pioneer Ministries Records.

41. James S. Bielo, *Emerging Evangelicals: Faith, Modernity, and the Desire for Authenticity* (New York: New York University Press, 2011).

42. Ann Burlein, *Lift High the Cross: Where White Supremacy and the Christian Right Converge* (Durham, NC: Duke University Press, 2002); Jodi Eichler-Levine, *Suffer the Little Children: Uses of the Past in Jewish and African American Children's Literature* (New York: New York University Press, 2013).

43. Anne Higonnet, *Pictures of Innocence: The History and Crisis of Ideal Childhood* (New York: Thames and Hudson, 1998).

44. Jason Bivins, *Religion of Fear: The Politics of Horror in Conservative Evangelicalism*

(Oxford: Oxford University Press, 2008); Sara Moslener, *Virgin Nation: Sexual Purity and American Adolescence* (New York: Oxford University Press, 2015).

45. Todd M. Brenneman, *Homespun Gospel: The Triumph of Sentimentality in Contemporary American Evangelicalism* (New York: Oxford University Press, 2014).

46. "Letter from Orien Johnson."

47. "Camp Cherith Echoes . . . 1952."

48. "Rescued from a Trash Can," *Hitchin' Post*, October 1954, box 2, folder 20, Pioneer Ministries Records.

49. "Camp Cherith Echoes . . . 1952." Underline in original.

50. Anna Strhan, *The Figure of the Child in Contemporary Evangelicalism* (Oxford: Oxford University Press, 2019), 2.

51. Everett to Raley, August 4, 1973.

52. "Letter from Orien Johnson."

53. Van Slyck, *Manufactured Wilderness*.

54. *Pioneer Girls Trail Book*, 8th ed. (Chicago: Pioneer Girls Inc., 1950), 155.

55. Bunny Eide, Lois Lorand, and Marion Perrigo, "Judges Announce Camp Contest Winners," *Hitchin' Post*, December 1952, box 2, folder 19, Pioneer Ministries Records.

56. Dorothy Knox, "You and the Early Church: Colonist Morning Watch" (Pioneer Girls Inc., 1973), box 4, folder 26, Pioneer Ministries Records.

57. Robert Murray, "My Morning Watch" (Camp Cherith, 1978), box 1, folder 20, Pioneer Ministries Records.

58. Eunice Russell, "Morning Watch," *Trails*, December 1964, box 1, Pioneer Ministries Records; Shirley McKay, "Morning Watch," *Reflection*, December 1973, box 8, folder 1, Pioneer Ministries Records; Bunny Eide and Diane Watson, "Camp Cherith Writing Contest," *Hitchin' Post*, October 1951, box 2, folder 18, Pioneer Ministries Records.

59. Short, "How Janet Gave Away."

60. Everett to Raley, August 4, 1973.

61. "Young Life Leadership: Orientation."

62. "The Decision and Follow-Up" (Young Life, n.d.), box 1, leadership material folder, Barbara Priddy papers.

63. *Pioneer Girls Trail Book*, 155. The seemingly out-of-nowhere nod to Abraham's wealth was not out of place for the Pioneer Girls; the organization frequently pointed to wealth and power, in particular in its discussions of patriarchs and presidents, in order to highlight those traits' compatibility with implied American values.

64. *Pioneer Girls Trail Book*, 155.

65. John P. Bartkowski, *Remaking the Godly Marriage: Gender Negotiation in Evangelical Families* (London: Rutgers University Press, 2001); Kate Bowler, *The Preacher's Wife: The Precarious Power of Evangelical Women Celebrities* (Princeton, NJ: Princeton University Press, 2019); Sally K. Gallagher, *Evangelical Identity and Gendered Family Life* (New Brunswick, NJ: Rutgers University Press, 2003).

66. "Objectives of the Adolescent Period" (Young Life, n.d.), box 1, Barbara Priddy papers.

67. Of course, coed camps involved more gender segregation in theory than in practice, as Sandra Fox has shown in her discussion of Jewish summer camps employing campers' sexual interest in each other toward marriage-oriented ends. However, the materials I work with here do

not include how this gender segregation actually shook out, and therefore I focus on the goals of summer camp homosociality rather than its lived experience. See Fox, *Jews of Summer*.

68. Knox, "You and the Early Church."

69. Knox, "You and the Early Church."

70. Catherine Driscoll, *Girls: Feminine Adolescence in Popular Culture and Cultural Theory* (New York: Columbia University Press, 2002); Marnina Gonick, *Between Femininities: Ambivalence, Identity, and the Education of Girls*, Second Thoughts (Albany: State University of New York Press, 2003); Paris, "Adventures of Peanut."

71. Knox, "You and the Early Church."

72. "Decision and Follow-Up."

73. "Kay to Barbara Priddy," July 21, 1962, box 1, Barbara Priddy papers.

74. Eide and Watson, "Camp Cherith Writing Contest."

75. E.g., "Letter from Dick Langford," fundraising letter, April 27, 1949, box 70, folder 19, Herbert J. Taylor papers; "letter from Martin Walt," fundraising letter, April 27, 1949, box 70, folder 19, Herbert J. Taylor papers.

76. "Eaglet Counsels in German Camp," *Hitchin' Post*, December 1957, box 2, folder 21, Pioneer Ministries Records.

77. "Young Life Leadership: Orientation."

78. "Giving Myself to God and Others" (Camp Cherith, 1978), 46, box 1, folder 20, Pioneer Ministries Records.

79. Eide, Lorand, and Perrigo, "Camp Contest Winners."

80. "Tom Raley to Jacky Everett," August 21, 1973, box 1, Barbara Priddy papers.

81. Robert Murray, "Reaching Up and Out" (Camp Cherith, 1978), box 1, folder 20, Pioneer Ministries Records.

82. "Orientation"; "Head Girls Counselor" (Young Life, n.d.), box 1, folder 50, Barbara Priddy papers.

83. Murray, "My Morning Watch"; "Camp Cherith Echoes . . . 1952."

84. "Letter from Orien Johnson."

85. "Judy," "Cherith Memories . . .," *Hitchin' Post*, October 1953, box 2, folder 19, Pioneer Ministries Records.

86. "Betsy to Barbara Priddy," n.d., box 1, Barbara Priddy papers. Underline in original.

87. Everett to Raley, August 4, 1973.

88. *Pioneer Girls Trail Book*, 158.

Myth and the Dismal Swamp Maroons

RYNE BEDDARD

In his 1853 novel, *Clotel; or, The President's Daughter*, William Wells Brown creatively rewrites history to connect the 1831 enslaved rebellion led by Nat Turner in Southampton County, Virginia, to the Great Dismal Swamp, a region of southeast Virginia and northeast North Carolina with a long reputation of harboring people who had escaped from slavery called maroons. "Here runaway negroes usually seek a hiding place, and some have been known to reside here for years," Brown writes, adding that Turner and his band were joined in the swamp by a revolutionary maroon leader named Picquilo.[1] By fictionally linking the Southampton rebellion to the Great Dismal Swamp in the figure of Picquilo, Brown initiated an abolitionist literary myth of militant Dismal Swamp maroons. In the tumultuous 1850s and 1860s, this myth was adapted and retold by some of the most influential American writers of that time: Martin Delaney, Frederick Douglass, Harriet Jacobs, and Harriet Beecher Stowe among them. What these authors have in common, I argue, is not just that they told stories about maroons in the Dismal Swamp but that they each, in their own way, deployed the myth of the Dismal Swamp maroons in their strategic efforts to use literature as an affective tool for dismantling slavery.

By "myth" I do not mean to imply, as with the common usage of the term, the idea of a story that is untrue, or a lie. Following Bruce Lincoln, I think of myth broadly, as a primarily narrative mode of discourse that, through its recitation, "may effectively mobilize a social grouping." Like claims to a special ancestral lineage or political slogans, as Lincoln observes, myth's power comes from its capacity to generate shared perceptions of the relationship between the past, present, and future.[2] It is precisely this capacity that the abolitionist authors I discuss here sought to harness in their mythologization of the Dismal Swamp maroons.

I refer, here, to the myth of the Dismal Swamp maroons in the singular, though this should not be taken as an indication that the myth is homogeneous and static. It is deployed in different ways, and with different goals in mind, by different authors. In the case of Brown, we even see how the myth was strategically redeployed over time by a single author. He published four different versions of *Clotel* between 1853 and 1867, modifying the story each time, adapting it to his changing social and political ambitions.[3] In each version, the chapter in which Picquilo briefly emerges is repeated almost word for word, and yet, as discussed below, in each version the potential implications of his emergence differ in important ways. I highlight the dynamism and complexity of the myth of the Dismal Swamp maroons to suggest that myths are effective social mobilizers precisely because of their malleability to urgent social problems. By exploring these variations, I foreground the elastic process through which the myth gained discursive force in the 1850s and 1860s.

To be clear, the presence of maroon communities in the Dismal Swamp was more than a myth. In recent years, archaeologists have found compelling evidence that historical maroon communities persisted in the Dismal Swamp throughout the colonial and antebellum periods. However, most of the authors under consideration here likely did not have access to reliable information about these highly secretive communities but instead invented fictional communities inspired by colonial and antebellum rumors and legends. In what follows, I will briefly summarize relevant archaeological and historical findings. This will provide useful context for my discussion of four mid-nineteenth-century fictional accounts of the Dismal Swamp maroons— William Wells Brown's *Clotel*, Martin Delaney's *Blake*, Frederick Douglass's *The Heroic Slave*, and Harriet Beecher Stowe's *Dred*—and one brief nonfictional account found in Harriet Jacobs's autobiographical *Incidents in the Life of a Slave Girl*.

HISTORY OF DISMAL SWAMP MARRONAGE

For centuries, people who escaped from slavery on southern plantations fled to the Great Dismal Swamp of southeast Virginia and northeast North Carolina. They built and maintained spaces of Black autonomy through efforts to "rework and reclaim geographic refuse."[4]

These communities—like many communities throughout the Greater Caribbean who escaped from slavery into inhospitable environments like swamps, forests, or mountains—came to be known as maroons. *Maroon* came into English around the middle of the seventeenth century from the Spanish *cimarrón*, which came to refer to self-ruled Indigenous people and escaped slaves living in the *montes*—wild, hilly spaces associated with communal land engagement.[5] While exact numbers are impossible to surmise, the historian J. Brent Morris has recently argued that "the aggregate population of the Great Dismal Swamp Maroon communities at any given time after the early eighteenth century likely numbered in at least the hundreds, and likely the thousands."[6]

Roughly the size of Delaware prior to the late eighteenth century, the Dismal Swamp was the home of a variety of maroon communities. Some communities were short-term while others endured for decades, maybe even centuries. Some were small and nomadic, others relatively large and permanent. Some remained on the peripheries of the swamp, staying in contact with loved ones on nearby plantations; others lived deep in the interior, minimizing any connection to the outside.[7] Archaeologists have found evidence of relatively permanent deep interior communities who erected raised living structures, dug cooking and water-catchment pits and trenches, cleared plots of land for subsistence gardening, and built defensive structures.[8] Archaeologists found that, in their efforts to remain detached from the outside world, these deep interior maroons tended to rework and transform artifacts like stone tools that had been left by previous Indigenous peoples rather than relying on outside materials.[9] And at one site archaeologists found evidence of several fire pits but no clearly identifiable living structures, which "may have served as a central gathering point or a communal space" for maroons dispersed throughout that region of the swamp.[10]

Most maroon communities rejected and avoided the world beyond the swamp, but some groups were more militant, organizing raids on nearby plantations.[11] Some maroons in the Dismal likely even sought to organize across and beyond the swamp for widespread revolt. For example, historian Kathryn Benjamin Golden argues that after the enslaved revolt planned by Gabriel Prosser (whose name is later considered "sacred" and a "talisman" by maroons in Delaney's *Blake*) was discovered, and Prosser executed, many of his coconspirers fled into the Dismal Swamp where they were instrumental in plotting the revolt that's come to be known as the Easter Conspiracy of 1802.[12] Through both their rejection of plantation society and their subversive plotting against it, generations of maroons successfully transformed the Dismal Swamp into an "insurgent ecology," an environment "rich with opportunities and possibilities for resisting slavery."[13]

As a sanctuary from slavery, the Dismal Swamp was a sacred space, an expression of the fugitive sacred.[14] I theorize sacred spaces as charged social sites, pulsing with the possibility of transformation and even destruction.

They are sites where the fixed categories and identity markers that govern the day-to-day, profane world of social relations (like, for example, "master" and "slave") become fluid, unstable, and threaten to melt away altogether.[15] The Dismal Swamp as sacred exceeds the order of plantation society; it is incompatible with the mundane market logics governing the circulations of capital and "property." As a site of the fugitive sacred it "disturbs the everyday."[16]

INCIDENTS, 1861

Of all the authors discussed in this essay, only Harriet Jacobs spent any time as a fugitive hiding in the Great Dismal Swamp. It should then come as no surprise, perhaps, that her account of the swamp is far less romanticized than the other representations discussed here. It is also the only nonfictional account discussed in detail here. Jacobs was enslaved in Edenton, North Carolina, a small port town on the Albemarle Sound near the southern boundary of the Dismal Swamp. Around 1842, she escaped to Philadelphia and then New York, where she worked as a live-in servant for a wealthy family and managed an antislavery reading room with her brother. She befriended the well-connected Quaker abolitionist Amy Post, who encouraged her to publish her story. Unsure in her writing ability, Jacobs had Post ask Harriet Beecher Stowe to write her story in 1852. In a letter that Jacobs felt was dismissive and demeaning, Stowe said she wouldn't write her story but asked if she could include the material in the *Key to Uncle Tom's Cabin*, which she was rushing to publication. Disappointed, Jacobs decided to write her story herself.[17]

Eventually, and with some help from the abolitionists Lydia Maria Child and William C. Nell, Jacobs published her story in 1861 in Boston under the title *Linda: Or, Incidents in the Life of a Slave Girl. Written by Herself.*[18] She chose to publish pseudonymously, as Linda, in order to protect her identity, and that of her family, as a fugitive from slavery. *Incidents in the Life of a Slave Girl*, as the text is conventionally referred to in scholarly literature, was so popular that Jacobs would publish a British edition, called *The Deeper Wrong*. Pirated reproductions quickly seized on the popularity, however, undermining the novel's commercial success during Jacobs's lifetime.[19]

In a key moment in her narrative, when Linda is onboard a northbound ship, finally escaping from Edenton, she passes by the Dismal Swamp, or the "snaky swamp" as she calls it, and Jacobs gives her readers two quick depictions of the wetland—first from the ship captain and then from Linda—which, taken together, express the ambiguity at the heart of the myth of the Dismal Swamp maroons.[20]

For Linda, the "snaky swamp" evokes dread, as she reflects on her brief time of hiding in the swamp years before. "I passed a wretched night," she remembered, "for the heat of the swamp, the mosquitos, and the constant terror of snakes. . . . I dreaded to enter this hiding space. But I was in no situation to choose." [21] This dismal swamp was not a romanticized city of refuge but a precarious "loophole of retreat."[22] "But even those large, venomous snakes," wrote Jacobs, who had a terrible fear of snakes after being bitten by one while hiding in the woods from slave patrols, "were less dreadful to my imagination than the white men in that community called civilized."[23]

The second perspective on the swamp Jacobs gives readers, that of the unnamed captain, has a different tone. Pointing out toward the swamp, the captain remarks to Linda: "There is a slave territory that defies all the laws."[24] That this territory belongs to enslaved people (or more accurately formerly enslaved maroons) in this captain's perception, highlights the effectiveness with which the swamp allowed them to defy the laws of plantation society.

Interestingly, this acute expression of the myth of the Dismal Swamp maroons is presented to readers by the white ship captain and underground railroad conductor and not by Linda. Jacobs lived near the Dismal Swamp her whole life, briefly sheltered there, and certainly knew about the maroon communities (perhaps more than she lets on), yet a reader of her narrative might easily assume that she had never heard of these maroon communities until the worldly captain mentioned them. Framing it this way is in line with the influence of Nell, who followed the popular abolitionist William Lloyd Garrison's dogmatic insistence on responding to slavery with moral persuasion rather than direct action. As the author's preface makes explicitly clear, Jacobs hoped to use moral suasion to "arouse" white, Christian "women of the North" to take up the cause of abolition. For this audience, Linda's innocence is highlighted, and the multiple incidents of the protagonist's hiding in woods or swamps (or below floors, in attics, on ships, or even costumed in plain sight) lose their subversive undertones. Nevertheless, Jacobs does evoke, however briefly, the myth of the Dismal Swamp maroons, and in doing so raises the possibility that the fugitive modes of place-making that Linda uses throughout the text might harbor radical social alternatives.

The "snaky swamp" in *Incidents* is a sanctuary from the violence of slavery, but it is itself dangerous.[25] The two perspectives Jacobs offers on the swamp in the falling action of one of her novel's most dramatic scenes express the ambiguity of the sacred: not all the radical potentialities the Dismal Swamp might portend are just or desirable. This ambiguity, or tension, appears as a minor theme in all the literature I consider here, nowhere more clearly than in Frederick Douglass's novella *The Heroic Slave*.

THE HEROIC SLAVE, 1853

Douglass's *The Heroic Slave* was his only published fictional writing. It first appeared in *Autographs for Freedom*, an abolitionist fundraising volume published in Boston and London that was edited by Julia Griffiths, the managing editor of his newspaper, in 1853. A couple of months later, Douglass released a serialized version of the novella in *Frederick Douglass' Paper*. The story fictionalizes the life of Madison Washington, who had escaped slavery in Virginia by fleeing to Canada, returned to Virginia to free his wife, and was captured and loaded on a slaving ship. In October of 1841, the *Creole* set sail from Richmond toward the busy slave port of New Orleans. While at sea, Washington led an enslaved mutiny, took control of the ship, and redirected her toward the Bahamas, where all the formerly enslaved on board were eventually formally freed by the British government.

As William Wells Brown did that same year with the Nat Turner insurrection in *Clotel*, Douglass artfully weaves the historical facts of Washington's *Creole* mutiny into his fictional narrative. Douglass was living as a fugitive from slavery in Boston, where he had just been hired as a public speaker for William Lloyd Garrison's Massachusetts Anti-Slavery Society, when Washington commandeered the *Creole*. His interest in Madison Washington only grew when Douglass moved to Rochester, New York, and got to know the abolitionists Hiram Wilson and Lindley Murray Moore, who had harbored Washington prior to his recapture in Virginia. He even made plans to travel to Nassau in early 1852, hoping to meet and interview Washington in order to write a nonfiction account of the rebellion, though the plans fell through.[26] As Douglass himself admits, Washington's real life can only be seen in "glimpses" and in "marks, traces, possibilities, and probabilities."[27] Nevertheless, through his eloquent fiction, Douglass breathes new life into this history, adapting it strategically toward his own abolitionist ends.

The story opens in Virginia on a Sunday morning in the spring of 1835. A white traveler from Ohio, Mr. Listwell, has wandered into the woods to find a creek for his horse to drink from when he overhears Madison Washington, who believes himself to be alone, engaged in a monologue consisting of "scathing denunciations of the cruelty and injustice of slavery," "heart-touching narratives of his own personal suffering," "prayers to the God of the oppressed," and "presentations of the dangers and difficulties of escape." Yet each impassioned speech ends with "an emphatic declaration of his purpose to be free."[28]

Listwell is deeply moved by Washington's monologue. "From this hour," he declares to himself, "I am an abolitionist." He sees in Washington "a child of God" who has shunned "the church, the altar, and the great congregation of Christian worshippers," which refuses to recognize his humanity, and who has instead turned to a "gloomy forest, to utter in the vacant air complaints and griefs, which the religion of his times and his country can neither console nor relieve."[29] The sanctuary provided by these unnamed woods represented an implicit critique of the Christian society beyond it that protected the interests of slaveholders. Opposing the planter's churches, built by human hands, Douglas presents a wild sanctuary of the Creator's own making. In this wild sanctuary Listwell hears, and is converted by, the truth that cannot be expressed in the slaveholders' churches.

Shortly after his monologue in the gloomy forest, Washington makes an escape from his plantation. He intends to make a run for freedom in the North but becomes disoriented and decides to shelter in the Dismal Swamp instead, to remain near his enslaved wife. Washington later describes the swamp as a "city of refuge" for "many a poor wandering fugitive."[30] This language echoes an essay from five years prior in the *North Star,* an abolitionist newspaper published by Frederick Douglass and Martin R. Delany. In a story (which was a reprint of a piece which originally ran in the *Zions Herald,* a weekly newspaper published in Boston between 1823 and 1828) titled "Slaves in the Dismal Swamp," the swamp is called a "city of refuge" for the enslaved, an allusion to sanctuary cities prescribed in the Hebrew Bible.[31] By linking the Dismal Swamp to "cities of refuge," Douglass and Delany purposely connect marronage with both the promise of salvation from oppression and the messianic hope for liberation, a theme they would both develop and intensify in the decade that followed.

For the next five years, Washington lives as a maroon in the Dismal Swamp, where he remains hidden during the day and "wander[s] about at night with the wolf and the bear."[32] The invocation of his harmonious (or at least sustainable) relationships with wolves and bears in the swamp is a departure from how Douglass describes the "wild beasts" of the wilderness in his *Narrative* eight years before. "In the *Narrative* nature is a paralyzing wilderness," writes Lance Newman, "while in the novella the forests of Virginia are theatres of self-emancipation." Newman argues that, while working for Garrison, Douglass was "pressured to tell the story of his life in conformity with [the Anti-Slavery Society's] increasingly doctrinaire program of nonresistance that rejected political action in favor of moral suasion."[33] The depiction of the wilderness as a place in which the fugitive from slavery is threatened on all sides, and powerless without the help of benevolent Northern abolitionists, fits more neatly with Garrisonian abolitionism's reliance on moral suasion than a depiction of the wilderness as an independent "city of refuge" from slavery and a site of Black autonomy.

The swamp that sheltered Madison Washington nevertheless remains a precarious home in the novella. If the Dismal Swamp was a sacred sanctuary from slavery, for Douglass, it was a dangerous one where the very forces that sustained you might quickly turn on you and overwhelm you if you were not careful. Washington learns this lesson the hard way when his swampy refuge catches fire. He later describes the "awful conflagration" in vivid detail to Listwell:

> It was horribly and indescribably grand. The whole world seemed on fire, and it appeared to me that the day of judgement had come; that the burning bowels of the earth had bust forth, and that the end of all things was at hand. . . . The very heavens seemed to rain down fire through the towering trees; it was by the merest chance that I escaped the devouring element. Running before it, and stopping occasionally to take breath, I looked back to behold its frightful ravages, and to drink in its savage magnificence. It was awful, thrilling, solemn, beyond compare.[34]

This description of the fire that Douglass places on the lips of his fictional maroon poetically evokes the tension that, I argue, propels the myth of the sacred swamp. It represents an ambiguously "dangerous force, incomprehensible, intractable but eminently efficacious."[35] On the one hand, the swamp represents a relatively safe harbor from plantation violence. On the other hand, because it could harbor maroons who, like Nat Turner and Madison Washington, were willing to use militant means to gain their freedom, the Dismal Swamp also represents the threat of revolutionary violence. This powerful tension was only amplified three years later with the emergence of the nineteenth century's most well-known fictional Dismal Swamp maroon: Harriet Beecher Stowe's Dred.

DRED, 1856

Harriet Beecher Stowe's *Dred; A Tale of the Great Dismal Swamp*, depicts its titular character, Dred, as a zealously religious maroon who spends the better part of the novel plotting an enslaved rebellion in the Dismal Swamp. Though it would eventually fade into popular obscurity, *Dred* was one of the most popular books of the nineteenth century, and it carried the myth of the Dismal Swamp maroons to a broad audience. "From the mid-1850s," writes historian J. Brent Morris, "the name 'Dred' became a kind of shorthand to reference the Dismal Swamp Maroons."[36]

Dred is the fictional son of Denmark Vesey, but he is primarily based on Nat Turner.[37] In August of 1831, an enslaved preacher named Nat Turner and around seventy other African Americans violently revolted against plantation society in Southampton County, Virginia. Allegedly inspired by an apocalyptic vision from God, Turner's revolt was an impactful moment in the history of the Dismal Swamp, and the history of the plantation South more broadly. The historical Turner did not head to the Dismal Swamp after the violence broke out, but during the time he was on the run, many white people in the region feared that he would, and they spoke and wrote openly about their concerns.

A letter to the editor of the *Richmond Enquirer* reported on August 26 that the rebellion was initiated by about 250 maroons "from a Camp Meeting about the Dismal Swamp."[38] Camp meetings, in this context, referred to the widely popular Christian revival meetings that were sweeping through the South in the first half of the nineteenth century. It was already well known that Turner was considered a preacher by his fellow bondspeople, and one strategy that defenders of slavery would use to make sense of Turner's revolt was to blame it on what they considered quasi-religious or superstitious fervor. By suggesting that Turner's revolt stemmed from what planter society considered improper and dangerous expressions of religion, this editorial evoked the memory of the enslaved and maroon uprising that had taken place decades before in Saint-Domingue. Carried by traders and Black watermen, reports had spread throughout the Greater Caribbean of maroons taking part in a revolutionary, African-inspired ritual ceremony, known as Bwa Kayman (sometimes written as "Bois-Caïman").[39]

Commentors could not help but see shadows of Caribbean revolutions in Turner's revolt. One concerned white commenter argued that, if Nat Turner and his band did make it to the Dismal Swamp, they would find in it "as secure a retreat as did the almost inaccessible mountains of St. Domingo to their black brethren of that land." That fear of a Haitian style revolt lingered on the minds of local whites decades later highlights the constant fear of uprising that shaped life in the plantation South. The white commentator went on to say, "Similar scenes of bloodshed and murder might our brethren at the South expect to witness, were the disaffected Slaves of that section of the country but once to gain the ascendency: In a 'General Nat,' they might find a wretch no less disposed to shed innocent blood, than was the perfidious Dessalines [from whom] little mercy could be expected."[40]

This fear, that in "General Nat" the Dismal Swamp maroons might find a leader to overthrow plantation society, spread quickly and left a powerful impression on how Americans imagined the swamp. Although Turner never did

flee to the Dismal Swamp, the panic over Dismal Swamp maroons that his rebellion fomented forged a powerful association between the infamous swampy
wilderness and violent enslaved rebellion in the minds of white folk in the region.[41] Or, as a newspaper editor from Petersburg, Virginia, wrote nearly four
decades after the revolt, "The Virginia Swamp has a historical memory clinging to it. . . . To the whole south, it seemed that in those horrid recesses of nature the avenging genius of slavery crouched but for a moment before covering the land with desolation."[42]

Stowe attached the *Confessions of Nat Turner* as an appendix to *Dred*, where
she reveals that "one of the principal conspirators in this affair was named
Dred."[43] Like Turner, Dred is portrayed as being motivated by quasi-religious
zeal. For example, he carries with him his father's Bible and he seems to have
special access to African-inspired spiritual power. Stowe describes Dred's
maternal grandfather as a reputed African conjurer who taught Dred snake
charming and "had possessed his mind from childhood with expectations of
prophetic and supernatural impulses."[44] Dred speaks with prophetic authority.
Many of the arguments against slavery made in Nat Turner's confessions are
directly expressed throughout the novel. Dred's affective power draws from the
lingering memory connecting Nat Turner with the Dismal Swamp.

Stowe's inclusion of the *Confessions* as an appendix was motivated by criticisms of her earlier novel, *Uncle Tom's Cabin; or, Life Among the Lowly*, published in 1852. Defenders of slavery argued that her story was an utter fabrication with no meaningful connection to real-life slavery. In response, Stowe
published *The Key to Uncle Tom's Cabin* the following year, which included
source materials that she claimed inspired the action in her first novel. In
Dred, she sought to get out in front of that criticism by including historical materials like the *Confessions* as appendixes.

Dred was also written partly in response to Black critics of *Uncle Tom's
Cabin*, who saw the passive acceptance of life under slavery by Uncle Tom as
demeaning. Martin R. Delany was among the most outspoken. Although Frederick Douglass reviewed Stowe's first novel positively, he also published Delany's criticisms of Stowe in his new newspaper, *Frederick Douglass's Paper*.[45] The
1856 publication of *Dred*, with its rebellious maroon title character, seems to
have changed Delany's perception of Stowe. In spite of his earlier criticism,
Delany included quotes from Stowe as epigraphs at the beginning of parts one
and two of his publication of *Blake*.[46]

BLAKE, 1859–1862

Passing through the South like "a thief in the night," Henry Blake stops only briefly in South Carolina, the state "which of all he most dreaded." He stops on the outskirts of town at the home of an elderly Black couple, former confidants of Denmark Vesey. Blake tells them that he is traveling through the South in an attempt to plot his own widespread revolt, organizing enslaved and free Black people to overthrow white supremacist rule. Upon hearing this news, the old man begins weeping and praising God, and then declares that he has "been prayin'" that the Lord would send them another leader like Denmark Vesey.[47]

Leaving South Carolina, the fictional protagonist of Martin R. Delany's *Blake; or, The Huts of America* heads into northeast North Carolina, where he encounters old allies of Nat Turner who embrace him as a "harbinger of better days." These old militants lead Blake into "the mystical, antiquated, and almost fabulous Dismal Swamp," where they introduce him to Gamby Gholar, the "noted high conjurer and compeer of Nat Turner, who for thirty years had been secluded in the swamp."[48] Gamby Gholar is one of the fictional high conjurors of the Dismal Swamp, a secretive council of seven wise and practiced elderly men who are known, collectively, as the "Head." Hidden deep in the swampy interior, the Head works their ritual craft, recruits new maroons from nearby plantations, and keeps alive the memory of Black revolutionaries.

Both Blake and the narrator seem skeptical of the Head's craft. Nevertheless, Blake accepts the ritual object—the "charm bone of a tree frog"—that Gamby Gholar offers him for protection. And he does not object when the Head ceremonially inducts him into their high council, making him a "conjuror of the highest degree known to their art."[49] He recognizes their strategic importance for his plan, and is eager to work with them. After his departure, it will fall to them to organize the maroons of the swamp and await Blake's instructions.

Maudy Ghamus, another member of the Head, tells Blake that within the Dismal Swamp there are enough maroons to "take the whole United States," if only Blake can convince other enslaved populations across the South to realize their own strength and join in the revolt. Delany describes these maroon communities as "some of Virginia and North Carolina's boldest Black rebels." Under the leadership of the Head, "the names of Nat Turner, Denmark Veezie, and General Gabriel [Prosser] were held by them in sacred reverence; that of Gabriel as a Talisman." The members of the Head often delight in retelling the stories of these Black revolutionaries, "whom they conceived to be the greatest men who ever lived."[50]

For Delany, more than any other abolitionist author, the myth of the Dismal Swamp maroons takes center stage. Within a decade of Brown introducing Picquilo, Delaney presents to readers a secretive maroon council of esteemed conjurers who maintain sophisticated networks of communication, negotiate a ritually complex world, and who revere as sacred the names of well-known Black revolutionaries. Moreover, he connects this council-led maroon army in the swamp to other pockets of resistance to slavery throughout the South and the Caribbean.

In 1839, two decades before the publication of *Blake*, Delany traveled throughout the US South to gain a broad perspective on the conditions faced by Black people in the region. The son of an enslaved man and a free woman in Virginia, Delany was born free and understood the limits and promises of moving throughout the region as a Black man. This experience seemed to have solidified, for him, the necessity of agitating for drastic political and social transformation. Delany, who named his son Toussaint L'Ouverture in an homage to the leader of the Haitian Revolution, clearly saw the struggles of Black people throughout the Americas as interconnected.[51]

Blake was published serially on two separate occasions, both times in abolitionist publications for a primarily Black audience. The original twenty-six-chapter version ran in the *Anglo-African Magazine* in 1859–1860, and a more complete, seventy-four-chapter version appeared in the *Weekly Anglo-African* in 1861–1862. As a novel, it was not well received at the time of its initial publications, even by Black reviewers. But, as McGann argues, "Delany was not a novelist—he was a polemicist, even a kind of prophet, who deployed various conventions of traditional fiction to make an argument about what black emancipation in America meant and how it was to be achieved."[52]

The final chapters of the later publication of *Blake*, unfortunately, either were not completed or are missing. From the narrative development it is reasonable to assume that Delany intended for Blake to carry the insurrections of the Caribbean back to the plantations he visited in the South.[53] How he would do so, and what would become of the more general revolution throughout the Greater Caribbean that he hoped to incite, is a question left unanswered in Delany's narrative. Whatever the explanation for the missing final chapters may be, their absence opens up other ways of reading the narrative that foreground not the actions of revolution but the process of marronage and the possibility of flight.

"For black authors in the nineteenth century," writes Judith Madera, the work of the novel was not only a tool for making sense of social dynamics, "it was also about unfolding space—to get across."[54] Delany provides his readers with tools for negotiating the dangers of emancipating themselves. The narrative regularly provides information on important river crossing sites and the names of certain captains. And Blake teaches enslaved people to read a compass, to feel for moss on the sides of trees to find north, and how to find and follow "the slave's great guide to freedom!": the north star.[55] For the latter,

Blake draws them a map of the stars and gives them clear instructions for using it. A publisher's note in the *Weekly Anglo-African* version of the story promises that "a beautiful diagram of Ursa Major, or the Great Bear, drawn by the
author" will be included if the story is published as a book.[56] In sharing knowledge useful for slipping through cracks in the plantation surveillance apparatus, Delany hoped to fatally disrupt the kino-politics of slavery and help foster
fugitive networks of resistance.[57]

What makes the Dismal Swamp so threatening, what gives its mythic maroons discursive power, in *Blake*, is that it is arranged as a "site of intensity"
within an underground network that spans the South and connects to Cuba.[58]
Delany gives novel form to the kind of underground community building he
had done across the South decades before. The Dismal Swamp, with its maroon armies and high conjurers patiently awaiting word from Blake, becomes
a "textual outworking of a rhizomatic geography from under the expanse of
the national landscape."[59] It exposes the limitations of plantation society, opens
the possibility of alternative topographies of Black place-making, and offers
strategies for negotiating these landscapes of possibility. Perhaps more than
any other author, Delany tests the limits of the abolitionist myth of the Dismal
Swamp maroons inaugurated by the figure of Picquilo in *Clotel*.

CLOTEL, 1853, 1860–1861, 1864, 1867

Widely considered the first African American novel, William Wells Brown's
1853 *Clotel; or, The President's Daughter: A Narrative of Slave Life in the United
States* was first published in London. Brown, who adopted his middle and
last name from an Ohio Quaker who helped him escape from slavery into
Canada in 1834, had been living in Europe since the summer of 1849. He
originally traveled there to promote the publication of European editions of
his popular autobiographical *Narrative of William W. Brown* (1847), but the
passage of the Fugitive Slave Act of 1850 made returning to the United States
especially dangerous for a now famous fugitive. In his second book, *Three
Years in Europe* (1852), Brown wrote that the Fugitive Slave Law has converted
the entire country, North and South, into one vast "hunting-ground."[60] In
Clotel he uses this imagery again, portraying parts of Mississippi as human hunting grounds. Published for a British audience, *Clotel* sought to "aid in bringing British influence to bear upon American slavery."[61] Brown understood that
London was the cultural hub of the English-speaking world in the 1850s and he
hoped to push the British public to exert more pressure on the United States to
abolish slavery, as Britain had done throughout its colonies with the 1834 Slavery Abolition Act.

In a pivotal moment in the novel, Brown discursively draws on the historical memory clinging to the Dismal Swamp when he creatively rewrites history
to place Nat Turner and his compatriots there among the "many thousands
of acres of wild land" and the "runaway Negroes."[62] This is where Brown introduces Picquilo, the armed Dismal Swamp maroon. The features of Brown's description of Picquilo—his Afro-Carribeanness, his militancy, the ease with which
he lives in and moves through his inhospitable environment —solidified into a
trope of a Dismal Swamp maroon that other abolitionist authors adapted and responded to in their own novels.

Born on a generic African coast, Picquilo embodied the ritual power and authority of his native home. Brown did not specify Picquilo's ethnicity, which,
given "the marks on his face" (the ritual scarification which marked his belonging in his native community), would have been all important to him.[63] Enslaved
in Cuba from the age of fifteen, prior to being smuggled into Virginia, he also embodied the restless "common wind" that carried maroon strategies of resistance
throughout the Greater Caribbean.[64] In his creation of Picquilo, Brown pulls from
John Reilly Beard's biography of Toussaint L'Ouverture, the legendary leader
of the Haitian revolution.[65] Picquilo's role as a leader among the maroons, as
demonstrated by his military adornments displaying his hunting prowess, implies
the existence of alternative social structures to those of plantation society and the
United States.

A figure like Picquilo would have been terrifying for white southern audiences
who might discover the novel. He makes a sword for himself out of the blade
of a stolen scythe, and "from revenge imbrued his hands in the blood of all the
whites he could meet."[66] While the Dismal might represent a sacred sanctuary for
a maroon like Picquilo, it evoked dread from plantation society. He moves freely
through the swamp "with the activity of a cat," upsetting plantation societies "politics of mobility" which sought always to bend the circulation of capital, goods,
and bodies to the will of planter elites.[67] Even if the plantation surveillance apparatus with its passes and patrols made movement beyond the swamps difficult
for enslaved people and maroons, in *Clotel*, the Dismal Swamp brings the distant
threat of Haitian style enslaved revolution close to home.

While Turner and the other maroons find a refuge from oppression in the Dismal, the results of the insurrection are disastrous for the novel's "mulatta" protagonist. Clotel's white husband, Horatio Green, keeps her, and their daughter Mary,
hidden from the public. Green's political ambitions lead to him marrying a white
woman from a politically powerful family. His new wife, upon discovering Mary
and Clotel and realizing Mary was her new husband's daughter, has Clotel sold
out of Virginia and enslaves Mary as her house servant. Clotel escapes and returns

to Virginia to rescue her daughter, but her return coincides with the immediate aftermath of the Southampton rebellion, and she is captured. She escapes but tragically commits suicide to prevent recapture.[68]

In 1860, Brown began serially publishing a new version of the story of Clotel—renamed *Miralda; or, The Beautiful Quadroon: A Romance of American Slavery Founded on Fact*—in the *Weekly Anglo-African*, a New York–based abolitionist paper that cost four cents an issue and was targeted primarily to African Americans.[69] New installations of the story appeared on the front page of the abolitionist publication every Saturday, in sixteen installments running from December 1860 to March 1861. In the context of this abolitionist weekly, "the fiction [of *Miralda*] was embedded in abolitionist material," writes Christopher Mulvey, "reversing the construction of *Clotel* which embedded abolitionist material in the fiction."[70]

Much of the text of *Clotel* appears word for word in *Miralda*, although there are important differences. For example, names of characters are altered and the latter edition is shorter, as Brown apparently felt comfortable dropping much of the abolitionist documentary materials that he included in *Clotel* for a publication which was already situated in an abolitionist weekly. Perhaps the most noticeable difference, however, is the title character's relationship to the former US president, Thomas Jefferson. In the 1853 version, Clotel is the daughter of Thomas Jefferson and an enslaved woman named Currer. In 1860, Clotel becomes Isabella, and her daughter Mary becomes the titular Miralda. Miralda is described not as Jefferson's granddaughter but more generically as "a descendant of Thomas Jefferson," and the 1853 subtitle "or, The President's Daughter" is also replaced in the new edition. By shifting the focus away from the role of Jefferson—a "founding father" in the United States' popular myth of its own development—as an enslaver who took sexual license with the women he enslaved, Brown subtly downplays the critique of the United States as a whole that characterized the 1853 version.[71]

Other than changing the names of the characters, the chapter in which Picquilo appears remains basically unchanged in the 1860–1861 version, with one notable exception. Right before describing the Nat Turner insurrection and the fictional Picquilo's role in it in the 1853 version, Brown writes that "the Free states are equally bound with the Slave States to suppress any insurrectionary movement that may take place among the slaves." He adds that northerners "are bound by their constitutional obligations to aid the slaveholder in keeping his slaves in their chains."[72] In the 1860–1861 version, however, these lines are omitted.

Written in the aftermath of the Fugitive Slave Act of 1850, the 1853 version casts Turner and Picquilo's revolutionary violence as an indictment of the whole United States, North and South, for its ongoing role in upholding slavery. The 1860–1861 version, on the other hand, was written in a context where Southern states had already began seceding from the Union, Lincoln had been elected president and taken office, and civil war seemed inevitable. Picquilo's appearance, here, is an indictment of Virginia and the other Southern states for whom the defense of slavery was becoming central to their political identities. Amid the chaotic urgency of an impending war, Brown takes sides, subtly modifying his deployment of the myth of the Dismal Swamp maroons to align it with the political necessities of the moment. Whereas the Northern states had been presented to English readers as sharing in culpability for slavery in 1853, in 1860–1861, the culpability is focused on Southern enslavers for African American readers amid a national crisis.

By 1864, anxiety over the threatened violence of enslaved rebellion that underpinned the figure of Picquilo and the myth of the Dismal Swamp maroons had given way to the violence of civil war. Once again, Brown adapted his 1853 novel to fit the urgency of his moment. In 1864, Brown's *Clotelle: A Tale of The Southern States* was published by James Redpath, who had already helped shape public perceptions of Dismal Swamp maroons. In his 1859 book, *The Roving Editor: or, Talks with Slaves in The Southern States*, Redpath describes the Dismal Swamp as a "Canada in the Southern States" for self-emancipators, and he includes an account from a former Dismal Swamp maroon named Charlie, which he tells readers was recorded "verbatim" by "Mrs. Knox, of Boston."[73] "Dar is families growed up in dat ar Dismal Swamp dat never seed a white man," Mrs. Knox records Charlie as saying, "an' would be skeered most to def to see one."[74]

The 1864 version of *Clotelle* was a part of Redpath's new series of dime novels targeted to Union soldiers: *Redpath's Books for The Camp Fires. Clotelle* was shorter than both *Clotel* and *Miralda* and lacked the abolitionist-oriented historical materials of the previous versions, focusing instead on the romantic drama. This version ends with a note from Redpath: "The author of the foregoing tale was formerly a Kentucky slave. If it serves to relieve the monotony of camp-life to the soldiers of the Union, and therefore of Liberty, and at the same time kindles their zeal in the cause of universal emancipation, the object both of its author and publisher will be gained."[75] Whatever other ambitions Brown harbored for his now multifaceted novel over the decades, in 1864 he seems to be content with its new publication aiding the Union army in its small way.

The final version of Brown's evolving narrative was printed in 1867 by the popular Boston publishing house Lee and Shepard as *Clotelle; or, The Colored*

Heroine. They used the same printing plates as used by Redpath in the 1864 version, only replacing his editorial note at the end with four new chapters.[76] In the previous three versions, Mary/Miralda/Clotelle finds happiness in Europe, with George in 1853 and with Jerome in 1860–1861 and 1864. But for a postwar, postemancipation readership, Brown uses the four new chapters to bring Clotelle and Jerome back to the United States. When Jerome dies fighting for the Union in the Civil War, a heartbroken Clotelle feels moved to help Union soldiers trapped in Confederate prisons. Passing as a white Confederate lady, she cares for Union prisoners at a prison camp in Georgia and helps many of them escape. After the war, Clotelle returns to the Mississippi plantation—Polar Farm—on which she had once been enslaved, purchases the property, and establishes a Freedmen's School.[77]

While the 1860–1861 and 1864 versions had been resolute in their criticism of the South, the 1867 ending is more ambiguous. Though he hated the white racism that existed before and after the fall of the Southern slavocracy, Brown always felt a strong attachment to the South. This ambiguous relationship is best expressed in his last book *My Southern Home*, published in 1880. According to Mulvey, "He lived in Boston because he had to live in Boston, but he dreamt of living happily on Polar Farm where he had once lived unhappily. The 'Conclusion' of 1867 fabricates for his heroine that improbable dream."[78] Nevertheless, Brown never ceased being critical of race relations in the South. He never returned to live there, and in *My Southern Home*, he decries "the bloody hands of the Ku-Klux and White Leaguer" who "through fear, intimidation, assassination, and all the horrors that barbarism can invent" take away "every right of the negro in the Southern States."[79] Rereading the 1867 ending through the lens of this final work, the figure of Picquilo and the myth of the Dismal Swamp maroons evokes a vision of a different South that never materialized, a South in which the sacred forces coalescing in the swamp undermined the stranglehold of white supremacy in ways that civil war had failed to do..

CONCLUSION

Myth, as Lincoln argues, has historically been deployed "more often and more effectively by those who seek to mystify and preserve exploitative patterns of social relations than it has by those who would reform or radically restructure such relations."[80] Planters seeking to consolidate their political power, for example, often deployed their own myth of the Dismal Swamp maroons as wild and savage threats to society that needed to be brought under proper planter control. But, as Lincoln points out, "the instrumentality [of myth] is not restricted to the reproduction of those social relations of which it is itself the product."[81]

Authors like William Wells Brown, Martin R. Delany, Frederick Douglass, Harriet Jacobs, and Harriet Beecher Stowe developed and deployed the ambiguous fear and promise evoked by the myth of the Dismal Swamp maroons as a discursive weapon against the social relations which sustained American slavery.

If, as I have argued, historical maroons transformed the Dismal Swamp into a site of the fugitive sacred, then abolitionist authors tried to harness this ambiguous sacred potency by submitting it to the logics of story structure (rising action, climax, and resolution, for example) and the determinations of editors, publishers, and markets. Through these literary and paraliterary mechanisms, the authors considered here sought to package this sacred potency as myth and deploy that myth to generate shared perceptions of the relationship between the past, present, and possible futures, perceptions from which to ground collaborative political action.

And while this tool-ification of the sacred (as Bataille might describe it) through literary myth sought to authorize political action, the texts considered here often relied on the authority of history to authorize that myth, as we see with, for example, Stowe's inclusion of the *Confessions* as an appendix to *Dred*. However, because the maroons of the Dismal Swamp so effectively evaded the authorities and record keepers of plantation society, the details of their lives could not be corroborated by the historiography of the dominant white supremacist institutions.[82] Nevertheless, rumors and legends could also serve to authorize myth, especially those as gripping as legends of militant swamp maroons in the aftermath of Nat Turner's Rebellion. In this way abolitionist authors sought to harness that historical memory clinging to the Dismal Swamp and deploy its affective power.

For these authors, how the myth is deployed, for whom, and why was shaped by their various, often disagreeing views on how best to confront slavery, and by the urgencies of their contexts. Nevertheless, they share the discursive terrain of the literary Dismal Swamp as a site for staging that confrontation. From the shaky ground of the swamp, the terrain of the slavocracy appears unstable. From this perspective, and in the context of the 1850s and 1860s, the myth of the Dismal Swamp maroons represents an urgent truth. Though the archive of slavery restricts or erases the subjective agency of swamp maroons, through their mythmaking the abolitionist authors considered here transformed these archival silences into charged sites for imagining and enacting life beyond subjugation.

NOTES

1. William Wells Brown, *Clotel; or, The President's Daughter: A Narrative of Slave Life in the United States* (Partridge and Oakey, 1853), 213.

2. Bruce Lincoln, *Discourse and the Construction of Society: Comparative Studies of Myth, Ritual, and Classification*, 2nd ed. (Oxford: Oxford University Press, 2014), 23.

3. I follow the lead of Christopher Mulvey who has argued that, although the four versions of *Clotel* were published under different titles by different publishers, "a great deal is to be gained by treating the novel as an evolving whole, and a great deal is to be lost by reading any one version in isolation." See Christopher Mulvey, "Clotel: Four Versions of the Novel," in William Wells Brown, *Clotel*, electronic scholarly ed., ed. Christopher Mulvey (University of Virginia Press, 2006).

4. Celeste Winston describes "geographic refuse" as "spaces that have been refused incorporation into dominant geographies and development, and sites where the people, land uses, and material environment are cast as marginal to the workings of racial capitalism's ecologies." See Celeste Winston, *How to Lose the Hounds: Maroon Geographies and a World Beyond Policing* (Durham, NC: Duke University Press, 2023), 3.

5. Alternatively, according to Gabriel de Avilez Rocha, *cimarrón* originated from a Taino word, *simara*, describing the flight of an arrow, signifying purpose and direction. *Cimarrón* was "forced into the language" of the Spanish colonizers he says, "through the strength of Native and Black insurrection." See Gabriel de Avilez Rocha, "Maroons in the Montes: Toward a Political Ecology of Marronage in the Sixteenth-Century Caribbean" in *Early Modbegetern Black Diaspora Studies: A Critical Anthology*; ed. Cassander L. Smith, Nicholas R. Jones, and Miles P. Grier (Cham: Palgrave Macmillan, 2018), 17.

6. J. Brent Morris, *Dismal Freedom: A History of the Maroons of the Great Dismal Swamp* (Chapel Hill: University of North Carolina Press, 2022), 95.

7. On the varieties of marronage from the perspective of an archeologist, and from that of a historian, see, respectively, Daniel O. Sayers, *A Desolate Place for a Defiant People: The Archaeology of Maroons, Indigenous Americans, and Enslaved Laborers in the Great Dismal Swamp* (Gainesville: University of Florida Press, 2014), 105–8; and Morris, *Dismal Freedom*, 93–136.

8. Sayers, *Desolate Place*, 116–35.

9. Sayers, *Desolate Place*, 172–75; Becca Peixotto, "Wetlands in Defiance: Exploring African-American Resistance in the Great Dismal Swamp," *Journal of Wetland Archeology* 17, no. 1 (2017): 22.

10. Peixotto, "Wetlands in Defiance," 30.

11. For example, in 1782 the overseer of the Dismal Plantation (owned by the Dismal Swamp Land Company) wrote a letter to a funder complaining that he had been "plagued" by maroons raiding the plantation to steal corn and rice. Jacob Collee to David Jameson, December 12, 1782, letter copy in Dismal Swamp Land Company Records (DSLC), box 7, folder 51, David M. Rubenstein Rare Book and Manuscript Library, Duke University, Durham, NC.

12. Kathryn Benjamin Golden, "'Armed in the Great Swamp': Fear, Maroon Insurrection, and the Insurgent Ecology of the Great Dismal Swamp," *Journal of African American History* 106, no. 1 (Winter 2021): 14–21.

13. Golden, "Armed in the Great Swamp," 10.

14. For a theorization of the "fugitive sacred" relevant to my discussion here, see Barbara Andrea Sostaita, "The Fugitive Sacred," in *Sanctuary Everywhere: The Fugitive Sacred in the Sonoran Desert* (Durham, NC: Duke University Press, 2024), 1–29.

15. My understanding of the sacred builds on, and reimagines, the work of anthro-

pologists of religion like Georges Bataille, Roger Caillois, and Mary Douglas. It is worth emphasizing that, for these theorists, nothing is *inherently* sacred. The sacred and profane distinction, then, does not describe some timeless and essential duality. It refers to an active social operation. Or, said otherwise: the profane is the register of human experience in which a group's commonsense language and experience map, more or less, neatly onto each other. It is the register in which things make sense within, and can be readily described by, the logic or discourse which governs the relations of a given social grouping. The sacred, on the other hand, refers to the forces which cannot be mapped neatly onto the socially normative circulation of discourse because it exceeds (and therefore calls into question) the very categories and assumptions which govern that circulation. See Georges Bataille, *Theory of Religion*, trans. Robert Hurley (New York: Zone Books, 1992); Roger Caillois, *Man and the Sacred*, trans. Meyer Barash (Urbana: University of Illinois Press, 2001); and Mary Douglas, *Purity and Danger*, 1966 (London: Routledge, 2002).

16. Sostaita, *Sanctuary Everywhere*, 7.

17. On Amy Post and the dispute between Harriet Jacobs and Harriet Beecher Stowe, see Jean Fagan Yellin, "Written by Herself: Harriet Jacobs' Slave Narrative," in Harriet Jacobs, *Incidents in the Life of a Slave Girl*, 2nd Norton critical ed., ed. Frances Smith Foster and Richard Yarborough (W. W. Norton: 2019), 213–16.

18. Jacobs, *Incidents*, 216–19.

19. Francis Smith Foster and Richard Yarborough, introduction to Jacobs, *Incidents*, vii.

20. Reflecting on the "terrible days" she had spent in the "snaky swamp" Linda thinks "though it was not called Dismal Swamp, it made me feel very dismal as I looked at it." This comment seems to suggest that the "Snaky Swamp" is not a pseudonym for the Dismal Swamp, but I suggest that we should understand it as the same place. Because Jacobs is writing as a fugitive from slavery, she regularly uses pseudonyms to prevent incriminating loved ones who are still enslaved or fugitives themselves. Moreover, In the early 1840s when Jacobs boarded the northbound ship, there was only one swamp along the route between Edenton and Philadelphia that might evoke the description of "a slave territory that defies all the laws": the Great Dismal Swamp. Thus, because Jacobs explicitly claims this "slave territory that defies all the laws" is the same "snaky swamp" in which she sheltered, it is most reasonable to interpret the "snaky swamp" as the Dismal Swamp.

21. Jacobs, *Incidents*, 96–97.

22. Jacobs used this phrase to describe the small garret in her grandmother's home where she hid from her enslaver while staying near her children. See Jacobs, *Incidents*, 97–100.

23. Jacobs, *Incidents*, 97.

24. Jacobs, *Incidents*, 133.

25. Snakes were not the only dangerous animals a human might encounter in the Dismal Swamp. Moses Grandy, for example, confronted this uncomfortable reality in an immediate way while hiding in the Dismal Swamp. An enslaved man who later bought his own freedom, Grandy fled to the swamp where he built himself a rudimentary shelter in which he could hide and recover from a brutal beating at the hands of a plantation overseer. He was awakened in horror from his sleep one night by the breath of a large predator on his face— in the intensity of the moment he could not decide whether it was a bear or a panther—

which he fortunately startled away in waking. Grandy's terrifying encounter highlights the reality that all Dismal residents lived with: the presence of swamp predators much stronger and faster than humans, for whom humans could and sometimes did serve as sustenance. *Narrative of the Life of Moses Grandy, Late a Slave in the United States of America*, transcribed by George Thompson (London: Charles Gilpin, 1844).

26. See Robert S. Levine, John Stauffer, and John R. McKivigan, introduction to Frederick Douglass, *The Heroic Slave*, 1853, cultural and critical ed., ed. Robert S. Levine, John Stauffer, and John McKivigan (New Haven, CT: Yale University Press, 2016), xxiii–xxiv.

27. Douglass, *Heroic Slave*, 4–5.

28. Douglass, *Heroic Slave*, 7–8.

29. Douglass, *Heroic Slave*, 9.

30. Douglass, *Heroic Slave*, 18.

31. Douglass and Martin R. Delany, *The North Star*, March 31, 1848; see also Marcus P. Nevius, *City of Refuge: Slavery and Petit Marronage in the Great Dismal Swamp, 1763–1856* (Athens: University of Georgia Press, 2020), 89–90. For references to cities of refuge in Hebrew Bible see Numbers 35, Deuteronomy 4:41–43, and Joshua 20.

32. Douglass, *Heroic Slave*, 192.

33. Lance Newman, "Free Soil and the Abolitionist Forests of Frederick Douglass's 'The Heroic Slave,'" *American Literature* 8, no. 1 (March 2009), 128.

34. Douglass, *Heroic Slave*, 17.

35. Caillois, *Man and the Sacred*, 22.

36. Morris, *Dismal Freedom*, 157.

37. Denmark Vesey was a formerly enslaved Charleston-based carpenter and lay-preacher-turned-rebel. In 1821, he and his still enslaved collaborators began planning a revolt, but the widespread plot was difficult to keep secret, and Vesey was discovered and executed. See Douglas Egerton, "Abolitionist or Terrorist?," opinion, *New York Times*, February 26, 2014. See also Robert L. Paquette, "From Rebellion to Revisionism: The Continuing Debate about the Denmark Vesey Affair," *Journal of the Historical Society* 4, no. 3 (Fall 2004): 291–334.

38. *Richmond Enquirer*, August 26, 1831. Quoted in Judith Louise Kemerait, "Routes of Freedom: Slave Resistance and the Politics of Literary Geography" (PhD diss., Louisiana State University, 2004), 23.

39. Crystal Nicole Eddins, *Rituals, Runaways, and the Haitian Revolution: Collective Action in the African Diaspora* (Cambridge: Cambridge University Press, 2022), 293–95; Laurent Dubois, *Avengers of the New World: The Story of the Haitian Revolution* (Cambridge, MA: Harvard University Press, 2004), 99–102.

40. Samuel Warner, *Authentic and Impartial Narrative of the Tragical Scene Which Was Witnessed in Southampton County (Virginia) on Monday the 22d of August Last* (New York: Warner and West, 1831), 30–31. Jean-Jacques Dessalines was a key figure in the Haitian Revolution and the first emperor of Haiti.

41. See Kemerait, "Routes of Freedom," 18.

42. *Petersburg Index*, October 1, 1869; Morris, *Dismal Freedom*, 92.

43. Harriet Beecher Stowe, *Dred; A Tale of the Great Dismal Swamp* (Boston: Phillips, Sampson, 1856), 338, transcription accessed through Documenting the American South, University Library, University of North Carolina at Chapel Hill, 2025. After Nat Turner was

arrested, while awaiting his trial and eventual execution, a white lawyer named Thomas Gray was sent to record his confessions. The product of this exchange, published by Gray as *The Confessions of Nat Turner*, is a vexing document, torn between Turner's alleged recounting of his rebellious plot and its motivations, and Gray's authorial intent to discursively limit the radical potential contained therein. For more on the fraught power dynamics behind *The Confessions*, see Eric Sundquist, *To Wake the Nations: Race in the Making of American Literature* (Cambridge, MA: Harvard University Press, 1993), 27–55; and Mark Simpson, *Trafficking Subjects: The Politics of Mobility in Nineteenth-Century America* (Minneapolis: University of Minnesota Press, 2004), 1–20.

44. Stowe, *Dred*, 7.

45. See Robert S. Levine, "Uncle Tom's Cabin in Frederick Douglass' Paper: An Analysis of Reception," *American Literature* 64, no. 1 (March 1992), 78–82.

46. Martin R. Delany, *Blake; or, The Huts of America*, 1861–1862, corrected ed., ed. Jerome McGann (Cambridge, MA: Harvard University Press, 2017), 3, 163.

47. Delany, *Blake*, 112–13. The protagonist of Delany's Blake is called Henry Holland in part 1 and Henry Blake in part 2. For the sake of simplicity, I will only refer to him as Henry Blake.

48. Delany, *Blake*, 113.

49. Delany, *Blake*, 114–16.

50. Delany, *Blake*, 114.

51. Jerome McGann, introduction to Delany, *Blake*, xi.

52. McGann, introduction, xv–xvi.

53. As Hugo Leaming points out, the final chapters must have connected "the Caribbean insurrection with that planned in the Southern United States, or else Part One would have no meaning in relation to Part Two." See Hugo Prosper Leaming, *Hidden Americans: Maroons of Virginia and the Carolinas* (New York: Garland, 1995), 381.

54. Judith Madera, *Black Atlas: Geography and Flow in Nineteenth-Century African American Literature* (Durham, NC: Duke University Press, 2015), 13.

55. Delany, *Blake*, 133–36.

56. See Delany, *Blake*, 324n122.

57. My use of "kino-politics," draws on the work of the philosopher Thomas Nail, who argues, "The power of the sovereign is first and foremost [the power] to move and make stop: kino-power." See Thomas Nail, *Lucretius I: An Ontology of Motion* (Edinburgh: Edinburgh University Press, 2018), 46.

58. Madera, *Black Atlas*, 17.

59. Madera, *Black Atlas*, 17.

60. William Wells Brown, *Three Years in Europe; or, Places I Have Seen and People I Have Met* (London: Charles Gilpin, 1852), 243.

61. Brown, *Clotel* (1853), 5.

62. Brown, *Clotel* (1853), 212.

63. On "country marks," see Michael Gomez, *Exchanging Our Country Marks: The Transformation of African Identities in the Colonial and Antebellum South* (Chapel Hill: University of North Carolina Press, 1998).

64. See Julius Scott, *The Common Wind: Afro-American Currents in the Age of the Haitian*

Revolution (London: Verso, 2018); David Cecelski, *The Waterman's Song: Slavery and Freedom in Maritime North Carolina* (Chapel Hill: University of North Carolina Press, 2001).

65. Sarah Jessica Johnson, "Outlyers: Maroons and Marronage in Eighteenth and Nineteenth-Century Literature" (PhD diss., University of California, Berkeley, 2018).

66. Brown, *Clotel* (1853), 213.

67. See Simpson, *Trafficking Subjects*, xiii–xiv.

68. Through Clotel, Brown deploys what scholars often call the "tragic mulatta" motif. This motif has received critical scrutiny for the ways in which it endorses biases based on skin complexion, as well as, as Jean Fagan Yellin has argued, "the patriarchal ideology of true womanhood in relation to women of color. See Jean Fagan Yellin, *Women and Sisters: The Antislavery Feminists in American Culture* (New Haven, CT: Yale University Press, 1989), 73. More recent scholarship has nuanced this criticism, shifting focus away from judgment and toward, as Hazel V. Carby writes, "a detailed analysis of its historical and narrative function." See Hazel V. Carby, *Reconstructing Womanhood: The Emergence of the Afro-American Woman Novelist* (Oxford: Oxford University Press, 1987), 89. "It was a strategy of the times," writes Ann duCille, which relied on "pointing out the mutability of race and the absurdity of white society's color codes." See Ann duCille, "Where in the World Is William Wells Brown? Thomas Jefferson, Sally Hemmings, and the DNA of African-American Literary History," *American Literary History* 12, no. 3 (2000): 454. And Eve Allegra Raimon argues that Brown manipulates the trope in an attempt to "unsettle the very categories of identity at work in the construction of founding U.S. ideologies of national origin and identity." See Eve Allegra Raimon, *The "Tragic Mulatta" Revisited: Race and Nationalism in Nineteenth Century Antislavery Fiction* (New Brunswick, NJ: Rutgers University Press, 2004), 63–64.

69. William Wells Brown, *Miralda; or, The Beautiful Quadroon: A Romance of American Slavery Founded on Fact*, published serially in the *Weekly Anglo-African* (New York, 1860–1861). Also see Mulvey, "Four Versions."

70. Mulvey, "Four Versions."

71. On the relationship between Thomas Jefferson and Sally Hemmings, a woman he enslaved, see Mulvey, "The African American Relations of Thomas Jefferson," in Brown, *Clotel*, electronic scholarly ed.

72. Brown, *Clotel* (1853), 219.

73. James Redpath, *The Roving Editor: or, Talks with Slaves in The Southern States* (New York: A. B. Burdick, 1859), 288.

74. Redpath, *Roving Editor*, 293.

75. William Wells Brown, *Clotelle: A Tale of the Southern States* (Boston: James Redpath, 1864), 104.

76. See Michael Winship, "Bibliographical Description of the 1867 Text," in Brown, *Clotel*, electronic scholarly ed.

77. William Wells Brown, *Clotelle; or, The Colored Heroine* (Boston: Lee and Shepard, 1867), 114.

78. Mulvey, "Four Versions."

79. Brown, *My Southern Home: or, The South and Its People* (Boston: A. G. Brown, 1880), 166.

80. Lincoln, *Discourse*, 48.

81. Lincoln, *Discourse*, 48.

82. This problem intensifies an underlying issue with the archives of slavery that historians have recognized and wrestled with for decades: that what gets recorded as "history" is overwhelmingly determined by people and institutions who refuse to recognize the full humanity of enslaved people. Enslaved and formerly enslaved people are instead most often rendered legible in these archives in either the forms of a commodity or a corpse. Nevertheless, I draw on methods developed by historians for reading these archives for, as Sadiya Hartman has written, "contrary purposes." Sadiya V. Hartman, *Scenes of Subjection: Terror, Slavery, and Self-Making in Nineteenth-Century America* (Oxford: Oxford University Press, 1997), 11. See also Marisa J. Fuentes, *Dispossessed Lives: Enslaved Women, Violence, and the Archive* (Philadelphia: University of Pennsylvania Press, 2015); Ann Laura Stoler, *Along the Archival Grain: Epistemic Anxieties and Colonial Common Sense* (Princeton, NJ: Princeton University Press, 2009); and Michel-Rolph Trouillot, *Silencing the Past: Power and the Production of History*, 20th anniversary ed. (Boston: Beacon, 2015).

Divine Duality in the Oneida Community

KIT HERMANSON

The Oneida Community, a perfectionist commune in Upstate New York, rattled American sensibilities for more than three decades in the mid-nineteenth century. The Community and its more than three hundred members became famous for their metal goods and infamous for their sexual practices. Contemporaries compared their system of "complex marriage," in which all members were considered married to one another, to the secular free love movement and Mormon polygamy; as such, it was frequently decried for licentiousness and biblical perversion. Scholarship on the Community in the nearly two centuries since has similarly focused on this aspect of its existence with particular attention paid to the practices effect on the commune's women. However, complex marriage was far from the only Oneida practice that reformulated the gender conventions of Victorian America: at the center of the community's perfectionist theology was their belief in a bigendered God. Oneida members imagined God as a bodiless but fully gendered being in whom stereotypical masculine aspects, like rationality and strength, were equally combined with feminine ones, like gentleness and love. This theological tenant was foundational to Community members' religious practices and daily life, effecting their dress, work, prayers, and social lives. Oneida members, like many Christians, strove to improve their souls through being and acting more God-like. In this case, this necessitated developing a sensibility around and performance of gender that reflected God's androgynous nature regardless of their gender assigned at birth.

Gender sensibility in the Oneida Community centered on affective gendered *expression* and *conduct*; not necessarily *what* one did, but the gendered connotations of *how* they did it. This sensibility, I argue, is more important than the heretofore scholarly focus on "gender roles" in which the terms of material access and divisions of emotional and physical labor are considered paramount to understanding gendered realities and experiences of Community members. Gender sensibility was actively sought and developed through prayer, self-assessment, and communal enforcement and, to the members themselves, differentiated the Oneida Community from the outside world far more than differences in gender roles, such as gendered division of labor. Community forms of gender expression were means to spiritual betterment and an expression of sectarian identity through the gendered body (and soul) in every action of their daily lives. Conforming to theologically determined social ideals held importance to each member. Each instance of gender performance was an immediate and urgent spiritual matter. While theological claims underpinned the gender and social mores of all Americans, for the Oneida perfectionists, their theological interpretations explicitly and solely defined the parameters of acceptable gendered expression and sociality.

Oneida Community members fundamentally changed the ways in which they thought about and performed gender based on the Oneida theological model of the divine androgyny defined by their image of God as bigender.[1] In Judith Butler's famous formulation of gendered subject formation in *Gender Trouble*, they state:

> The rules that govern intelligible identity . . . operate through *repetition*. . . . Indeed, when the subject is said to be constituted, that means simply that the subject is a consequence of certain rule-governed discourses that govern the intelligible invocation of identity. The subject is not *determined by* the rules through which it is generated because signification is *not a founding act, but rather a regulated process of repetition* that both conceals itself and enforces its rules precisely through the production of substantializing effects . . . The question is not: what meaning does the inscription carry within it, but what cultural apparatus arranges this meeting between instrument and body, what interventions into this ritualistic repetition are possible?[2]

The Oneida Community's approach, unexpectedly, anticipated Butler's proposed problem and answers their rhetorical question without disturbing the matrices of gender hierarchy or compulsory heterosexuality. Community members intentionally remade their gendered subjectivities and performances toward embodying a divine, internally androgynous ideal of human perfection through iterative religious practice. Unlike the gender performativity of Butler's theory (which they later clarified in *Bodies that Matter* is not necessarily an agential, *chosen* act as *Gender Trouble* readers generally assumed), performing and internalizing hyperlocal Oneida Community gendered subjectivities was purposeful, structured, and ritualized. Most importantly, perfectionist theology identified the gendered dynamics of interpersonal life as an aspect of the self and soul that was changeable and separate from biological sex. Gender performance, that is, could and must be intervened on through alternative forms of ritualistic repetition and new cultural apparatuses. In this case, religiosity and a certain imagining of the materiality, gender, and function of the human spirit tangibly enabled a reimagining and reformation of gendered subjectivity. In short, Oneidans' religious beliefs *created* the gender and sexual deviance of the Oneida Community, rather than simply providing "an excuse" for it as has often been claimed. The "interventions into this ritualistic repetition" practiced by Oneida Community to reform nineteenth-century American gender norms were, in fact, rituals themselves.

This chapter explores the Oneida Community's theological discursive and practiced revision of the relationship between gender, sex, and the soul in efforts to develop and codify this new gender sensibility. God was, Oneida members believed, both male and female, masculine and feminine, active and receptive within a single divine "body." Members extrapolated this concept of a "dual Godhead" to subject formation practices, requiring members to commit to broad reevaluations of the nature of and relationship between men and women in terms of sociality, sexuality, economics, and religious practice. These practices negotiated the theologically important concept of an interior gender duality of the spirit while retaining the perceived fact of biological sexual dimorphism, constantly fluctuating between transgressing and upholding the gender and sexual norms of the nineteenth-century United States.

That is to say that although Oneida's practices were explicitly about changing social practices of gender they were not necessarily practices of protofeminism, equality, or liberation either in a historical retrospective or nineteenth-century contemporary framework. By not focusing on either women or the question of liberation, we can more easily see how ideals and reality of Community life were interpreted as coherent and promising by its members, as opposed to the vast historiography of Oneida that has interpreted the Community exclusively as a story of either the victimization or liberation of women. To live in a world where God was both male and female fundamentally changed the social experience of gender for Community men and women; perfectionism promised different, if not to today's normative standards "better," ways of living.

While we could also trace the importance of this theological claim in Oneida's other practices—such as stirpiculture and Community women's "short dress"—in this chapter I focus on complex marriage, mutual criticism, and the concept of submission. Complex marriage is the most popular aspect of the Oneida Community for scholars. In particular, historians have generally approached the Oneida Community in terms of its liberatory or oppressive effect on women members beginning in the era of gender studies' establishment with Richard DeMaria's *Communal Love at Oneida* in 1978 and closely followed by Louis J. Kern's *An Ordered Love* in 1981 and Lawrence Foster's *Religion and Sexuality* in 1984, both of which compared the status of women (as determined by sociosexual arrangements) in Mormon, Oneida, and Shaker communities.[3] Since then, the dozens of academic writings on the Oneida Community have rehashed the issue and, in doing so, have obscured analysis of *gender*, as a broad functional aspect of sociality, in the Community behind the specific question of complex marriage's (proto)feminist potential. By contrast, mutual criticism—a practice for which ample amounts of archived materials exist and was thoroughly steeped in concerns about gender—has very rarely been written about.[4] My intent in focusing on the most popular aspect of the community alongside a lesser-known Community practice is to demonstrate the breadth of the perfectionist reformulation of gender ideals' applicability as well as the potential for further study for the spaces in between.

Throughout this chapter I narrate how to Oneida Community members gender was religious and spiritual itself—disconnected though entangled with biological sex. This disconnect demonstrates evidence of nineteenth-century engagements with gender and sexuality as a mutable and manipulable social concept that differently imagined the social implications of scientific biological determinism that bear an affinity to queer and trans imaginings of sex, gender, and sexuality today. By recognizing the centrality of combinatory androgyny and sexuality to Oneida theology, and by taking theology and religious practice seriously as a mode of gendered self-making, we can see more deeply into one of the many ways in which nineteenth-century Americans critically engaged with and created alternatives to the rapidly concretizing landscape of cisnormativity in American scientific and cultural discourse. Approaching historical gender dynamics in this way allows for, first, a focus on the social phenomenon of *gender* as a subject of analysis rather than as an academic euphemism for *women* and, second, to see the ways in which historical subjects actively and intentionally engage with gender, sex, and sexuality as malleable concepts rather than passively inherited truths before and outside of the twentieth-century advent of gender studies and queer theory. In the case of the Oneida Community, and doubtless many other historical groups, this approach particularly emphasizes the ways in which theological claims can themselves be critical analyses and result in social modifications of gender as such far before theories of social constructionism.

GOD'S DUAL NATURE

The peculiar customs of the Oneida Community stemmed from the community's founder and religious leader, John Humphrey Noyes (1811–1886). As early as 1833, Noyes began gaining followers to the sect that became informally known as Putney perfectionism. Like other forms of perfectionism, Putney perfectionism was based on the pugilist idea that the human soul could and *should* be perfected in mortal life. Mainline American Protestants, to Noyes, basely misinterpreted many of the basic biblical tenants, from the purpose of Christian marriage to the timing of the promised Second Coming of Christ. Noyes also claimed that nonperfectionists misunderstood the nature of their very own bodies *and* the body of God.

Noyes looked to Genesis to understand *what* people were, particularly in terms of biological sex. Like theologians from Augustine of Hippo to Swedenborg, Noyes found himself deeply interested in the moment of human creation and what the story of Adam and Eve said about the nature of sex and gender. The long history of this question, reviving cyclically throughout Christianity's tenure, generally centered on the bodily sex of Adam and, by extension, the bodily sex—or lack of sex—in the postresurrection state.[5] Noyes approached the question of "the two sexes'" creation very differently. Late eighteenth- and early nineteenth-century scientists had largely discredited the possibility of the bisexed, nonsexed, or "truly hermaphroditic" body by the 1830s, despite its persistence in the popular imagination. All deviations from the imagined perfect male or female body were generally understood to be malformed men or women that could be correctly identified and "fixed" through medical and social intervention. Noyes prided himself on his scientific mind and engagement with recent developments in the field and, given his interest in sex and the body, would have been very aware of the state of the field regarding nonbinary sex. Intersex bodies never figure into Noyes's assertions. In his 1847 theological treatise titled *The Berean* he stated, "The distinction between male and female is as universal as vitality, and all visible evidence goes to prove that it is the indispensable condition of reproduction, i.e. of vital creation."[6] To Noyes, the contrasting yet complementary natures of the male and female (conventionally construed) constituted a foundational truism of human existence.

This primary belief next prompted Noyes to reflect on the sexed and gendered nature of God himself. Given observable and assumed universal necessity of male-female combination for procreation, the Putney perfectionists were "led to the simple conclusion, that the uncreated Creator, the Head of the universe, like the head of mankind and the head of every family, though one, is yet 'twain;' (Mark 10:8;) in a word, that the creation has a Father and a Mother."[7] Unlike

Mormon and German pietist theology in which the feminine aspect of divinity was personified in a separate entity (the Holy Mother and Sophia, respectively), perfectionist theology collapsed the feminine into the preexisting conception of God's masculine existence. God, then, was *both* male and female. Returning again to the apparently indisputable natural fact of sexual dimorphism, Noyes asked, "If we find two elements [male and female] in all the streams of life, why should we not infer that the same two elements are in the Fountainhead?"[8] If creation, imagined here in terms of heterosexual reproduction in both the spiritual and mundane worlds, required male and female participation, then God himself must have and be capable of both.

For the perfectionists, the gender duality of God also solved the theological problem of the diversities of human form all being created "in His image." The perfectionists asked:

For what, is the human form? Is it the form of man? or of woman? Nay; it is certainly the form of all that enters into the constitution of human beings, i.e. it is the form of both man and woman. To call a male form alone, the human form, is as absurd as it would be to call the right half of the human body the human form, or to call the odd half of a pair of shears' the shear-form. . . . We are quite willing that the indication of the created universe should be true—that woman as well as man should have her archetype in the primary sphere of existence—that the receptive as well as the active principle, subordination as well as power, should have its representative in the Godhead.[9]

By extension, God himself is always-already perfect, interlocked in and of his own male and female parts and essences, not only the Creator but the *Procreator* of all life. This imagery reflects earlier imaginings of the "true hermaphrodite" who had complete sets of male and female genitalia and was capable of self-impregnation. Noyes noted in many writings and sermons that sexual shame should itself be considered sinful: male and female genitalia were "the most perfect instruments of love and unity," not only perfect in themselves as a reflection of God's body but perfect in their mutually corresponding design for interlocking sexual fit.[10] The perfection of heterosexual bodily correspondence since the creation of the first humans provided proof that God's intention for sex to occur as a means for reuniting the male and female halves into an androgynous whole.

In creating Adam and Eve, the perfectionists believed, God created two sexes from his own sexual and spiritual duality. In the first pages of the lengthy 1847 theological treatise *The Berean*, Noyes and the perfectionists proclaimed:

"We believe not in the Trinity, nor in the Unity, but in the *Duality* of the Godhead; and that Duality in our view, is imaged in the two-fold personality of the first man, who was made 'male and female' (Gen 1:27)."[11] Despite establishing this God's own androgyny, however, Noyes and his Community did not change the masculine language traditionally used to refer to God in Christianity. Rather, Noyes asserted that since the masculine was "naturally" more dominant than the feminine, it was the "higher" masculine principle that believers should directly reference: "As Adam was to Eve, so is the Father to the Son; i.e. he is the same in nature, but greater in power and glory."[12] Thus, while both masculine and feminine principles were from the same divine source, hierarchy persisted.

"The constitutional distinctions and offices of the sexes," Noyes wrote in *Bible Communism* (1853), "belong to their original paradisaical state; and there is no proof in the Bible or in reason, that they are ever to be abolished, but abundance of proof to the contrary . . . so the sexes, though one in their innermost life, as members in Christ, yet retain their constitutional differences."[13] The "constitution" of the sexes in their bodily differences underscored the "offices" of the sexes in which woman was always-already subordinate to man, both theologically and biologically. Furthermore, this quote emphasizes the perfectionist belief that all people would retain sexual distinctiveness in the resurrected and heavenly states, as opposed to the harmonists, Zoarites, Swedenborgians, and Shakers who predicted that heavenly bodies would have no physical sex at all, in the way of angels in the Christian tradition. Brought together, perfectionist reimaginings of sex across Christian states (mortal and postresurrection) required followers to understand themselves differently and urged them toward a different way of being Christian. The urgency with which Noyes referred to both paradise and the glorified image of the "primitive church" assured followers that in the face of the imminent Second Coming, radical alterations to self, community, and religion were necessary.

The idealization of the primitive church was a popular theological justification among many Christian separatist groups that practiced communitarianism in the nineteenth century. Like these other groups, members of the Community surrendered their own personal wealth and possession to community ownership upon entrance as well as the practice of any past profession. Unlike many other nineteenth-century intentional communities, however, this system of shared labor had the secondary goal of the abolishment, or at least the revision, of gender-role based divisions of labor, which was seen as another way in which men and women were misled into improper, un-Christian life paths. For example, Noyes claimed that women, who God gave the "largest muscular developments in the lower part of the trunk, about the legs," were "adapted by nature, even better than men, to out-door employments and sports—to running, leaping, &c."[14] Furthermore, the Community objected to the normative separation of men and women into domestic and public labor spheres: "In the current system, the woman keeps the house, and the man labors abroad. . . . When the partition between the sexes is taken away, and man ceases to make woman a propagative drudge, when love takes the place of shame, and fashion follows nature in dress and business, men and women will be able to mingle in all their employments, as boys and girls mingle in their sports; and then labor will be attractive."[15] Although many women continued to choose jobs in the community traditionally coded as feminine, so did many men. Even if unsuccessful, the attempt to eliminate compulsory gendered labor roles reflected a desire for an effective approach to communal economics that furthered the theological goal of broadly reorienting gendered and sexual sociality.[16] Upon joining, Oneida members committed to a total subjective transformation in order to become closer to the dual Godhead through radical processes of self-perfection.

However, radical and androgynous by no means meant egalitarian. The Oneida Community was organized into a system known as "ascending fellowship" that measured degree of spiritual perfection to determine each member's hierarchical position in the community. Oneida's theological commitment to androgyny, however, should not be too generously read as an abolishment of patriarchal social control. While men and women held equal potential for perfection, in any dynamic between a man and woman of the same spiritual degree, the male would rank higher by default. This system augmented traditional patriarchy with the conviction that masculine and feminine spiritual energy could be found, and externalized, in each person's soul regardless of sex and furthermore restricted women's access to the kinds of domestic and spiritual authority that was often afforded them in more mainstream Christian American settings. However, the system did mirror Noyes' interpretation of Paul's chain of authority that incorporated the internal gender duality of God in ways that actively lateralized gendered access to social positions unique to the community itself. The more spiritually perfect (usually older or longtime members) had authority over all those of any gender who were less perfect. This authority played out in all practical aspects of Community life. Heads of work departments, people in charge of communicating with customers and partners outside of the community, and council members were almost always selected with a basis in their high position in the fellowship.

Among high-ranking members, women and men were about equally represented. Gaining position in the chain of fellowship required a complete transformation of their character, behavior, and ideals from what they held in the outside world to Community standards. The processes involved in living in the community inculcated a capacity for experiencing gender, body, and faith differently. Any individual's proper gender performance as understood by community members—whether to be deferential or firm, to guide or submit to guidance—was based on each person's position within the fellowship; thus, each member was expected to be fully capable of socializing both femininely and masculinely regardless of their own gender and to develop a new kind of sensibility around gender that would allow to them take on variously rank-based submissive or authoritative roles in interactions with other community members. These modifications were seen as spiritual as well as social because, for the members of the Community, a separation between the two could not exist. All aspects of life, from work to worship to leisure, were connected through the proximity.

Oneida Community members sought to *live differently* in a world where they saw false religion, unjust wealth distribution, and unsatisfying gender dynamics led Americans away from Christian traditionalism. Their seemingly new and innovative approaches to Christian life were in fact, to the members, a return to form, an earnest desire to be closer to their androgynous God than they thought was possible in the world at large. This image of God was thoroughly and intentionally extrapolated on and applied every aspect of commune social life.

COMPLEX MARRIAGE

Noyes and his followers maintained that bodily sex was an essential aspect of one's mortal and heavenly life. For a group of believers striving to become more like an androgynous God, however, the eternality of sex posed a problem: humans, as lesser reflections of God, each person could only take on either the male or female nature of God in their bodies. Humans, in their reasoning, could only be male *or* female whereas God was both at once. The solution to the immutable nature of sex could, however, be achieved through heterosexual union in which two sets of body and soul "became one." Complementarianism—the idea that man and woman were essentially different, designed for one another, and thus through union made up for each other's physical and spiritual deficiencies—had traditionally manifested as marriage in the Christian tradition. In Oneida, the act of sexual intercourse itself took marriage's place as the literal and metaphysical union of the masculine and feminine essences of the soul that reflected the internal unity of God.

Beginning in 1844, the perfectionists replaced the husband-wife foundation of the traditional heteronormative family unit with a system they called "complex marriage." In this arrangement, all adult members of the community were considered married to one another and encouraged to pursue sexual intercourse for pleasure—in Community terms "amative relations"—with a variety of community partners so long as no "special attachments"—exclusive romantic—relationships developed. "The Communities insist," the *Handbook of the Oneida Community* stated, "that the heart should be kept free to love all the true and worthy, and should never be contracted with exclusiveness or idolatry, or selfish love in any form."[17] Community members saw complex marriage as a method of modeling their lives after the biblical postulations on postresurrection state that "they neither marry nor be given in marriage" without relinquishing the God-given pleasure of sexual intercourse. Although members were (even aggressively) heterosexual, their spiritual and personal commitments to the system of complex marriage constituted a kind of sexual identity without necessary reference to gender. To have and show a "community spirit" was constitutive of a way of being gendered and sexual in the world that differentiated members from nonmembers.[18] This approach to sex and relationships reflected the perfectionist interpretation of Genesis: in the moment of sex, the entangling of male and female bodies most perfectly reflected the body of God.[19] Through sex and attraction, members could positively influence one another spiritually as well as maintain the counternormative social dynamics of the Community.

Noyes and leading Community members insisted that the desire for increased spiritual connection between participants seeking to perfect themselves should lay at the center of all sexual interactions. In contrast to mainline Christians of the period, procreation was the least important function of sex in Oneida. Besides creating a reflection of the body and spirit of God, the most important aspect of sex was the spiritual effect of the physical and metaphysical unification of two spirits in "fellowship." At an evening meeting in the Oneida Community Mansion House in 1875, Noyes preached that "all fellowship is of the nature of sexual intercourse. Within ourselves, aside from the connection of the sexes, there is the duality of male and female in our powers and passions. We are every one of us both male and female." Noyes asserted that the male and female essences, active and receptive respectively, should be equally balanced in each Community member regardless of external sex, one dominating the other only when certain social relations called for it. This reimagining did not tamper with what Noyes and others of the nineteenth century saw as the biological immutability of the difference between male and female bodies or attempt to deconstruct the practice of assigning gender based on sex even as it asserted that these external realities must be negotiated through a recognition and embracing of each soul's internal duality.[20]

Noyes's assertion that a dual-gendered spirit dwelled within every sexed individual demonstrates an Oneidan understanding of the *separation* of interior gender from physical sex that in many ways prefigures late twentieth- and twenty-first-century queer and trans understandings of gender/sex/sexuality distinctiveness. This is not to say that gender itself was able to be chosen (Oneida members never seem to have questioned normative cisgender interpretations of the body), but that identifying and changing the gender-associated attributes of social interaction (what we might call gender performance) was imminently possible and necessary for perfection. The externalization of gender through speech, action, countenance, and style was entirely mutable through the exercise of religious self-improvement even if bodily sex was stagnant. The soul's gender duality, in this formulation, did not undermine heterosexual attachment but rather reflected it and reified its importance to everyone's constitution and their relationships with opposite-sexed bodies. Finding an appropriate balance of the masculine and feminine within the self was a process of internalizing the perfectionist interpretation of sexual union in which two distinct forms, each with both masculine and feminine essences, met to form a singular connection in the image of God.

Members especially encouraged one another to "get into the highest and best activity of the receptive part of your nature—the female part" to increase the connection "between our hearts and the control of the spiritual world."[21] Jesus Christ, Noyes noted in *The Berean*, was the most perfect example of divine androgyny, manifesting his dual nature on Earth through exalting his feminine power through passion for God and his personal conduct while exerting masculine power through his leadership of his followers.[22] The invocation of Christ in the Community writings often referenced his perfectly harmonious embodiment of the two genders. We can see the members' internalization of this theological assertion in the diary of Community member Harriet Matthews, who wrote in her diary in 1856 that she "pray[ed] for the meekness of Christ—for a true womanly spirit and a spirit that esteems others better than myself."[23] Following the path of countless other Christian sects, members of the Community sought to be like Christ, though their attempts to mimic him took on gendered forms that set a combinatory androgynous ideal at their center. Living in the Oneida Community was not simply about adhering to a belief in perfectionist theology. One must seek perfection, must develop a *capacity* to live and find pleasure in a lifestyle modeled after the duality of God.[24]

In his text *The Berean*, Noyes indicated that the post-Fall, singular division of the sexes had been detrimental to human life itself: "The good elements of life are distributed to the two sexes in such a manner that man by himself is deficient in those beautiful affections which abound in woman, and woman by herself lacks the strength of heart and head which belongs to man. The condensation of any two characters into one, would improve both; and the more diverse the two might be, the greater would be the improvement."[25] As perfectionists, this suggestion of improvement was not just a theological abstraction. To strive for a kind of proper dual balance in which the masculine and feminine were balanced and condensed within each person while maintaining male social superiority, was a practical basis for many of the practices of the Oneida Community.

Perfectionist theological "duality" abounds with queerness, as defined as deviation from traditional sex and gender norms, while also maintaining hierarchical power and compulsory heterosexuality. While feminine and masculine attributes were equal aspects of God, each had a complementary role predicated on their presupposed nature, with masculine aspects being the more encompassing, stronger, and active of the two. "The female capacity is in its very nature negative," *The Berean* states, "Weakness makes room for strength. Deficiency embraces fullness." Noyes, and many Christians in the nineteenth century and today, extrapolated this inferiority from 1 Corinthians 11:13: "The head of every man is Christ, and the head of the woman is the man, and the head of Christ is God" (KJV). What differentiates Noyes's theology is that rather than an ascending line of increasing masculinity toward the male God, this chain leads toward divine androgyny in the form of the dual Godhead.

In this theological assertion, masculinity and femininity fold into one another within individual beings who are physically divided into two sexed categories: "The distinction of male and female creates a duality consisting of an inner and outer life. As the Father is the inner fullness of Christ, and as Christ is the inner fullness of the universal sphere of the redeemed, so man is the inner fullness of woman. This is said, not of the relations of individual men and women, but of the relation of the whole man-spirit to the whole woman-spirit."[26] Perfection required members to strive for relational duality that reflected the at once male and female nature of God and pre-Fall Adam: "Before [unity with heaven] can be attained every spirit must rejoice to be not only male to a sphere without, but female to a sphere within. In the whole succession of spirits the 'weaker vessels' must consent to be filled by the stronger."[27] In practice, this framing required multidirectional submission and leadership depending on each interlocutor's position in the system of ascending fellowship, which did not at any time necessarily correspond to their own external gender.

MUTUAL CRITICISM

The "frank criticism of each other's character for the purpose of improvement," Noyes claimed, was how he himself came to the theology of perfectionism, taken from his congregationalist training at Andover Theological Seminary.[28]
In response to contemporary outsiders who struggled to understand how a society could function without formal government, the Community publication *Bible
Communism* humorously stated: "Here is the whole secret of government among
us. Our government is Democratic, inasmuch as the privilege of criticism is distributed through the whole body, and the power which it gives is accessible to any
one who will take the pains to attain good judgment. It is Aristocratic, inasmuch
as the best critics have the most power. It is Theocratic, inasmuch as the Spirit of
Truth alone can give the power of genuine criticism."[29] Beyond regulating Oneida
as a social body, mutual criticism was the means through which members mediated interpersonal problems and spiritual failings—the former always taken as a
sign of the latter. In a mutual criticism meeting, a member to be criticized would
sit in the center of a semicircle and silently listen as eight to ten other community
members (or in cases of severe disapprobation, the entire community) sat around
them and discussed their behavior in detail, giving the criticized member both rep-
robation and praise. These meetings often took the form of conversation between
the criticizing members that the criticized person simply witnessed, but sometimes criticizing members were represented in meetings by anonymous or signed
notes. Beginning in the early 1870s, the roles of criticizers were made exclusive to
an elected, rotating council of critics that was usually made up of older men and
women who held high positions in the system of ascending fellowship. The subject of criticism was allowed to dispute facts but not opinions. As such, both quib-
bling and silence on any point was seen as an admission of guilt of any given of-
fense. This process was emotionally intense, even traumatic, and was the reason
that many people declined joining or even left Oneida throughout the decades.
"Those who cannot bear this ordeal are unfit for Community life and ought not to
attempt it," Noyes wrote in 1875.[30] Those who remained despite, or in some cases
because of, this difficult-to-endure ritual consented to being gradually remade as
a subject, to give their speech, actions, and reputation over to the norms of the
community.

Scholars have deeply investigated the role of charismatic authority in mutual criticism, its possibility to a nonstate form of government, and the emotional trauma it inevitably produced. The significance of gender to mutual
criticism, however, has been little examined. Against scholarly claims that mutual criticism was primarily "a system of conflict reduction" that "failed to do
away with a number of social tensions that affected the OC" or an "effectively

combined peer pressure with self-examination . . . [not] regarded primarily as a rite of worship," records of and about criticism sessions show that the practice *was* both ritualized and a direct outgrowth of the theologically mandated task of spiritual betterment at the root of the Community's perfectionist beliefs.[31] Mutual criticism, as a religious practice and method of subject (re)making, aimed to orient community members toward an appropriate balance of everyone's internal masculine and feminine essences, a mission that, secondarily, was trusted in as the most effective means of regulating communal sociality.

As I have outlined, Noyes's theology and prescribed practices manifested as a tension between a strongly held belief in the masculine-feminine nature of every human soul and the desires of promoting heterosexual intimacy and hierarchically differentiating the roles of men and women. In the surviving notes and transcriptions from mutual criticism sessions, we can see the difficulty of seriously reconciling these apparently contradictory points but nevertheless a pervasive commitment to doing so. The theological emphasis on gender and sexuality pervading the religious and social thinking of members resulted in critiques of gender performance becoming one of the key modes in which members expressed concern and dissatisfaction with one another.

Mutual criticism functioned as ritualized gender policing that aimed to produce members hyperaware of their own gender performance, deeply connected to their spiritual salvation, and capable of actively changing it. This is particularly significant and unique in a period when almost all forms of human behavior and sociality were increasingly prescriptively attached to binary sex characteristics and often utilized as evidence for making a selection of "true sex" of actual intersex people. Thus, while the Oneida Community saw the binary division of the sexed bodies as permanent, natural, and divinely gifted to allow for carnal union, their theology figured *gender* in a similar way that queer theorists and popular culture have begun to see it since the late twentieth century: an aspect of the social self mapped onto the sexed body that is performed and potentially malleable.[32] Mutual criticism was a tool that allowed members to modify the gendered dynamics of interpersonal interaction and foster a specific gendered self-conceptualization through religious language and theological intervention. Mutual criticism was the medium through which gender was retaught and relearned by members upon entering into fellowship with the community and enforced a hyperlocal normative gendered comportment oriented toward an internalized combinatory gender ideal while maintaining practical sexual dimorphic identities.

Despite the dual, androgynous nature of the soul in their theology, it is the feminine, receptive aspect that was most often called on to be improved and fostered. "Getting into the feminine aspect" was a prerequisite for effective reception of criticism. We can also see through the excerpts of sessions published in their public-facing materials that the Community wanted the outside world to know that this was the case, likely as a counter to public concerns about the abuse of women inside the community. The pamphlet *Mutual Criticism* (1876) provides twenty-seven anonymized excerpts from mutual criticism sessions. Critique in these sessions covers the complete gambit of community life, including complaints about a young woman laughing too much and too loudly, a young man who is too inquisitive about others' business, a variety of personal vanities, superficiality in interpersonal connections, and lack of earnestness in labor and business; the list goes on. Four of these excerpts specifically advise men to cultivate feminine aspects of their character. "S. has a great deal of what is usually termed manliness," one entry states: "He has encouraged the stern side of his nature, and discouraged the gentle side. He seems to be ashamed to show the softness and tenderness that he feels. He needs to know that these two phases of character are not irreconcilable. That are in fact necessary complements of each other. . . . No one can be like Christ without having both the lion and the lamb in his character."[33] References to an androgynous ideal in this statement and the reference to Christ's perfection reassert the centrality and divinity of dualistic androgyny in Oneida. A more extensive criticism notes that "the generic fault with A. is that he is too *masculine*. He would be a better man if he were a little more of a woman: *i.e.*, if his life instead of running so much into strength, ran more into delicacy, affection, amiability—qualities which particularly belong to the feminine nature."[34] The maintenance of essential binary gender traits—strength with masculinity, delicacy with femininity—is here uncoupled from the normative form of binary logics through explicit encouragement of transgendered cultivation. This cross-association of affective gendered sensibility did not threaten the importance of heterosexual intimacy and hierarchy to community members; rather, the cultivation of men's "feminine" inclinations were expressed as desirable by community men and women alike.

Unpublicized transcriptions and notes from mutual criticism sessions also reflect this pattern, demonstrating that the intentional feminization of community men was not simply to assuage cultural critics. Oneida member J. B. Herricks, one of the core businessmen of the community, noted during a criticism of E. Foder that "the female side of his character I like very much. So long as he is receptive to masculine spirits which are above him, he is a beautiful man, but when he attempts to perform a part which he is not qualified by nature or grace he becomes exceedingly tiresome."[35] Herricks in turn was criticized during a time when he struggled with fully separating from his wife, who did not join the community with him. The criticizer stated: "I think Mr. H is a feminine character a very lovable nature but truth of the Gospel of Christ compels me to say that I think his wife is the strongest character and that apart from Christ she will have the mastery of him but with Christ he can have the victory."[36] We can see here how proper gender performance, especially the cultivation of a prescriptive form of femininity that encouraged willing subordination, was seen as vital to the stability of the community and the spiritual betterment of its members.

Critiques of women in available archival evidence rarely invoked the same degree of specifically gendered language in cultivating their own masculinity. Rather, critics generally found that women were also wanting in their feminine character. Most rely on tropes of correct Christian feminine performance (such as encouraging quietness at dinner or less time spent on beautifying), which were equally a part of Oneida's gendered ideals. A few exceptions demonstrate, however, at the very least an admiration for the industrious, public-facing typifications of American cultural masculinity. One woman was commended during a criticism session for her interest in smithing: "This is beautiful thing in a woman, to be able to interest herself in the labor of man [is] indicative of a lady like character."[37] Acceptable gender deviations of women away from traditional American femininity were an ingrained part of women's lives in the Oneida Community (from dress to work to forms of leisure); while lauded generally, they less often manifested themselves as problems to be addressed through criticism.

Mutual criticism sessions, however, could just as easily enforce sexism as they could undermine it. In a mutual criticism of Lily Hobart on November 7, 1876, Alfred Barron noted that her "spirit of irreverence and insubordination to men we have felt so much lately. This is a point on which I have for a considerable time had a good deal of feeling. If women—especially young women— were to come up and go along without respect for a man as her head, this community would become intolerable. . . . When I think of a woman without religion and without a deep reverence for man as her head and superior . . . it passes me like whoredom."[38] He goes on to note that the particular problem with Lily Hobart is her apparent to "[attract] men who can't be serious with her," vacating the vital spiritual element of her sexual life. This criticism from Barron reflects both the reality of freedom of expression and sexuality that communal life allowed girls and young women brought up there (Hobart was known to have many sexual partners, which does not appear as a problem itself within the criticism session) as well as the seriousness with which the gendered aspects of ascending fellowship were taken. Likewise, a community woman named Elmira Higgins stated during an 1888 criticism of Marcus L. Worden that "I think Mr Worden has a strong desire for the truth and is anxious for improvement and has a loving heart. He has too much of the feminine spirit has too much sympathy for his children and worldly relations."[39]

In these two cases we can see a striving for a gender normativity that largely aligns with American contemporary standards. However, it is also clear in these cases that the basis for critique of gender deviance from community standards was often couched in the language of concern for the community itself. Alfred Barron is anxious that Oneida's young women will become too outspoken and threaten the established ascending fellowship model; Elmira Higgins is concerned that Marcus L. Worden's "sympathies" and paternal feelings draw him away from the Oneida way of life. In these examples, we can see how the maintenance of male-dominated gendered hierarchy was in a very real way as important as the radical reformation of gender itself. Furthermore, the constant appearance of explicitly gendered and gendering words (feminine, masculine, female, male, etc.) in mutual criticism discourse demonstrates a shared constructed understanding of the essence of each gender as well as its perceived importance to all aspects of life. Thus, by critiquing another's gender performance through suggesting an increase or decrease of masculinity or femininity in their actions would have been understandable to the listener as a practicable set of instructions that did not necessarily threaten their gender identity or sex.

The community social hierarchy model of ascending fellowship, discussed above, was also often invoked through speaker-listener relationships during mutual criticism sessions. Ascending fellowship formalized a model in which the more perfect of women were recognized without sacrificing patriarchal dominance. The theological perception that those higher in fellowship were also more perfect and closer to God rendered critiques given by those in higher positions of fellowship as God-sent by extension. This was not an enthusiastic or possession practice in which God appeared *through* members' bodies but rather the casual assumption that God always acted through the model of ascending fellowship, criticism, and the unseen omnipresence of God in the physical body. This idea underscores the actual, physical presence of the dual God in each human body (as I explore subsequently) as well as the ways in which the human interior reflected God's nature in being able to give, receive, and act on criticism based on one's masculine or feminine relational position to their interlocutor. Thus, in the example above, high-ranking women like Elmira Higgins had the authority to tell lower-ranking men like

Marcus Worden to be less masculine and Worden was expected to not only listen but follow her instructions. According to the logics of fellowship and mutual criticism, Worden's position in the fellowship required a receptive (explicitly labeled "feminine") attitude toward her critique that resulted in a broader change in his gender performance.

Receiving this kind of criticism, however, was not always easy. In a recorded evening meeting that the transcriber entitled "The Way to Take Criticism," Noyes and others high in the fellowship discussed the practice of receiving criticism in gendered, sexed, and even romantic terms. Noyes noted that:

> The only way for God to get into us is by criticising us, and when he has gotten us into a certain state so that we rejoice in our criticism—how shall he get deeper? Not by flattery or fondling, as a mother does her baby—but by suggesting ways in which we can improve by setting us to work of self judgment. . . . The course of true love is said to never been smooth. God's way of courting is not like the world's, the world's way is by flattery, God's by criticism and by starting an appetite for improvement. . . . A man cannot get into full fellowship with a woman in the first instance, at least, without hurting her, no more can God get into full fellowship with man without enlarging and causing him pain.[40]

Noyes's statement implies that all human souls (though particularly those of men, who seem to have been the target audience for this talk) are penetrated by God's love not unlike penetrative vaginal sex. As with breaking the hymen, there is temporary pain on the part of the receiver, but the act ultimately increases the love, the fellowship, between the two participants. Furthermore, God *enlarges* himself in order to properly achieve this penetration, a description that notably lends God both imaginable scale and relatable sexual corporeality. The romanticism of this idealization of primary sexual encounter is telling of the ways in which, unlike mainstream American cultural values that lauded virginity and feminine purity, the Oneida Community held deep religious appreciation for the postvirginal state in which one could be in "full fellowship" with other community members and God.

Another member at the same meeting—whose initials are unfortunately illegible on the transcription—spoke after Noyes, stating, "It is criticism that bores us out and makes tubes of us so that our inner surface can be exposed to the spirit of truth and inspiration."

"Yes," Noyes replied, "it is opening the vagina. It may take God thirty or forty years to break into our virginity. Consider how you would like to have a woman think and feel toward you under such circumstances. You would like her to not make any more fuss than was necessary, and not to think evil of you as though you were cruelly hurting her, as though you were a monster trying to kill her. So God likes you to be quiet as possible under his judgments and not to think evil of him."[41] Noyes's erotic metaphor here is telling of Community expectations of the receptive party in two settings: the mutual criticism session and the bed of a woman's introductory penetrative experience. In their theological writings, Noyes and other members of the community constantly wrote in erotic metaphors about each other, Christ, and God that similarly evoked expected comportment during sexual encounters. Noyes himself most frequently uses the very literal anatomical language and sexual imagery in his writing that we see above, but penetrative sex and its affective and physical realities appear throughout Oneida members' writings. The image of the intertwined couple was often metaphorically invoked to express the desired balance of feminine and masculine within an individual's character as well as the divinely sanctioned inferiority of women within an otherwise equivalently spiritual encounter.

Archival evidence generally points to a relative difficulty among men coming into Community life to subject themselves to a lifestyle in which individualism and traditional models of masculine house-heading were seen negatively, inhibiting some of the public-sphere privileges they would have otherwise enjoyed. Conversely, women were often encouraged to be more serious, studious, or hard-working (masculine-coded traits), which was practicable for the labor needs of a communistic setting. However, *all* members, regardless of gender, were encouraged to be femininely *receptive* to the authority of those above them in the system of ascending fellowship, which was topped by John Humphrey Noyes himself. This fact has led some scholars to see mutual criticism solely in terms of a method of control and domination. Exclusive attention to the *function* of mutual criticism, however, is reductive of the lived gendered experience of members whose subjects were formed through mutual criticism and, importantly, discounts the significance of the queer logics that went into rendering Oneida gender norms.

The remaking of the sexual and gendered self through attending to the instructive advice from mutual criticism was essential to the Oneida theology of perfectionism. In addition to attaining a perfect, sinless existence within their own lifetimes, "the aim was to internalize values of sexual self-control so that individual impulses could be sublimated to the goals of the larger community."[42] This goal was pervasive to all aspects of community life. Given the constant proximity and open style of communication of interpersonal relationships in the community, critiques of gender performance, or of any social actions that could or had been perceived in terms of masculinity or femininity, likely extended past mutual criticism sessions themselves to many other reminders in the criticized member's daily life. Mutual criticism and communal gender reformation was not restricted to metaphor

In the practice of mutual criticism, we can see how gender was actively worked on as a malleable form of individual capacity that should be reoriented for the greater good of the community and the perfection of the individual. We can see in individual narrations of member experiences of mutual criticism and of other forms of Oneida religiosity that the cultivation of androgynous interiority was a very real experience requiring intense investment of emotional and intellectual labor of community members beyond the kind of top-down, authoritarian narration of Oneida's history that has often been emphasized. The ways in which members altered their own understandings of their own and others' gender and sexuality, in fact, mirror the kinds of self-work called for by queer and feminist theory in their logics and experience despite arriving at vastly different conclusions about how gender should be thought about and practiced.

SUBMISSION AND LIBERATION

> *Now which liberty will you choose—the liberty of independence, or the*
> *liberty of union?—the liberty of an insect to fly off into darkness and iso-*
> *lation, or the liberty of Children of God to come into Communism with*
> *him and with one another—the liberty to be alone, or the liberty that*
> *makes a happy home?—"Liberty."*
> —John Humphrey Noyes, *Home-Talks*, p. 347

The Oneida Community struggled between "the family" as it existed in its heteronormative, bound form in the United States and their own expanded reimagining of the family as an extended network of kinship mediated through shared belief, shared labor, and a network of erotic encounters. From their own writing we can see that they fully intended to liberate members from what they saw as the illogical, un-Christian realities and constraints of monogamous, sexist, capitalist American cultural norms. From these same writings, however, we can also see a commitment to maintaining patriarchal hierarchy and the constant reification of compulsory heterosexuality, even if that form of heterosexuality was not heteronormative.

On February 14, 1879, a meeting of lawyers, reporters, and mainstream Protestant clergy invited from around the country met at the Hall of Languages at Syracuse University with the aim of once and for all eliminate the Oneida

Community that laid less than thirty miles east of the city. The *New York Her-ald* reported that Professor John W. Mears of Hamilton College led the meeting, opening with a description of the Community and its practices: "In the Oneida Community men and women live together in a sort of concupiscence. No woman has a husband of her own, and no man has a wife of his own. They declare that they live the resurrection life, in which 'they neither marry nor are given in marriage.' They are not allowed the right of choice. . . . Their institution is an outgrowth of vile passion."[43] Mears and his fellows insisted on that the Oneida was abusive and despotic despite reports from the Community's hundreds of annual visitors who claimed that the Community and its people were "delightful," "happy," and "industrious" and the general acceptance of the Community by the villages immediately surrounding it (not to mention their economic reliance on it as a source of employment). Mears protested that a person going through this community sees nothing there to offend because "all is secret. Our students who visit the place say that the men look passably well, but that the women have a dejected look, and how such women can be mothers of an excellent stock of men is one of the problems which the students discuss."[44] As in movements against the multitudes of religious Others throughout American history from the eighteenth century until today, "saving the women" became a lens and strategic entry point for Mears and his colleagues. The reading of the "dejected look" of Oneida women, regardless of (and notably without) women's opinions on their own condition became a justification for intervention in and of itself. In a religious lecture by Reverend J. H. Hartley in Cincinnati, Ohio, that was typical of the anti-Oneida campaign by the fall of that same year, he characterized the "free-love notions" of the Community as "hateful to the extreme, and inimical to any true progress" and ended the gathering with "an earnest plea for the upholding of the sanctity of the marriage relation." A summary of the lecture was printed in the *Cincinnati Commercial* alongside notices of suicides, grain shortages, and the spread of gambling addiction in New York City.[45] Although others had tried to disrupt the Community dozens of times since its establishment in 1848, including Mears himself, the lingering drama of the recent Supreme Court case that criminalized Mormon polygamy and emerging knowledge about the Oneida's sexual initiation methods for young people instigated widespread outrage and boycotts against the community. Mainly in the form of polemical publications and letter-writing campaigns, activism against the Community began to draw high levels of negative attention and criticism, leading the police to charge Noyes with incest, kidnapping, and statutory rape and gradually unraveling member allegiance.[46]

The rhetoric of sexually and socially vulnerable, religiously duped women utilized by Mears's campaign and the writings of feminist scholars since are similar in that they do not interest themselves in the gender significance of Oneida theology and practices themselves, only in how women in the Oneida Community differed too much (or too little) from American feminine norms. Regarding the community practices already discussed, we can see that even within the Oneida Community itself there was a tension between a desire to free women from certain material restrictions of nineteenth-century womanhood and the insistence on the internal coherency of the category of womanhood in terms of body, ability, and inferiority. The limitations of the community to live up to their egalitarian ideals in many cases, however, does not detract from the interesting work their theology and practices did to reimagine the gendered landscape of their physical and spiritual worlds.

In fact, in the Oneida Community practices described in this chapter, we can see a general willingness of members and potential members to submit to restrictions in efforts to achieve a gender sensibility grounded in Community standards. Submission of self to the community, of personal pride to spiritual perfection, and of mainstream gender roles to idealized androgyny were all part of the greater mission of salvation. Members identified and lived toward new aspirations that intentionally detracted from the religious and social norms of their time, down to the basic understanding of what gender was. The process of forming a Community gender sensibility was difficult, at times even traumatic. Oneida was in most ways not the space of complete harmony and perfection that it aimed to be, but it was a space in which gender and religion were approached with acute awareness. The Community was infamous for "destroying" traditional gender relations in the popular press. Members who were attracted to the Community must have had at least some inclination to participate in that destruction, whether through having multiple sexual partners, fostering "opposite" gendered aspects of themselves, or worshipping the dual God. The discipline, sexual training, and general lack of independence and individuality in the Community were intentional and never claimed to be feminist or liberatory in nature; they were crucial aspects not only of their communitarianism but of their religious beliefs. Perfectionism, as a theological discourse and practiced system of subject formation, sublimated the individual into the community itself by requiring adherents to remake themselves against normativity.

Beyond the self, perfectionism demanded that the social and cultural roles of gender at large be remade through spiritual logics while maintaining contemporary scientific theories of sex. For example, women's God-given strong legs suiting them for outside work, or the desire for women's and men's dress to reflect the similarity of their bodily forms. Noyes maintained that body and role are and should be linked but that the normative mode of this link in the nineteenth-century United States was based on erroneous assumptions about the body that were rooted in a pollution of both science and religion by erroneous understandings of gender. Traditional gender roles, in the Community view, had been misread ever since the end of the primitive church. God's, Adam's, Christ's, and the human soul's gender was dual in male and female essence. While the Oneida Community still undercut many American gender norms, they upheld a specific ideal of binary bodily sex that was entangled with traditional understandings of gender. This theological duality's logical reliance on natural observable sexual difference also provided a means and justifications for certain logical extensions of the mundane to the divine: male and female genitalia interpreted as designed "interlocking" parts extended to a belief that intercourse was natural and thus spiritual. That sex was spiritual meant that who one had sex with had the potential for massive influence over the spirit and mind of the participants, meaning sexual partner selection must be intentionally controlled. Sex and gender, in perfectionist theology, were central to (re)creating a hierarchy that at once proclaimed spiritual and scientific truth.

The Oneida Community is one of many examples that demonstrate that the establishment of religious, gender, and sexual norms in the nineteenth century was a multidirectional battle featuring intellectual vitality, self-awareness, and experimentation; in Foucault's terms, a "tactical polyvalence of discourses."[47] He states: "We must not imagine a world of discourse divided between accepted discourse and excluded discourse, or between the dominant discourse and the dominated one; but as a multiplicity of discursive elements that can come into play in various strategies."[48] Oneida Community perfectionism, as a discourse, is an example of the complex dynamics of power at play that cannot be easily categorized as dominating or dominated, subversive or traditional. Growing off countless ongoing discourses around gender, religion, science, and sexuality, it developed its own logics of the relationship between categories of sex, gender, and sexuality based in a shared member desire to live outside of sociosexual normativity.

NOTES

1. By "androgyny," I am referring to what we might now called bigender; that is, the combination of two genders (here male and female) in a single person or entity. I have chosen this term because (1) "androgyny" was used during the nineteenth century in this way as opposed to today's understanding of androgyny as the absence of identifiable binary gender (for example, an androgynous bathhouse was one that tended to male and female clients), (2) it places the emphasis of analysis on gender and the social rather than embodiment, and (3) *nonbinary* and *bigender* usually do not work well as nouns.

2. Judith Butler, *Gender Trouble: Feminism and the Subversion of Identity* (New York: Routledge, 1990), 198.

3. See Richard DeMaria, *Communal Love at Oneida: A Perfectionist Vision of Authority,
Property, and Sexual Order* (New York: E. Mellen Press, 1978). Louis J. Kern, *An Ordered Love:
Sex Roles and Sexuality in Victorian Utopias: The Shakers, the Mormons, and the Oneida Com-
munity* (Chapel Hill: University of North Carolina Press, 1981). Lawrence Foster, *Religion
and Sexuality: The Shakers, the Mormons, and the Oneida Community* (Urbana: University of
Illinois Press, 1984).

4. Writings on mutual criticism tend to be confined to academic articles or sections
of book chapters. Mutual criticism rarely, if ever, makes an appearance in popular media
accounts of the Oneida Community. See Jason Vickers, "'That Deep Kind of Discipline of
Spirit': Freedom, Power, Family, Marriage, and Sexuality in the Story of John Humphrey
Noyes and the Oneida Community," *American Nineteenth Century History* 14, no. 1 (March
2013): 1–26. Leigh Gialanella, "Discord in Utopia: Reconciling Perfectionism with Human
Nature in the Oneida Community," *Communal Societies* 35, no. 2 (December 2015): 185–211.
Anthony Wayne Wonderley, *Oneida Utopia: A Community Searching for Human Happiness
and Prosperity* (Ithaca, NY: Cornell University Press, 2017).

5. See Leah DeVun, *The Shape of Sex: Nonbinary Gender from Genesis to the Renaissance*
(New York: Columbia University Press, 2021).

6. John Humphrey Noyes, *The Berean: A Manual for the Help of Those Who Seek the Faith
of the Primitive Church* (Putney, VT: Office of The Spiritual Magazine, 1847), 87.

7. Hubbard Eastman, *Noyesism Unveiled* (Brattleboro, VT: Reverend Hubbard Eastman,
1849), 324.

8. Noyes, *Berean*, 490.

9. Noyes, *Berean*, 87.

10. Oneida Community, *Bible Communism: A Compilation from the Annual Reports and
Other Publication of the Oneida Association and Its Branches* (Brooklyn, NY: Office of the
Circular, 1853), 54.

11. Noyes, *Berean*, v.

12. Noyes, *Berean*, v.

13. Oneida Community, *Bible Communism*, 27.

14. Oneida Community, *Bible Communism*, 61.

15. Oneida Community, *Bible Communism*, 61.

16. The basis of normative domestic economy's single-family unit was difficult to
maintain without individual or family-held property, and many of the marks of middle-class
nuclear familial success became either meaningless or explicitly undesirable in this new
theological context. As a result, domestic duties in communistic groups were often reformed
in ways that shared them among all women (or all adults), relieving women from the full-
time domestic reproduction activities so that they could contribute to the community in
other ways. In the Oneida Community, ideals of femininity and motherhood were intentionally alienated from the domestic material consumption and anxious maternalism that came
to define middle-class womanhood in nineteenth-century American culture. Community
children were expected to have no special (or in Community terms, "sticky") connection
to their biological parents and, after weaning at around one year old, lived separately from

the adults-only Mansion House in a building known as the Children's Department, where adults, though mostly still women, worked as caretakers and teachers.

17. *Handbook of the Oneida Community* (Brooklyn, NY: Office of the American Socialist, 1871), 51.

18. In all cases I can find of discussions of complex marriage, it is never stated that all men were married to all women of the community. Rather there is a consistent language that all adult members were married to each other. Rather than this necessarily intimating same-sex relational possibility, however, the silence around the sexual possibilities of women or men being married among themselves seems to be an oversight stemming from their own heteronormative assumptions around sex. Similarly, the possibility of nonbinary sex is never raised in their theology or practice. Sexed bodies, in perfectionism, were tangibly divided and designed as a complementary male-female pairing for intercourse by God, despite the internal flexibility accompanying the dual nature of the soul.

19. Over the decades of the Community's existence, this denial of shame was made practical. On one occasion, an evening dance performance by some young women members during which twirling resulted in their dresses flying up above the waist, a member named Mr. Hamilton rose concern about modesty stating that "the spirit about the 'dancer's petticoats' was unpleasant to him." In an evening meeting soon after, a note from Mr. Noyes contradicted this sentiment: "Men like to see up there," he wrote, "and it is right they should sometimes; do let them. It was a pleasant sight. I liked it very much and there is no need to be squeamish about it. It wasn't near as bad as what is going on the stage in the world all the time. I like to see women's bottom once in a while, it is one of the legitimate sights. But there was no real exposure about it, and if anybody criticized it, I shall commend it." In dancer Harriet Worden's diary entry that night she wrote that "after this was read, everybody laughed and that was all." On another occasion, Noyes joked that one day in the future, when the member's minds and hearts were more thoroughly perfected from their outside world prudishness, it may even be enjoyable for some members to have exhibitionary sex for the group, though it seems it never came to fruition.

20. Within this reimagining of the nature of gender and the body, *who* a member had sex with became a spiritual concern. When Noyes stated that "all fellowship was in the nature of sexual intercourse," he emphasized the importance of sex as a physical and spiritual mediation between two souls. Sexual intercourse was an important practice of spiritual betterment itself; having sex with a member who had achieved a higher degree of spiritual betterment acted on and bettered one's own spirit. This also extended to other social interactions between male and female Community members.

21. "Home Items—Wallingford." *Oneida Circular* 12, no. 33 (August 3, 1875), 261. Harriet M. Worden, the editor of the *Oneida Circular* for many years, began this particular edition of the publication with the following note:

> We devote considerable space in this week's issue to a subject which we regard as the key-stone to immortality—viz., the Ascending Fellowship. It is a doctrine of the greatest importance to every Christian believer, and yet there are few who rightly understand the term, and much less the practical bearing it has on our daily life. We ourselves only comprehend it in part, but we feel assured herein lies the hope of mankind for the future, and we

are striving to know its deepest meaning. Victoria Woodhull claims to have found the secret of immortality, and yet she is a staunch advocate of the Individual Sovereignty principle. We feel safe in assuring her and all who adhere to this principle, that they can not eat their cake and keep it too—they can not have both Individual Sovereignty and immortality. If they desire immortality, they must find a way to reconcile an immortal God and all the Heavens with this world. (260)

22. Noyes, *Berean*, 79.

23. Harriet Matthew's diary, February 1, 1856, Oneida Collection, Special Collections Research Center, Syracuse University, Syracuse, NY.

24. The act of developing gendered capacities for worship and belief, in this case, closely reflects the intention (if not the substance) of Muslim women of the piety movement discussed in Saba Mahmood, *Politics of Piety: The Islamic Revival and the Feminist Subject* (Princeton, NJ: Princeton University Press, 2005).

25. Noyes, *Berean*, 492.

26. Noyes, *Berean*, 490.

27. Noyes, *Berean*, 490.

28. Oneida Community, *Mutual Criticism* (Oneida, NY: Office of the American Socialist, 1876), 5.

29. Oneida Community, *Bible Communism*, 85.

30. Oneida Community, *Mutual Criticism*, 4.

31. "System of conflict reduction": Gialanella, "Discord in Utopia," 188; "failed to do away . . .," "effectively combined peer pressure . . .": Wonderley, *Oneida Utopia*, 80.

32. Noyes, *Berean*, 55–56.

33. Oneida Community, *Mutual Criticism*, 54.

34. Oneida Community, *Mutual Criticism*, 49–50.

35. Criticism of Mr. E Foder," box 16, Oneida Collection.

36. "CSJ criticism session on Oct 4, 1866," box 16, Oneida Collection.

37. "March 27—1862," criticism of a woman working in the children's house, written by her on reflection of the session, unsigned, box 16, Oneida Collection.

38. Entry [letter?] by Alfred Barron, November 7, 1876, reflecting on criticism of Lilly Hobart, box 16, Oneida Collection.

39. Undated criticism of Marcus L. Worden by Elmira Higgins, box 4, Oneida Collection.

40. "The Way to Take Criticism," unpublished transcription of home-talk, box 70, Oneida Collection.

41. "Way to Take Criticism."

42. Foster, *Religion and Sexuality*, 237.

43. "Oneida Community. Episcopal and Presbyterian Bishops and Priests in War Paint. A Religious Crusade. No Quarter to Be Shown to Followers of Noyes. Theories of Marriage. A System of Organized Fanaticism and Lust," *New York Herald*, February 15, 1879, 3.

44. "Oneida Community," *New York Herald*, 3.

45. "The Oneida Communism and Complex Marriages—Lecture by Rev. J. H. Hartley," *Cincinnati Commercial*, November 17, 1879, 5.

46. See Doyle, *Ministers' War.*

47. Michel Foucault, *The History of Sexuality* (New York: Vintage Books, 1988), 100–102.

48. Foucault, *History of Sexuality,* 100.

The Cryptic Dramaturgies of
Christian Performance

Robyn Lee

Signs of political and cultural division in the United States were quite visible
from the highways and byways that took me from my home in Buffalo, New
York, to Poolville, Texas, where I traveled to attend *Independence Trail*, an immersive theatrical portrayal of events leading to the Revolutionary War that
was created and staged by the Christian production company Capernaum
Studios. Much like the performance I was traveling to attend, many of the
roadside political signs along the route combined symbols of US patriotism
and Christian ideology. On the outskirts of Memphis, the seventy-two-foot-
tall Statue of Liberation through Christ loomed over a busy intersection (see
figure 1).

In lieu of her customary tablet and torch, this statue holds aloft a cross and
clutches tablets reminiscent of those carried by Charlton Heston as Moses in
Cecil B. DeMille's *The Ten Commandments*.[1] A single tear is visible on the statue's cheek, and her base is inscribed with the plea, "America Return to Christ." At
a busy intersection in Tennessee, a man on foot wove through the cars while wearing a sandwich board that read, "Coming Soon: More Pandemics, Economic Collapse, Extraterrestrial Deception, Mark of the Beast 666." In Arkansas, a billboard
announced that the Ozark Patriots were seeking new recruits who were "willing to
FIGHT to oppose those who would detract from, or erase, our steadfast belief in
God, our faith in our Country, our pride in our culture and our trust in our heritage."[2]

One message appeared repeatedly along the route, plastered on billboards,
hand-painted road signs, and bumper stickers, and printed on the T-shirts and
mugs sold in gas stations and souvenir shops: "Stand for the Flag, Kneel for the

Figure 1. Ryan Bessant, "Statue of Liberation through Christ," World Overcomers Church, Memphis, Tennessee, photographed by the author, June 28, 2022.

Cross." While it is difficult to pinpoint the origin of the phrase, it gained wide-spread popularity after Colin Kaepernick and other athletes knelt during the national anthem at sports games to protest racial inequality and violence in the United States. It can be read as a pointed and racially charged political critique or as easily as an innocuous expression of patriotism and faith. The potent symbols of the cross and the flag are marked by an excess of feeling and seem to defy civil discourse, debate, and critique. They command narrative attention and draw focus from gaps and elisions that demand narrative completion from the reader. The rhetorical effect of an object, discourse, or performance is contingent on the particularities of audience, time, and circumstances, and disparate publics close such gaps with personalized contextual understandings. And because "rhetorical legibility is predicated in publicly recognizable symbolic activity *in context*," it naturally follows that as the audience size and diversity of their cultural contexts increases, the universal legibility of ideological messaging decreases.[3] Through its narrative gaps and potent symbols, a billboard reading "Stand for the Flag, Kneel for the Cross" becomes cryptic. The outward message is legible to all audiences, declaring duty and devotion to country and Christ, but certain contextual understandings unlock secondary messages, and for those readers, the slogan is read as an indictment of those who participate in or support certain forms of political protest as un-Christian and anti-American.

It seems logical that in-group cohesion would benefit from clear boundaries delineating where the in-group ends and the out-group begins. As a seminal media studies text argues, "awareness of the symbolic boundaries of our culture and their dramatization in their performance is a precondition for the making and holding of community."[4] However, the illegibility of cryptic messages coupled with potent symbols allows a range of ideological positions to believe that a message speaks directly to their own in-group values and beliefs. As Barbara Kirshenblatt-Gimblett suggests, "little dramas of hiding and showing structure our perception and attention."[5] In this way, cryptic messages and ensuing acts of alignment shape not only what we believe but how we believe. And unlike a clearly defined message, the very act of decoding and interpreting cryptic messages prompts choice and action in the listener. In essence, they prompt performance.

Just as billboards use potent symbols to communicate to publics, pioneering evangelicals have long used performance—on the radio, on television, and in theaters—to communicate to new and larger publics beyond the closed community of a traditional congregation and their attendant shared cultural history and language.[6] Like the road signs I encountered along the way, the performances I attended were ostensibly designed for public consumption.

Similar to the road signs, the messaging and symbols I encountered within these performances sometimes seemed pointedly cryptic, leaving me to wrestle with ambiguous or contested meanings. Noting the effectiveness of the cryptic billboard, I am left with the question of whether ambiguity is a type of frequency loss that occurs from scaling a message to large audiences or if it is something more intentional. Are cryptic dramaturgies a bug or a feature of Christian performance?

While a theater event is the subject of this research, performance studies is the methodological lens through which I explore this event within its larger cultural context. Performance studies is an interdisciplinary field that examines performance in its broadest sense—as a mode of cultural expression, a site of identity formation, and a means of social intervention. As a methodological lens, performance studies foregrounds the ephemeral, affective, and relational dimensions of cultural expression, asking how meaning is made in the moment of enactment. This perspective challenges text-based or strictly representational analyses by privileging action, interaction, and the lived experience of both performers and audiences.[7] Throughout this chapter, I refer to *dramaturgy* or *dramaturgies*, a term that is sometimes used to describe the structure of a performance and is sometimes used synonymously with the act of analyzing theatrical works. I prefer Adam Versenyi's more dynamic definition of dramaturgy as "the architecture of the theatrical event involved in the confluence of components in a work and how they are constructed to generate meaning for an audience."[8] This definition extends the focus beyond what a performance is to the consideration of what a performance does. Further, Versenyi's use of the term *theatrical event* expands the analytical boundaries beyond the performance to encompass the event's larger context. This methodological approach is vital in the research of Christian theater, where performance events often do not fit neatly within a theatrical frame that begins when the lights go down and ends when the actors take their bows.

I use these methodologies to examine *Independence Trail* and similar performances that leverage the inherent untranslatability of performance for publics as a benefit rather than a struggle or hazard and strategically exploit the instability of rhetorical legibility to constitute and construct agonistically oppositional publics. I contend that the ideological slipperiness of cryptic dramaturgies is a key component of their coalition-building success. I explore how these performances communicate to various publics and how these theatrical offerings participate in the production and performance of a Christian American public identity. The central focus of the chapter is on the cryptodramaturgies of a performance at Capernaum Studios in Poolville, Texas. I attended

Capernaum Studios' first annual Independence Day Freedom Fest (hereafter referred to as Freedom Fest) on Saturday, July 2, 2022, which featured an immersive theatricalized portrayal of events leading up to the Battle of Lexington called *Independence Trail*. *Independence Trail* and Freedom Fest both enact history and perform a present-day call to arms for Christian militias, embodying an ideology that can be summarized in words attributed to Benjamin Franklin: "Rebellion to tyrants is obedience to God."

Both Freedom Fest and Capernaum Studios defy easy categorization. Capernaum's forty-acre campus in Poolville, Texas, serves as a Christian film studio, retreat venue, living history village, and venue of live, immersive theater. In their advertising material, Capernaum seems to eschew the label *theater*, instead calling their productions "live, immersive events" or "walk-through experiences."[9] The venue features a life-sized first-century village, replicas of Holy Land sites, and a thirty-thousand-square-foot sculpture garden with life-sized statues that depict scenes from Genesis to the crucifixion, accompanied by biblical text carved into stone walls. Capernaum is a 501(c)(3) ministry that first operated under the name Capernaum 1st Century Village and originally appeared to emphasize living history performances. Soon after, the name was shortened to Capernaum Village—a name that can still be found on some signage, including over the entrance to the venue. The most recent iteration of their name, Capernaum Studios, seems linked to the opening of a new sound stage in 2020 and the expansion of the movie production side of the organization. Capernaum's tagline, which has remained consistent throughout the company's evolution, is "Experience HIS-tory in History," promising Godly encounters in a historical setting or perhaps an encounter with history in a Godly setting.

It's difficult to pinpoint exactly when the organization was founded. It was built over a span of five years on a parcel of land gifted to Capernaum founder Tammy Lane by her father. Capernaum's first annual production, *The Passover Experience*, was performed during Easter in 2008. In subsequent years, the studio added the following live productions to its yearly roster: *The Star of Bethlehem Experience*, performed during the Christmas season, telling the story of Christ's birth; *The Crimson Experience*, an immersive passion play that dramatizes the events surrounding Christ's crucifixion; and Capernaum's take on the evangelical "hell house" genre, through a Halloween staging of the apocalyptic texts in Matthew, chapter 24, and Revelation, chapter 6, called *The Apocalypse Experience*.[10]

After leaving the Fort Worth metro area, most of the forty-mile drive to Capernaum Studios takes place on one road, flanked by ranchland on either

side, with few turnoffs or conveniences. The barren landscape is a marked
contrast to Capernaum's entrance gate and the enormous white statue, which
gleams in the Texas sun (see figure 2).

Figure 2. Yom Sim Pak, "Second Advent of Christ," Capernaum Studios, Poolville,
Texas, photographed by the author, July 1, 2022.

"The Second Advent of Christ" is carved in the statue's base; it depicts Jesus with outstretched arms surrounded by a single dove and five flying cherubim, two of whom point at a book that is open before them—presumably the
"book of life," referenced in the books of Ezekiel and in Revelation.[11] The scene
looks peaceful, but visitors conversant in the Bible's prophetic texts might imagine the elements just beyond the boundaries of the sculpture. They may picture the
"lake of fire and brimstone" into which the Antichrist and false prophet have been
cast to "be tortured day and night forever and ever." Perhaps some see those who
died prior to the Second Coming eagerly lining up to learn whether the cherubim
would locate their name in the book, all the while knowing that "whoever was not
found written in the book of life was cast into the lake of fire."[12] Recontextualized,
the statue's outstretched arms can be read as a symbol of judgment rather than

welcome; the left arm held aloft toward heaven and the right arm angled down toward the lake of fire and brimstone as a cryptic depiction of God's final judgment, separating the saved "us" from the damned "them."

There is no scholarly writing on Capernaum Studios, and media coverage is limited to a handful of promotional articles in the local paper, but Capernaum is no small-scale or amateur operation. On the day of Freedom Fest, the large, nearly full parking lot was bustling. Volunteers in red T-shirts emblazoned with the Capernaum logo and the words "Jesus is Alive" drove patrons in golf carts from the lot, past Capernaum Studio's sound stage and production office, to the visitor entrance. At the ticket booth—designed to look as if it was constructed of stone and wood, in keeping with the rest of the "first-century village" design—I presented proof of my online ticket purchase for the sold-out event and was given a glossy color map (see figure 3) of the grounds and a concert-style wristband marked with my ticket time for *Independence Trail*.

The performance, *Independence Trail*, was one of several events presented that day. A ten-dollar ticket provided entrance to Freedom Fest, which included access to the grounds and sculpture garden, vendors, food trucks,

Figure 3. Map of Capernaum Studios, Poolville, Texas.

special effects exhibit, "Patriot Speakers," two invited guests who gave talks on hot-button issues of interest to the political right, and Spy Game, an interactive, performance-based scavenger hunt game aimed at youth attendees.[13] A twenty-dollar ticket included entrance to Freedom Fest and a timed ticket to the *Independence Trail* performance. Tickets to a screening of the Capernaum-produced film *Washington's Armor* was a five-dollar add-on to either ticket price. *Washington's Armor*, based on books of the same name, makes an argument that George Washington and, thus, America received special protection from God during the Revolutionary War. The live *Independence Trail* performance utilized the set and costumes that had been built for *Washington's Armor* but did not follow the narrative of the movie; instead, *Independence Trail* staged "the scenes that launched the first battle of the Revolutionary War."[14]

The Capernaum Studios' film *Washington's Armor* makes a case for the special role that America plays across the prophetic timeline. Despite the cross-promotion between film and performance, George Washington was not a subject of *Independence Trail*. The performance focuses instead on lesser-known figures in the Revolutionary War: pastors Peter Muhlenberg and Jonas Clark. The two clergymen were part of what became known as the Black Robe Regiment: a group of influential pastors who exerted influence for the Patriot cause. While members of the Black Robe Regiment may be considered niche historical figures to some, they are well-known to many in conservative Christian circles; modern Black Robe Regiment groups have sprung up all over the country. One of the leaders of this current Black Robe Regiment movement is a pastor and two-term member of the Oklahoma House, Dan Fisher. Fisher dresses up as Muhlenberg, the only pastor known to have participated in the Battle of Lexington, and delivers performance-lectures across the country, in which he argues that pastors should prepare their congregations to fight in a battle to defend the Constitution and Judeo-Christian values.[15]

Fisher's rhetoric about battles and fighting is as slippery as in the *Independence Trail* performance. At its most innocent, this movement could be calling for a return to jeremiad, or Protestant political sermon—a form that was brought to America by the Puritans and revived by Jerry Falwell and other leaders in the conservative Christian political movement. Harding describes the jeremiad as a sermon that "laments the moral conditions of a people, foresees cataclysmic consequences, and calls for dramatic reform and revival."[16] However, Black Robe Regiment groups have been accused of "mustering Christian violence in service of the preexisting crisis in American evangelical Christianity."[17] What could be seen as ambiguous language in the political realm is not just reflected in *Independence Trail*, it is transformed into polysemous, multivalent performance. The performance could be understood as staging of a historical moment to impart a generalized moral message about the importance of standing up to fighting for freedom. Knowledge of the modern Black Robe Regiment movement serves as one key to unlocking a parallel performance that enacts a temporal transformation rich with doublings—modern Christians have a duty to take up arms, and even sacrifice their lives, to combat what Black Robe Regiment adherents see as federal overreach and attacks on Judeo-Christian principles.

Print and social media advertisements described not only the content of the *Independence Trail* performance but also *how* it would perform: "We believe that you will see many similarities in the freedom our founders were fighting to *obtain* and the freedom we are now trying to *maintain*. Most importantly, we believe that God will speak through this event to our responsibility in the fight against tyranny."[18] By denoting the pedagogical elements and investing the performance with God's authority, Capernaum primes audiences to engage with the event not as passive spectators but as semiotic-interpretive participants. The advertisement further emphasizes that God's message, communicated through *Independence Trail*, will require participants to engage in action that extends beyond the performance and into the public sphere.

After a friendly volunteer shuttled me to the performance staging area by golf cart, I joined the eleven other members of my group, who sat or stood in a small strip of shadow looking for an escape from the midday Texas sun, but the shade provided little relief from the ninety-eight-degree temperature. As we waited for our performance to begin, an explosion of gunshots from a concluding performance prompted nervous laughs from several members of our group. A volunteer crossed to the group to brief us on what to expect in the performance, including loud musket fire and walking on uneven terrain. After checking his watch, he began to read from a prepared statement that began with basic details about the Revolutionary War and ended with two points of emphasis: "Not many people know the colonists were fighting for their own banking system and government. They knew that whoever controlled the banking system would control the government. *Kind of like it is today.*" The scripted phrase, "kind of like it is today," was delivered as a theatrical aside; the performance convention, popularized in Elizabethan England, in which an actor turns from the action and breaks the fourth wall to speak directly to the audience. Shakespeare scholar Robert Weimann notes that an aside "assumes a moral function: the actor's rejection of illusion is turned into the character's honesty."[19] The metatheatrical promise of the aside is that the character breaks free of the story into which she has been scripted to impart a greater truth to the audience. The *Independence Trail* aside implied the speaker went off-script while providing prepared, factual remarks about the Revolutionary War to communicate some truer, more urgent message. But what exactly was that message? Unlike Elizabethan asides, in which character might express their motivation "rather baldly," the aside "kind of like it is today" performed paralipsis: a rhetorical device characterized by the deliberately concise, incomplete, or indeterminate treatment of a topic meant to draw greater attention to what was said, or rather, to what was left *unsaid*.[20]

In addition to the literary term *paralipsis*, one might call this kind of indirect rhetorical strategy dog-whistling, or to use cultural anthropologist Janet McIntosh's term, "alt-signaling," which she defines as "a kind of mirroring between form and content, where allusions to sinister, illicit, or conspiratorial dynamics . . . are couched in semiotically indirect, ambiguous, or cryptic forms."[21] A performance lens provides another clue to reading this moment. An aside is an embodied action. The off-the-cuff, just-between-you-and-me nature of the convention is partly communicated through vocal inflection, but the physical action from which the term derives its name—the physical movement of an actor *turning aside*, away from the action, to speak directly to the audience—is its defining characteristic.[22] While the Capernaum Studios volunteer who said "kind of like it is today" nailed the change in pitch and volume that suggests an aside, he did not, as a more seasoned performer might, look up from his script as he delivered the line. This minor deficiency in performance practice highlighted the strategic nature of the paraleiptic aside as dramaturgical conceit.

At the performance I attended, the volunteer's aside was met by several knowing chuckles and murmured assents, yet I wondered if all the audience members were laughing at the same joke. For some, the comment may have passed unnoticed or been perceived as nothing more than a benign truism akin to "money is power." Conspiratorially minded individuals may have inferred a reference to any number of shadowy figures, from George Soros to the Rothchild family to the World Economic Forum. Behind each of those figures lies another conspiratorial web of possible puppeteers, including globalists, political shadow states, Semitic cabals, the Antichrist, or any combination of perceived forces. The paraleiptic aside permits the speaker to evade the responsibility of backing up their allusion with a coherent or cogent argument while allowing the listener to draw whatever conclusion best fits their systems of belief. In this way, the paraleiptic aside differs from the "dog whistle," a rhetorical conceit in which key phrases or images communicate specific messages to intended audiences while eluding notice by out-groups. Dog whistles leave open the possibility of multivariate interpretations, that is, not built into the rhetorical design, which divides audiences more neatly into categories of those who are primed to hear the dog whistle and those who are not. Where the dog whistle separates, the paraleiptic aside builds coalition.

The volunteer continued, saying,

> Another important thing you should know about America is that the church played an important role in our battle for our independence. Pastors from across the colonies arose and led their congregations into battle for freedom. These pastors were called the Black Robed Regiment, and you will meet a few of them today. Politics were discussed in the church from the pulpit, and congregations were instructed what to do based on what the Bible said. It's time to get back to this way of doing church. It takes everyone to save a country.[23]

Following the speech, the group was led into a small, dark room, where we watched a short, animated, informational film (similar in animation style and learning level to the Crash Course YouTube series produced by PBS) covering the basics of the Revolutionary War. After the film, we were led out of the room and down a narrow pathway lined with stone walls that suddenly opened outdoors into what appeared to be a colonial town square—likely a set from the *Washington's Armor* movie. We were met by about two dozen actors in sumptuous period costumes who were gathered outside the steps of a small chapel singing "Amazing Grace." Many broke from their song and beckoned us individually to join them. By the time the actor playing pastor Peter Muhlenberg came through the church doors, the twelve audience members were dispersed evenly throughout the crowd of actors. Muhlenberg addressed the assembled congregation with a rousing sermon that concluded with a variation on the famous text from the book of Ecclesiastes,[24] saying: "There is a time for all things, a time for everything under the sun. There is a time for war, and there is a time for peace. There is a time to preach. And there is also a time . . . to fight! And now, friends, is the time . . . to fight!"[25] At this, the actor ripped off his black pastoral robe to reveal the uniform of the Continental Army and produced a musket which he held aloft, crying, "Now who will go with me? Be courageous!" He looked at each of us, imploring, "Will you join the fight? Will you stand against tyranny?" As a trio of drummers stuck up a march, I, along with the others in my group, joined in with the crowd, cheering "Freedom!" as the drummers led us marching out of the village green (see figure 4).

During Muhlenberg's speech, I was aware of the loud whirring of a drone

Figure 4. Trio of drummers from *Independence Trail*, Capernaum Studios, Poolville, Texas, photographed by the author, July 1, 2022.

flying low overhead, filming our group. Rather than pulling me out of time, I experienced Rebecca Schneider's assertion that "in the syncopated time of reenactments . . . then and now punctuate each other."[26] The drone comple-mented the ominous militarism of the performance, helping to collapse time and bringing the present to the past the past into the present. As I marched through the streets with my fellow patrons, most of whom were decked out in red, white, and blue, and was egged on by the actors to shout "Freedom" and demand our "God-given rights," I couldn't help imagining myself at an antimask protest or stop-the-steal rally, although it was unclear whether insurrectionist resonances were scripted for us.

A man who had been part of the crowd gathered our group as the rest of the cast marched on. After questioning us about our loyalties, he ushered us into one of the buildings and to a room designed to be the sitting room of Pas-tor Jonas Clark, who was in the midst of a clandestine meeting with Sam Ad-ams. Clark greeted us and explained to Adams that we were members of his congregation and he had been preparing us for battle. The pair were soon met by John Hancock, who balked at our presence and questioned our loyalty, just as our guide had done earlier. Clark assured Hancock, gesturing to us and say-ing, "In my preaching, I have trained them for this very hour. They will fight, John. And if need be, they will die."[27] Before long, Paul Revere rushed in to warn that the British were coming, and we were rushed out of the house and delivered to the care of Prince Estabrook, an enslaved man who fought and was wounded in the Battle of Lexington.

Estabrook invited us into his home, where we stood against the wall while he said goodbye to his mother and two young siblings. When his mother begged him tearfully not to go, he held his gun aloft, declaring, "It is my duty as a citizen of this country to fight!"[28] This line of dialogue struck me as spurious at the time; an enslaved man would not be considered a citizen under the law. Estabrook, a historical figure, is described by the National Park Service Minute Men Historical Site as "an enslaved man who stood with his white neighbors against the British Army on April 19, 1775."[29] He was injured in the Battle of Lexington and, following the battle, he is believed to have returned, or been returned, to his enslaver, with whom he spent the remainder of his life. This ahistorical narrative fits the modern white Christian nationalist movement's tokenizing of the minoritarian Other who professes gratitude for the "freedoms" they have been granted through American citizenship.[30]

Estabrook led us back into the streets, where our earlier guide charged us with the duty of carrying gunpowder across enemy lines. He handed each of us a small satchel and hurried us down a pathway leading to a strip of field, where five minutemen faced off against five British soldiers (figure 5).

As they discharged their weapons and rushed toward each other for

Figure 5. Battle scene from *Independence Trail*, Capernaum Studios, Poolville, Texas, photographed by the author, July 1, 2022.

hand-to-hand combat, a British Army soldier suddenly charged toward the spectators through the smoke-filled air and shouted at us to stand against the wall. Amid the chaos, the British officer was disarmed by a minuteman, who proclaimed, "Stand back sir, you shall be taking no prisoners today!" and then to the group said, "Remember, friends, freedom is not free. And it's worth fighting for. We shall never surrender to tyranny! Find your courage! Go!"[31]

The performance ended with members of the colonial militia collecting our "gunpowder" with words of thanks and a guide hurrying us away, this time out of the performance area. As I was, I could hear the actor playing Muhlenberg, on the other side of a wall, launching into his speech from the book of Ecclesiastes for the next audience group moving through the performance. This prompted the memory of hearing musket fire from the previous performance and how that occasioned the volunteer's approach and the beginning of our performance. I was experiencing the collapsing and folding of the cyclical time amid the incongruity of colonial Massachusettes imagined in present-day Texas. But one last segment of the performance remained that would attempt to direct our understanding of how these timelines touch and what we should take away from the experience.

As we moved toward what I thought was the exit, a door opened, and we were ushered into an unadorned room that stood in stark contrast to the theatrical world we had just left. The room was outfitted with metal folding chairs, two smiling church volunteers, and a table of religious materials. From my previous research on "hell house performance," I immediately recognized this as the "invitation room," the afterpiece to some evangelical performances in which the audience is invited to commit or recommit their lives to Jesus, or to "get saved."[32] While every Christian performance I attended for this project alerted audiences that cast members and staff were available for prayer following the performance, Capernaum Studios offered the only direct prayer intervention I encountered. It was particularly unexpected because, unlike hell house performances, which are salvific in nature, the Christian outreach in *Independence Trail* was surprisingly obscured. Following Muhlenberg's speech at the beginning of the performance, most of references to God that followed were of the "God-and-country" variety, the only exception being when Sam Adams called to our exiting group, "Remember, we serve no other king than King Jesus."[33]

Before the ministry portion of this encounter began, the volunteer pressed play on a video that attempted to bridge that gap and describe parallels between the "fight for freedom" in 1775 Massachusetts and a spiritual battle taking place here and now. Before any picture filled the large projection screen before us, ominous, pulsing music began to play from mounted speakers. Disorienting, slow-motion footage began to appear on the dark screen, fading between a close shot of a horse's mouth straining at the bit and of hooves thundering across a dusty field. The words of Revelation 22:12–13 flashed across the screen, over the images: "Look. I am coming soon! My reward is with me, and I will give to each person according to what they have done." The screen filled then with foreboding clouds and the rumble of thunder, and the text continued, "I am the Alpha and the Omega, the First and the Last, the Beginning and the End." The video then cut to a very close shot of a man wearing a black cowboy hat, looking directly into the camera. He did not introduce himself but immediately spoke with urgency about the performance of *Independence Trail*, specifically the moment when Pastor Jonas Clark promised John Hancock that the men of his congregation would fight and die for the revolution. The speaker explained: "America needs such men of God again today because our freedom is threatened by a force much more sinister than the British ever were. The forces of extreme immorality and perversion are threatening our children and our freedom. And if American churches do not answer the call, then I fear that the USA will soon pass into the dustbin of history. And our people as well."[34]

The screen then cut to black and an incongruously sunny, smiling blond volunteer stepped to the front of the room. She explaining that Capernaum put together the performance because "their heart is for the kingdom of God and freedom, and our country of course was founded on the biblical principles of the word of God and freedom."[35] She then asked if anyone among the group fought in the armed forces, and for a brief moment, I wondered if we were about to be ministered to or conscripted into the service of spiritual warfare. However, her questions served a segue from the video into her pitch for salvation as she shared her testimony, or conversion story, which involved her war-veteran grandfather. As invitation rooms are typically structured, this would be the point when the assembled are given a choice to leave the room or stay, and if they stayed, to either receive or participate in prayer. However, no such choice was offered at Capernaum—the volunteer requested that we bow our heads and pray with her, and she then recited a variation of the evangelical Sinner's Prayer that added one additional entreaty to God: "Use me in this very, very important time in history. Help me to be a history maker, not only for the United States but for the kingdom of God."[36] In July 2022, when I attended this performance, America was still embroiled in the culture wars that had come to define our political landscape. However, it was not an election year, and there were no significant events in the news that would explain why this was a "very, very important time in history" or who were the "sinister forces" that were threatening children, and country, the populous at large. Yet people in the room nodded their heads to these cryptic remarks. The performance was marked by a disjuncture between the definitive and the enigmatic. Did moments or references within this performance resonate differently for patrons already primed in conservative Christian ideology and rhetoric?

After the invitation room encounter, we filled out a response card by selecting "I received Jesus Christ today" or "I rededicated my Life to Jesus today," we were offered Christian literature, and then the group was released to enjoy the remaining events at Freedom Fest. As we left, a woman from my group spoke to me with seeming assuredness about the gravity and urgency of *Independence Trail's* message and said it was her belief that that Tammy Lane, Capernaum's founder, has special insight into future events. As evidence, she shared her experience attending the *Apocalypse Experience* in 2019, "before all this COVID stuff happened, and they actually did some scenes like, with the jab and stuff." She gave me a meaningful look under raised eyebrows before saying, "Of course, it's all in the Bible. The currency, the One World Order, and all that. It's all happening right now."[37] The conversation highlighted the temporal ambiguity of Christian performance. The eschatological tension of living on a prophetic timeline—what Jennifer Eyl calls "Kingdom time"—further complicates the temporality of historical reenactment and the performance of history.[38] It also complicates the ambiguous call to arms posed in the performance afterpiece. Does this performance call participants to prepare for a literal/physical or spiritual battle? When Christians read current events in biblical prophecy the physical and spiritual become as difficult to parse as the collapsed temporality of now and soon and past.

These temporal questions were further complicated when I attended the last of the four daily performances of Spy Game. The game took place in the courtyard of a walled recreation of a first-century village and inside the stone houses ringing the courtyard. Spy Game was not advertised as a performance, so it was surprising to encounter a set of costumed actors, different from those featured in *Independence Trail*, greeting a group of about thirty participants, most of whom appeared to be family groups. We were approached by an adult woman and two boys who appeared to be about ten and twelve years old, all in colonial dress. In a lilting Irish brogue, the woman introduced the young boys as her sons and herself as Lydia Darraugh. Casting a glance at the men dressed as British infantry who milled about the perimeter of the space, she explained that her oldest son was fighting under George Washington and he was a spy for the Continental Army. "In the challenge you're about to under-take," she told us, "you'll learn how I gathered intelligence." The game worked a bit like an escape room in which teams race to find and solve clues but with an added layer of interactive performance. Each clue would prompt us toward an improvisational interaction with a British officer who would provide infor-mation that led to the next clue. However, even if we had the right answers, the officers would not give us the information we sought unless we stayed in character and did not reveal our identities (figure 6).

Figure 6. Task # 3 from *Spy Game*, Capernaum Studios, Poolville, Texas, photographed by the author, July 1, 2022.

The game ended when the first team procured a "pass" from the British soldiers to carry wheat to a mill in an adjoining village, which is how the his-torical Lydia Darraugh was able to leave her British-occupied village to pass information to the Continental Army. The winning team received candy and bubbles as a prize, and Lydia Darraugh thanked us all for our service as we ex-ited through a gate.

Unlike *Independence Trail*, the Spy Game did not have an afterpiece with a call to action, and I almost chalked it up as a fun diversion with little to add to the analysis of this performance event. However, in a YouTube promotional video, Capernaum Studios' founder, Tammy Lane, said, "I found out from the Lord that he wants us to do three new live experiences," and in her description for the Independence Day event said, "Everyone had a role to play in the war for Independence. Not just men—women and kids—and I believe that's true

today too."[39] Lane's words prompted a deeper analysis into Spy Game and its performance temporalities. In *Independence Trail*, while the modern corollary with
the British is up for interpretation, generalized parallels are not difficult to imagine; the performance was only eighteen months removed from the January 6 at-
tack on the capital, after all.

However, the women and children characterized in Spy Game are subju-
gated to an enemy who controls their freedom of movement and restricts their
communication, all the while covertly assisting the men fighting in the Continental Army. It is not an allegory of contemporary cultural warfare; instead,
Spy Game presents a more apocalyptic vision: one of total Christian persecution, where women and children will need to hide their allegiances and live
among the enemy while acting as spies. It is an eschatological imaginary, similar to a plotline in the *Left Behind* series, in which, after having a child, Tribu-
lation Force member Chloe Steel stays behind to facilitate black market trade
among Christians as CEO of the International Commodity Co-op while her
husband fights forces aligned with the Antichrist. I say an eschatological imaginary rather than an apocalyptic future because it was clear that these Christian theater makers see this apocalyptic battle as already underway; the afterpiece for *Independence Trail* called Christians to engage militaristically in the
present tense, saying, "America needs such men of God again *today* because
our freedom is threatened by a force much more sinister than the British ever
were" (emphasis added).[40] Likewise, the day's "Patriot Speakers" discussed
present-day threats to Christian America: globalism, Marxism, and what was
framed in the talk as a government-engineered pandemic. Viewing the day's
performances through this lens upends the temporality of *Independence Trail*,
exemplifying the "tension of now and soon and past" that is central to Kingdom theology and prophecy belief.[41] The temporal loop doubles and triples on
itself, performing America's founding, current militia movements, insurrections, and apocalyptic comings.

Scott Magelssen and Ariaga Mucek's 2014 research on the Bible camp game
Romans and Christians reveals that a similar storyline has played out in evangelical storytelling for decades, even when the participants didn't understand
it as such. As they describe the game, campers "simmed" as persecuted Christians who sought spaces for secret worship. Magelssen defines simming as
"theatre and performance practices to stage environments in which participants played out a scripted or improvised narrative in order to gain or produce understanding of a situation and its context."[42] Magelssen and Mucek ask
whether the performance was an embodiment of sacred history, a rehearsal
for evangelizing in the world, or an allegory pitting the church against a sinful

world.[43] In 2014, they did have access to the ramping up of rhetoric about Christian persecution that occurred in the latter half of the decade. If they had, they might have drawn the conclusion that these simming experiences serve as rehearsal for a far more literal belief in a coming war and the Christian persecution and martyrdom that is promised in End Times narratives.

Biblical prophecies, like accounts of miracles, are built on "semantic risk or ambiguity, some sort of excess or gap that demands interpretive attention and engagement."[44] These gaps and excesses in Christian theater encourage exegesis beyond the bounds of the performance. Active and attuned perception and attention have real eschatological consequences in the End Times, when "many false prophets shall rise, and deceive many."[45] As Jill Stevenson notes, interpretation of biblical prophecy can "help people understand and navigate the geographies of the End."[46] I hesitate to put undue emphasis on the survivalist view because the Christian performances with apocalyptic messages I study do not emphasize the fear and violence present in some eschatological cultural products, like the *Left Behind* series or the hell house genre. Instead of using "a dramaturgy of threat to produce the future End-Time," the eschatological allusions in the Christian performances I study are framed as a reminder of the coming victory in Christ.[47] Even in *Independence Trail*, the dire warnings that follow the performance are tempered by the fact that the victorious ending— of both the historical Revolutionary War and the coming apocalypse—has already been written.

NOTES

1. Despite its shape, the tablets do not contain the Ten Commandments. They are inscribed, "The Law of Liberty James 1:25," a New Testament Bible verse that reads: "But whoso looketh into the perfect law of liberty, and continue therein, he being not a forgetful hearer, but a doer of the work, this man shall be blessed in his deed" (KJV).

2. "The Ozark Patriots: We Stand for Freedom," *Billboard* (Baxter County, AR), July 1, 2022.

3. Greg Dickinson, Carole Blair, and Brian L. Ott, "Introduction: Rhetoric/Memory/Place," in *Places of Public Memory: The Rhetoric of Museums and Memorials*, ed. Greg Dickinson, Carole Blair, and Brian L. Ott (Tuscaloosa: University of Alabama Press, 2010), 4.

4. Roger Silverstone, *Why Study the Media?* (London: Sage, 1999), 99.

5. Barbara Kirshenblatt-Gimblett, *Destination Culture: Tourism, Museums, and Heritage* (Berkeley: University of California Press, 1998), 255.

6. For research on evangelical performance across media spaces and in theater, see Tona J. Hangen, *Redeeming the Dial: Radio, Religion & Popular Culture in America* (Chapel Hill: University of North Carolina Press, 2002); Jeanne Halgren Kilde, *When Church Became Theatre: The Transformation of Evangelical Architecture and Worship in Nineteenth-Century America* (New York: Oxford University Press, 2002); and Daniel A. Stout and Judith M. Buddenbaum, *Religion and Mass Media: Audiences and Adaptations* (London: Sage, 1996).

7. This definition is adapted from the chapter "What is Performance Studies" in Richard Schechner and Sara Brady, *Performance Studies: An Introduction*, 3rd ed. (London: Routledge, 2013).

8. Cathy Turner and Synne Behrndt, *Dramaturgy and Performance* (New York: Bloomsbury, 2017), 22.

9. Capernaum Studios' avoidance of the label *theater* might reflect conservative Christianity's long history of antitheatricality, as noted by many scholars, including Claudia Durst Johnson, *Church and Stage: The Theatre as Target of Religious Condemnation in Nineteenth Century America* (Jefferson, NC: McFarland, 2008); Henry Bial, *Playing God: The Bible on the Broadway Stage* (Ann Arbor: University of Michigan Press, 2015), 12; Ann Pellegrini "'Signaling through the Flames': Hell House Performance and Structures of Religious Feeling," *American Quarterly* 59, no. 3 (2007): 911–35; and Matthew Avery Sutton, *American Apocalypse: A History of Modern Evangelicalism* (Cambridge, MA: Belknap Press of Harvard University Press, 2014), 114.

10. "Meet Tammy Lane of Tammy Lane Productions/Capernaum Village in West of Fort Worth," *Voyage Dallas* (website), June 20, 2018. *The Crimson Experience* is a live performance modeled on a Capernaum-produced movie, titled *The Crimson*, about Christ's crucifixion.

11. "And the dead were judged out of those things which were written in the books, according to their works" Revelation 20:12 (KJV).

12. Revelation 20:15 (KJV).

13. Jon Fleetwood, managing editor of the right-wing news network *American Faith*, gave a talk on Blackrock and the World Economic Forum and Dr. Richard Bartlett, West Texas physician and antivaccine advocate, was promoting his non-FDA approved treatment for COVID-19, a combination of nebulized steroids and zinc. One of these talks concerned the demonic Marxist intentions of the World Economic Forum. The other talk posited that the pandemic was a "plandemic" and offered information about ivermectin and other alternative treatments for COVID-19. That is how I interpreted the talks, but the speakers never drew concrete conclusions; they instead presented vague "evidence," made cryptic suggestions, paraliptic examples, and asked question that implied that the audience was all in on the answer.

14. Capernaum Studios, "Independence Day Experience," Facebook, April 19, 2022.

15. Dan Fisher, "Bringing Back the Black Robed Regiment" (website), accessed March 15, 2025.

16. Susan Friend Harding, *The Book of Jerry Falwell: Fundamentalist Language and Politics* (Princeton, NJ: Princeton University Press, 2001), 161.

17. Thomas Lecaque and J. L. Tomlin, "Pastors Claiming the Mantle of the 'Black-Robed Regiment' Get the History Wrong," *Washington Post*, October 15, 2021.

18. Capernaum Studios, "Independence Day Experience."

19. Robert Weimann, *Shakespeare and the Popular Tradition in the Theatre* (Baltimore: Johns Hopkins University Press, 1978) 232. Quoted in Jeremy Lopez, *Theatrical Conventions and Audience Response in Early Modern Drama* (Cambridge: Cambridge University Press, 2002), 58.

20. "Rather baldly" in Madeleine Doran, *Endeavors of Art* (Madison: University of Wisconsin Press, 1954), 254. Quoted in Lopez, *Theatrical Conventions*, 58.

21. Janet McIntosh, "Alt-Signaling: Fascistic Communication and the Power of Subterranean Style," Hot Spots, *Fieldsights*, April 15, 2021.

22. Lopez, *Theatrical Convention*, 58.

23. Field recording, *Independence Trail*, Capernaum Studios, Poolville, TX, July 2, 2022. (Capernaum Studios permits photography and recording during its performances, and I, along with other patrons, were openly documenting the event.)

24. Ecclesiastes 3:1–18: "To every thing there is a season, and a time to every purpose under heaven" (KJV).

25. Ecclesiastes 3:1–18: "To every thing there is a season, and a time to every purpose under heaven" (KJV). Capernaum Studios, *Independence Trail*, Poolville, TX, July 2, 2022. All subsequent references to *Independence Trail* are to this performance.

26. Rebecca Schneider, *Performing Remains: Art and War in Times of Theatrical Reenactment* (London: Routledge, 2011), 2.

27. Capernaum Studios, *Independence Trail*.

28. Capernaum Studios, *Independence Trail*.

29. Seymour, Pete, "Prince Estabrook of Lexington," Boston National Historical Park, Minute Men National Historical Park, National Parks Service website, May 2020.

30. This viewpoint aligns with several videos produced by Capernaum Studios and posted to their YouTube channel that pose oppositional arguments to the 1619 Project, the Black Lives Matter movement, and "critical race theory." Capernaum Studios, YouTube, accessed August 22, 2022.

31. Capernaum Studios, *Independence Trail*.

32. Robyn Lee Horn, "American Hells: Hell Houses, Abortion Frames, and Unsexed Women," in *Theatre and the Macabre,* ed. Meredith Conti and Kevin J. Wetmore Jr, Horror Studies (Cardiff: University of Wales Press, 2022), 237–50; John Fletcher, *Preaching to Convert: Evangelical Outreach and Performance Activism in a Secular Age* (Ann Arbor: University of Michigan Press, 2013), 162.; Jill Stevenson, *Feeling the Future at Christian End-Time Performances* (Ann Arbor: University of Michigan Press, 2022), 151.

33. Capernaum Studios, *Independence Trail*.

34. Capernaum Studios, video afterpiece, *Independence Trail*.

35. Capernaum Studios, invitation room, *Independence Trail*.

36. Offering the choice to pray is thematically aligned with hell houses performances—which dramatize a series of decisions and their earthly and eternal consequences—in a way that it was not aligned with *Independence Trail*. It is also true that public prayer is not uncommon at gatherings in many parts of the country. Yet, there was something unduly assertive about the involuntary nature of the prayer intervention, particularly because the Sinner's Prayer is considered by many evangelical Christians to have performative salvific qualities. Simply reciting the prayer, either aloud or silently, is considered by some to be the definitive moment of conversion and salvation.

37. *Independence Trail* audience member, conversation with author, July 2, 2022.

38. Jennifer Eyl, "Anachronism as a Constituent Feature of Mythmaking at the Biblewalk Museum," in *Christian Tourist Attractions, Mythmaking, and Identity Formation* (London: Bloomsbury, 2019), 124.

39. Capernaum Studios, "Introducing New Live Experiences," YouTube video, accessed August 22, 2022.

40. Capernaum Studios, afterpiece, *Independence Trail*.

41. Dave Jenkins, "Tension of Now and Soon and Past," Christian Blogger, *Christianity Today*, 2020.

42. Scott Magelssen, *Simming: Participatory Performance and the Making of Meaning* (Ann Arbor: University of Michigan Press, 2014), 3.

43. Scott Magelssen and Ariaga Mucek, "Romans and Christians: Bearing Witness and Performing Persecution in Bible Camp Simulations," *Performance Matters* 3, no. 1 (2017): 20.

44. Magelssen and Mucek, "Romans and Christians," 20.

45. Matthew 14:11 (KJV).

46. Stevenson, *Feeling the Future*, 8.

47. Stevenson, *Feeling the Future*, 8.

Bibliography

Albanese, Catherine L. "Introduction: Awash in a Sea of Metaphysics." *Journal of the American Academy of Religion* 75, no. 3 (2007): 582–88.

————. *A Republic of Mind and Spirit: A Cultural History of American Metaphysical Religion.* New Haven, CT: Yale University Press, 2007.

Alexander, Elizabeth. *The Black Interior: Essays.* Saint Paul, MN: Graywolf, 2004.

Allen, Jafari S. *There's a Disco Ball between Us: A Theory of Black Gay Life.* Durham, NC: Duke University Press, 2022.

Altman, Michael J. "Introduction: Something Someone Calls Religion Somewhere Someone Calls America." In *American Examples: New Conversations about Religion*, vol. 1, edited by Michael J. Altman, 10–13. Tuscaloosa: University of Alabama Press, 2021.

Anidjar, Gil. "Secularism." *Critical Inquiry* 33, no. 1 (2006): 52–77.

Asad, Talal. *Formations of the Secular: Christianity, Islam, Modernity.* Stanford, CA: Stanford University Press, 2003.

Bailey, Marlon M. *Butch Queen Up in Pumps: Gender, Performance, and Ballroom Culture in Detroit.* Ann Arbor: University of Michigan Press, 2013.

Baker, Mandi. *Becoming and Being a Camp Counsellor: Discourse, Power Relations and Emotions.* Cham, Switzerland: Palgrave Macmillan, 2020.

Barthes, Roland. *Mythologies.* Translated by Annette Lavers. New York: Hill and Wang, 2006.

Bartkowski, John P. *Remaking the Godly Marriage: Gender Negotiation in Evangelical Families.* London: Rutgers University Press, 2001.

Bataille, Georges. *Theory of Religion.* Translated by Robert Hurley. New York: Zone Books, 1992.

Bell, Catherine. *Ritual: Perspectives and Dimensions.* New York: Oxford University Press, 1997.

Bell, Catherine. *Ritual Theory, Ritual Practice.* New York: Oxford University Press, 1992.

Berry, Evan. *Devoted to Nature: The Religious Roots of American Environmentalism.* Oakland: University of California Press, 2015.

Bial, Henry. *Playing God: The Bible on the Broadway Stage.* Ann Arbor: University of Michigan Press, 2015.

Bielo, James S. *Emerging Evangelicals: Faith, Modernity, and the Desire for Authenticity.* New York: New York University Press, 2011.

Bivins, Jason. *Religion of Fear: The Politics of Horror in Conservative Evangelicalism*. Oxford: Oxford University Press, 2008.

Bowler, Kate. *The Preacher's Wife: The Precarious Power of Evangelical Women Celebrities*. Princeton, NJ: Princeton University Press, 2019.

Boym, Svetlana. *The Future of Nostalgia*. New York: Basic Books, 2001.

Brenneman, Todd M. *Homespun Gospel: The Triumph of Sentimentality in Contemporary American Evangelicalism*. New York: Oxford University Press, 2014.

Brooks, Daphne A. "Divas and Diasporic Consciousness: Song, Dance, and New Negro Womanhood in the Veil." In *Bodies in Dissent: Spectacular Performances of Race and Freedom, 1850–1910*, 281–42. Durham, NC: Duke University Press, 2006.

Brown, Elspeth H. *Work! A Queer History of Modeling*. Durham, NC: Duke University Press, 2019.

Brown, Jayna. *Babylon Girls: Black Women Performers and the Shaping of the Modern*. Durham, NC: Duke University Press, 2008.

Brown, William Wells. *Clotel*. Electronic scholarly ed., edited by Christopher Mulvey. University of Virginia Press, 2006.

———. *Clotel; or, The President's Daughter: A Narrative of Slave Life in the United States*. London: Partridge and Oakey, 1853.

———. *Clotelle: A Tale of the Southern States*. Boston: James Redpath, 1864.

———. *Clotelle; or, The Colored Heroine*. Boston: Lee and Shepard, 1867.

———. *Miralda; or, The Beautiful Quadroon: A Romance of American Slavery Founded on Fact*. Published serially in the *Weekly Anglo-African*. New York, 1860–1861.

———. *My Southern Home: or, The South and Its People*. Boston: A. G. Brown, 1880.

———. *Three Years in Europe; or, Places I Have Seen and People I Have Met*. London: Charles Gilpin, 1852.

Burlein, Ann. *Lift High the Cross: Where White Supremacy and the Christian Right Converge*. Durham, NC: Duke University Press, 2002.

Butler, Jon. *Awash in a Sea of Faith: Christianizing the American People*. Studies in Cultural History. Cambridge, MA: Harvard University Press, 1990.

Butler, Judith. "Gender Is Burning: Questions of Appropriation and Subversion." In *Bodies That Matter: On the Discursive Limits of "Sex,"* 121–40. New York: Routledge, 1993.

———. *Gender Trouble: Feminism and the Subversion of Identity*. New York: Routledge, 1990.

Butler, Octavia. *Parable of the Sower*. 1993. New York: Grand Central, 2019.

Cailliet, Émile. *Young Life*. 1st ed. New York: Harper and Row, 1963.

Caillois, Roger. *Man and the Sacred*. Translated by Meyer Barash. Urbana: University of Illinois Press, 2001.

Carby, Hazel V. *Reconstructing Womanhood: The Emergence of the Afro-American Woman Novelist*. Oxford: Oxford University Press, 1987.

Cashman, Ray. "Critical Nostalgia and Material Culture in Northern Ireland." *Journal of American Folklore* 119, no. 472 (2006): 137–60.

Cecelski, David. *The Waterman's Song: Slavery and Freedom in Maritime North Carolina*. Chapel Hill: University of North Carolina Press, 2001.

Chireau, Yvonne P. *Black Magic: Religion and the African American Conjuring Tradition*. Berkeley: University of California Press, 2003.

Christian, Barbara. "The Race for Theory." *Cultural Critique*, no. 6 (1987): 51–63.

Collier-Thomas, Bettye. *Daughters of Thunder: Black Women Preachers and Their Sermons*. San Francisco: Jossey-Bass, 1998.

Cox, Aimee Meredith. *Shapeshifters: Black Girls and the Choreography of Citizenship*. Durham, NC: Duke University Press, 2015.

Craig, Maxine Leeds. *Ain't I a Beauty Queen? Black Women, Beauty, and the Politics of Race*. Oxford: Oxford University Press, 2002.

Crain, Liz. *Food Lovers' Guide to Portland*. Portland, OR: Hawthorne Books, 2014.

Crockford, Susannah. *Ripples of the Universe: Spirituality in Sedona, Arizona*. Chicago: University of Chicago Press, 2021.

Cummings, Celeste, and Amara Williams. *Speaking in Tongues and Dancing Diaspora: Black Women Writing and Performing*. New York: Routledge, 2015.

Daniel, Yvonne. *Dancing Wisdom: Embodied Knowledge in Haitian Vodou, Cuban Yoruba, and Bahian Candomblé*. Urbana: University of Illinois Press, 2017.

Dawdy, Shannon Lee. *Patina: A Profane Archaeology*. Chicago: University of Chicago Press, 2016.

DeFrantz, Thomas F., ed. *Dancing Many Drums: Excavations in African American Dance*. Philadelphia: Temple University Press, 2002.

DeFrantz, Thomas F., and Anita Gonzalez, eds. *Black Performance Theory*. Durham, NC: Duke University Press, 2014.

Delany, Martin R. *Blake; or, The Huts of America*. 1861–1862. Corrected ed., edited by Jerome McGann. Cambridge, MA: Harvard University Press, 2017.

DeMaria, Richard. *Communal Love at Oneida: A Perfectionist Vision of Authority, Property, and Sexual Order*. Vol. 2. New York: E. Mellen Press, 1978.

Deren, Maya. *Divine Horsemen: The Living Gods of Haiti*. New Paltz, NY: McPherson, 1953.

Deutsch, Tracey. *Building a Housewife's Paradise: Gender, Politics, and American Grocery Stores in the Twentieth Century*. Chapel Hill: University of North Carolina Press, 2010.

Devereux, Paul. *The Ley Hunter's Companion: Aligned Ancient Sites; A New Study with Field Guide and Maps*. London: Thames and Hudson, 1979.

DeVun, Leah. *The Shape of Sex: Nonbinary Gender from Genesis to the Renaissance*. New York: Columbia University Press, 2021.

Dickinson, Greg, Carole Blair, and Brian L. Ott. *Places of Public Memory: The Rhetoric of Museums and Memorials*. Rhetoric, Culture, and Social Critique. Tuscaloosa: University of Alabama Press, 2010.

Dochuk, Darren. *From Bible Belt to Sunbelt: Plain-Folk Religion, Grassroots Politics, and the Rise of Evangelical Conservatism*. New York: W. W. Norton, 2011.

Doran, Madeleine. *Endeavors of Art*. Madison: University of Wisconsin Press, 1954.

Douglas, Mary. *Purity and Danger*. 1966. London: Routledge, 2002.

Douglass, Frederick. *The Heroic Slave*. 1853. Cultural and critical ed., edited by Robert S. Levine, John Stauffer, and John McKivigan. New Haven, CT. Yale University Press, 2016.

Doyle, Michael. *The Ministers' War: John W. Mears, the Oneida Community, and the Crusade for Public Morality*. Syracuse, NY: Syracuse University Press, 2018.

Drewal, Margaret Thompson. "The State of Research on Performance in Africa." *African Studies Review* 34, no. 3 (December 1991): 1–64.

———. *Yoruba Ritual: Performers, Play, Agency*. Bloomington: Indiana University Press, 1992.

Driscoll, Catherine. *Girls: Feminine Adolescence in Popular Culture and Cultural Theory*. New York: Columbia University Press, 2002.

Dubois, Laurent. *Avengers of the New World: The Story of the Haitian Revolution*. Cambridge, MA: Harvard University Press, 2004.

Du Bois, W. E. B. *Black Reconstruction in America, 1860–1880*. New York: Harcourt, Brace, 1935.

———. "Returning Soldiers." *The Crisis* 18 (May 1919): 13.

———. *W. E. B. Du Bois on Sociology and the Black Community*. Edited by Dan S. Green and Edwin D. Driver. Chicago: University of Chicago Press, 1978.

DuCille, Ann. "Where in the World Is William Wells Brown? Thomas Jefferson, Sally Hemmings, and the DNA of African-American Literary History." *American Literary History* 12, no. 3 (2000): 443–62.

Dym, Warren. "Scholars and Miners: Dowsing and the Freiberg Mining Academy." *Technology and Culture* 49, no. 4 (2008): 833–59.

Eastman, Hubbard. *Noyesism Unveiled*. Brattleboro, VT: Reverend Hubbard Eastman, 1849.

Eddins, Crystal Nicole. *Rituals, Runaways, and the Haitian Revolution: Collective Action in the African Diaspora*. Cambridge: Cambridge University Press, 2022.

Edwards, Laura F. *Gendered Strife and Confusion: The Political Culture of Reconstruction*. Urbana: University of Illinois Press, 1997.

Eichler-Levine, Jodi. *Suffer the Little Children: Uses of the Past in Jewish and African American Children's Literature*. New York: New York University Press, 2013.

Eyl, Jennifer. "Anachronism as a Constituent Feature of Mythmaking at the Biblewalk Museum." In *Christian Tourist Attractions, Mythmaking, and Identity Formation*, edited by Erin Roberts and Jennifer Eyl, 111–26. London: Bloomsbury, 2019.

Ferguson, Roderick A. *Aberrations in Black: Towards a Queer of Color Critique*. Minneapolis: University of Minnesota Press, 2004.

Fessenden, Tracy. *Culture and Redemption: Religion, the Secular, and American Literature*. Princeton, NJ: Princeton University Press, 2007.

Fletcher, John. *Preaching to Convert: Evangelical Outreach and Performance Activism in a Secular Age*. Ann Arbor: University of Michigan Press, 2013.

Foner, Eric. *Reconstruction: America's Unfinished Revolution, 1863–1877*. Updated ed. New York: Harper Perennial Modern Classics, 2014.

Foster, Lawrence. *Religion and Sexuality: The Shakers, the Mormons, and the Oneida Community*. Urbana: University of Illinois Press, 1984.

Foster, William Patrick. *Band Pageantry: A Guide for the Marching Band*. Minnesota: Hal Leonard Music, 1968.

Foucault, Michel. *The History of Sexuality*. New York: Vintage Books, 1988.

Fox, Sandra. *The Jews of Summer: Summer Camp and Jewish Culture in Postwar America*. Stanford Studies in Jewish History and Culture. Stanford, CA: Stanford University Press, 2023.

Fromont, Cécile. "Dance, Image, Myth, and Conversion in the Kingdom of Kongo, 1500–1800." *Journal of African History* 56, no. 2 (2015): 215–32.

Fuentes, Marisa J. *Dispossessed Lives: Enslaved Women, Violence, and the Archive*. Philadelphia: University of Pennsylvania Press, 2015.

Gallagher, Sally K. *Evangelical Identity and Gendered Family Life*. New Brunswick, NJ: Rutgers University Press, 2003.

Gialanella, Leigh. "Discord in Utopia: Reconciling Perfectionism with Human Nature in the Oneida Community." *Communal Societies* 35, no. 2 (December 2015): 185–211.

Gill, Sam. *Dancing Culture Religion*. Lanham, MD: Lexington Books, 2012.

Glissant, Édouard. *Poetics of Relation*. Translated by Betsy Wing. Ann Arbor: University of Michigan Press, 1997.

Golden, Kathryn Benjamin. "'Armed in the Great Swamp': Fear, Maroon Insurrection, and the Insurgent Ecology of the Great Dismal Swamp." *Journal of African American History* 106, no. 1 (Winter 2021): 1–26.

Gomez, Michael. *Exchanging Our Country Marks: The Transformation of African Identities in the Colonial and Antebellum South*. Chapel Hill: University of North Carolina Press, 1998.

Gonick, Marnina. *Between Femininities: Ambivalence, Identity, and the Education of Girls*. Second Thoughts. Albany: State University of New York Press, 2003.

Gottschild, Brenda Dixon. *The Black Dancing Body: A Geography from Coon to Cool*. New York: Palgrave Macmillan, 2003.

———. *Waltzing in the Dark: African American Vaudeville and Race Politics in the Swing Era*. New York: Palgrave Macmillan, 2000.

Graham, Kathleen, ed. *Stepping Stones*. 2nd ed. Wheaton, IL: Pioneer Girls Inc., 1977.

Grandy, Moses. *Narrative of the Life of Moses Grandy, Late a Slave in the United States of America*. Transcribed by George Thompson. London: Charles Gilpin, 1844.

Griffith, J'aime. "Historically Black College and University Dance Lines: Redefining and Identifying Elements to Determine Aesthetic Value." Master's thesis, University of Oklahoma, 2022.

Gross, Rachel B., *Beyond the Synagogue: Jewish Nostalgia as Religious Practice*. New York: New York University Press, 2021.

Hagens, Bethe. "The Divine Feminine in Geometric Consciousness." *Anthropology of Consciousness* 17, no. 1 (2006): 1–34.

Hahn, Stephen. *A Nation under Our Feet: Black Political Struggles in the Rural South from Slavery to the Great Migration*. Cambridge, MA: Belknap Press of Harvard University Press, 2003.

Hall, David D. *Lived Religion in America: Toward a History of Practice*. Princeton, NJ: Princeton University Press, 1997.

Hangen, Tona J. *Redeeming the Dial: Radio, Religion & Popular Culture in America*. Chapel Hill: University of North Carolina Press, 2002.

Harding, Susan Friend. *The Book of Jerry Falwell: Fundamentalist Language and Politics*. Princeton, NJ: Princeton University Press, 2001.

Hardt, Michael. "Affective Labor." *Boundary 2* 26, no. 2 (1999): 89–100.

Harker, Brian. "Louis Armstrong, Eccentric Dance, and the Evolution of Jazz on the Eve of Swing." *Journal of the American Musicological Society* 61, no. 1 (2008): 67–121.

Hartman, Sadiya V. *Scenes of Subjections: Terror, Slavery, and Self-Making in Nineteenth-Century America*. Oxford: Oxford University Press, 1997.

Hazard, Sonia, ed. "Religion and Material Texts in the Americas." Special issue, *Material Religion* 17, no 2 (2021).

Higginbotham, Evelyn. *Righteous Discontent: The Women's Movement in the Black Baptist Church, 1880–1920*. Cambridge, MA: Harvard University Press, 1993.

Higonnet, Anne. *Pictures of Innocence: The History and Crisis of Ideal Childhood*. New York: Thames and Hudson, 1998.

Hildago, Jacqueline. *Revelation in Aztlán: Scriptures, Utopias, and the Chicano Movement*. New York: Palgrave Macmillan, 2016.

Hilderbrand, Lucas. *Paris Is Burning: A Queer Film Classic*. Vancouver: Arsenal Pulp, 2013.

Hong, Grace Kyungwon. *The Ruptures of American Capital*. Minneapolis: University of Minnesota Press, 2006.

hooks, bell. "Is Paris Burning?" In *Black Looks: Race and Representation*, 145–56. Boston: South End, 1992.

Horn, Robyn Lee. "American Hells: Hell Houses, Abortion Frames, and Unsexed Women." In *Theatre and the Macabre*, edited by Meredith Conti and Kevin J. Wetmore Jr., 237–50. Horror Studies. Cardiff: University of Wales Press, 2022.

Hurston, Zora Neale. *Mules and Men*. Philadelphia: J. B. Lippincott, 1935.

———. *The Sanctified Church*. Berkeley, CA: Turtle Island Foundation, 1981.

Jacobs, Harriet. *Incidents in the Life of a Slave Girl*. 1861. 2nd Norton critical ed., edited by Frances Smith Foster and Richard Yarborough. W. W. Norton, 2019.

Johnson, Claudia Durst. *Church and Stage: The Theatre as Target of Religious Condemnation in Nineteenth Century America*. Jefferson, NC: McFarland, 2008.

Johnson, E. Patrick. *Appropriating Blackness: Performance and the Politics of Authenticity*. Durham, NC: Duke University Press, 2003.

Johnson, Jasmine Elizabeth. "Flesh Dance: Black Women from Behind." In *Futures of Dance Studies*, edited by Susan Manning, Janice Ross, and Rebecca Schneider. Madison: University of Wisconsin Press, 2020.

Johnson, Sarah Jessica. "Outlyers: Maroons and Marronage in Eighteenth and Nineteenth-Century Literature." Phd diss., University of California, Berkeley, 2018.

Jun, Helen Heran. *Race for Citizenship: Black Orientalism and Asian Uplift from Pre-Emancipation to Neoliberal America*. New York: New York University Press, 2011.

Kemerait, Judith Louise. "Routes of Freedom: Slave Resistance and the Politics of Literary Geography." PhD diss., Louisiana State University, 2004.

Kerby, Lauren R. *Saving History: How White Evangelicals Tour the Nation's Capital and Redeem a Christian America*. Where Religion Lives. Chapel Hill: University of North Carolina Press, 2020.

Kern, Louis J. *An Ordered Love: Sex Roles and Sexuality in Victorian Utopias: The Shakers, the Mormons, and the Oneida Community*. Chapel Hill: University of North Carolina Press, 1981.

Kilde, Jeanne Halgren. *When Church Became Theatre: The Transformation of Evangelical Architecture and Worship in Nineteenth-Century America*. New York: Oxford University Press, 2002.

Kirshenblatt-Gimblett, Barbara. *Destination Culture: Tourism, Museums, and Heritage*. Tourism, Museums, and Heritage. Berkeley: University of California Press, 1998.

Koerselman, Rebecca A. "'Invading Vacationland for Christ': The Construction of Evangelical Identity through Summer Camps in the Postwar Era." PhD diss., Michigan State University, 2013.

Kotz, David M. *The Rise and Fall of Neoliberal Capitalism*. Cambridge, MA: Harvard University Press, 2015.

Larsen, Timothy. "Pioneer Girls: Mid-Twentieth-Century American Evangelicalism's Girl Scouts." *Asbury Journal* 63, no. 2 (2008): 59–79.

Leaming, Hugo Prosper. *Hidden Americans: Maroons of Virginia and the Carolinas*. New York: Garland, 1995.

Lepselter, Susan. *The Resonance of Unseen Things: Poetics, Power, Captivity, and UFOs in the American Uncanny*. Ann Arbor: University of Michigan Press, 2016.

Levine, Robert S. "Uncle Tom's Cabin in Frederick Douglass' Paper: An Analysis of Reception." *American Literature* 64, no. 1 (March 1992): 71–93.

Lewis, Sydney Fonteyn. "'Everything I Know about Being a Black Femme I Learned from *Sula*': Or, Towards a Black Femme-inist Criticism." *Trans-scripts* 2 (2012): 100–125.

Lewis, William. "Marching to the Beat of a Different Drum: Performance Traditions of Historically Black College and University Marching Bands." *North Carolina Folklore Journal* 50, no. 1–2 (2003): 19–47.

Lincoln, Bruce. *Discourse and the Construction of Society: Comparative Studies of Myth, Ritual, and Classification*. 2nd ed. Oxford: Oxford University Press, 2014.

———. *Theorizing Myth: Narrative, Ideology, and Scholarship*. Chicago: University of Chicago Press, 1999.

Livingston, Jennie, dir. *Paris Is Burning*. New York: Off White Productions, 1990.

Lofton, Kathryn. *Consuming Religion*. Chicago: University of Chicago Press, 2017.

———. "Religious History as Religious Studies." *Religion* 42, no. 3 (2012): 383–94.

Lomax, Tamura. *Jezebel Unhinged: Loosing the Black Female Body in Religion and Culture*. Durham, NC: Duke University Press, 2018.

Lopez, Jeremy. *Theatrical Convention and Audience Response in Early Modern Drama*. Cambridge: Cambridge University Press, 2002.

Lorde, Audre. *Sister Outsider: Essays and Speeches*. Berkeley, CA: Crossing, 2007.

Lowe, Lisa. *Immigrant Acts: On Asian American Cultural Politics*. Durham, NC: Duke University Press, 1999.

Loyd-Sims, Lamont. "J-Setting in Public: Black Queer Desires and Worldmaking." Master's thesis, Georgia State University, 2014.

Lundberg, Björn. "Localized Internationalism: Camping across Borders in the Early Swedish Boy Scout Movement." *Journal of the History of Childhood and Youth* 15, no. 1 (2022): 75–92.

Madera, Judith. *Black Atlas: Geography and Flow in Nineteenth-Century African American Literature*. Durham, NC: Duke University Press, 2015.

Magelssen, Scott. *Simming: Participatory Performance and the Making of Meaning*. Theater: Theory/Text/Performance Series. Ann Arbor: University of Michigan Press, 2014.

Magelssen, Scott, and Ariaga Mucek, "Romans and Christians: Bearing Witness and Performing Persecution in Bible Camp Simulations." *Performance Matters* 3, no. 1 (2017): 19–38.

Mahmood, Saba. *Politics of Piety: The Islamic Revival and the Feminist Subject*. Princeton, NJ: Princeton University Press, 2005.

Malone, Jacqui. *Steppin' on the Blues: The Visible Rhythms of African American Dance*. Chicago: University of Illinois Press, 1996.

Manning, Susan, Janice Ross, and Rebecca Schneider, eds. *Futures of Dance Studies*. Madison: University of Wisconsin Press, 2020.

Martin, Asia N. *Legendary Loading . . . .* Self-published, 2021.

Martin, Joel W., and Mark A. Nicholas, eds. *Native Americans, Christianity, and the Reshaping of the American Religious Landscape*. Chapel Hill: University of North Carolina Press, 2010.

Mauss, Marcel. "Techniques of the Body." *Economy and Society* 2, no. 1 (1973): 70–88.

McGirr, Lisa. *Suburban Warriors: The Origins of the New American Right*. Princeton, NJ: Princeton University Press, 2001.

Meyer, Birgit, ed. *Aesthetic Formations: Media, Religion, and the Senses*. New York: Palgrave Macmillan, 2009.

Mikles, Natasha L., and Joseph P. Laycock, eds. *Religion, Culture, and the Monstrous: Of Gods and Monsters*. Lanham, MD: Lexington Books, 2021.

Mitchell, Angelyn, ed. *Within the Circle: An Anthology of African American Literary Criticism from the Harlem Renaissance to the Present*. Durham, NC: Duke University Press, 1994.

Mitchell, Kerry. *Spirituality and the State: Managing Nature and Experience in America's National Parks*. North American Religions. New York: New York University Press, 2016.

Mock, Janet. *Redefining Realness: My Path to Womanhood, Identity, Love & So Much More*. New York: Atria Books, 2014.

Moreton, Bethany. *To Serve God and Wal-Mart: The Making of Christian Free Enterprise*. Cambridge, MA: Harvard University Press, 2009.

Morris, J. Brent. *Dismal Freedom: A History of the Maroons of the Great Dismal Swamp*. Chapel Hill: University of North Carolina Press, 2022.

Moslener, Sara. *Virgin Nation: Sexual Purity and American Adolescence*. New York: Oxford University Press, 2015.

Muñoz, José Esteban. *Disidentifications: Queers of Color and the Performance of Politics*. Minneapolis: University of Minnesota Press, 1999.

Murphy, Emily A. *Growing up with America: Youth, Myth, and National Identity, 1945 to Present*. Athens: University of Georgia Press, 2020.

Nail, Thomas. *Lucretius I: An Ontology of Motion*. Edinburgh: Edinburgh University Press, 2018.

Nevius, Marcus P. *City of Refuge: Slavery and Petit Marronage in the Great Dismal Swamp, 1763–1856*. Athens: University of Georgia Press, 2020.

Newman, Hugh. *Earth Grids: The Secret Patterns of Gaia's Sacred Sites*. Glastonbury, UK: Wooden Books, 2008.

Newman, Lance. "Free Soil and the Abolitionist Forests of Frederick Douglass's 'The Heroic Slave.'" *American Literature* 8, no. 1 (March 2009): 127–52.

Newton, Richard. *Identifying Roots: Alex Haley and the Anthropology of Scriptures*. New York: Equinox, 2020.

Noyes, John Humphrey. *The Berean: A Manual for the Help of Those Who Seek the Faith of the Primitive Church*. Putney, VT: Office of the Spiritual Magazine, 1847.

———. *Home-Talks*. Vol. 1, edited by Alfred Barron and George Noyes Miller. Oneida, NY: Oneida Community, 1875.

Nyong'o, Tavia. *Afro-Fabulations: The Queer Drama of Black Life*. New York: New York University Press, 2018.

Ogbar, Jeffrey O. G. *Black Power: Radical Politics and African American Identity*. Baltimore: Johns Hopkins University Press, 2005.

Oneida Community. *Bible Communism: A Compilation from the Annual Reports and Other*

Publication of the Oneida Association and Its Branches. Brooklyn, NY: Office of the Circular, 1853.

———. *Handbook of the Oneida Community*. Brooklyn, NY: Office of the American Socialist, 1871.

———. *Mutual Criticism*. Oneida, NY: Office of the American Socialist, 1876.

Oneida Community Collection. Special Collections Research Center, Syracuse University, Syracuse, NY.

Ongiri, Amy Abugo. *Spectacular Blackness: The Cultural Politics of the Black Power Movement and the Search for a Black Aesthetic*. Charlottesville: University of Virginia Press, 2009.

Paquette, Robert L. "From Rebellion to Revisionism: The Continuing Debate about the Denmark Vesey Affair." *Journal of the Historical Society* 4, no. 3 (Fall 2004): 291–334.

Paris, Leslie. "The Adventures of Peanut and Bo: Summer Camps and Early Twentieth-Century American Girlhood." In *The Girls' History and Culture Reader: The Twentieth Century*, edited by Miriam Forman-Brunell and Leslie Paris, 84–108. Urbana: University of Illinois Press, 2011.

———. *Children's Nature: The Rise of the American Summer Camp*. American History and Culture Series. New York: New York University Press, 2010.

Peixotto, Becca. "Wetlands in Defiance: Exploring African-American Resistance in the Great Dismal Swamp." *Journal of Wetland Archaeology* 17, no. 1 (2017): 18–35.

Pellegrini, Ann. "'Signaling through the Flames': Hell House Performance and Structures of Religious Feeling." *American Quarterly* 59, no. 3 (2007): 911–35.

Penrose, Evelyn. "Dowsing." *Blackwood's Magazine* 232 (1932): 345–53.

Pike, Sarah M. 2004. *New Age and Neopagan Religions in America*. Columbia Contemporary American Religion Series. New York: Columbia University Press.

Pioneer Girls. *Cherith Chips*. 1st ed. Wheaton, IL: Pioneer Girls Inc., 1943.

———. *Pioneer Girls Trail Book*. 8th ed. Chicago: Pioneer Girls Inc., 1950.

Pioneer Ministries Records. CN 264, Evangelism and Missions Archives, Wheaton College, Wheaton, IL.

Priddy, Barbara. Papers. 2016-019, Evangelism and Missions Archives, Wheaton College, Wheaton, IL.

Promey, Sally, ed. *Sensational Religion*. New Haven, CT: Yale University Press, 2014.

Puglionesi, Alicia. *In Whose Ruins: Power, Possession, and the Landscapes of American Empire*. New York: Scribner, 2022.

Quashie, Kevin. *Black Aliveness, or a Poetics of Being*. Durham, NC: Duke University Press, 2021.

Raboteau, Albert J. *Slave Religion: The "Invisible Institution" in the Antebellum South*. Oxford: Oxford University Press, 2004.

Raimon, Eve Allegra. *The "Tragic Mulatta" Revisited: Race and Nationalism in Nineteenth Century Antislavery Fiction*. New Brunswick, NJ: Rutgers University Press, 2004.

Ramsey, Frederic, Jr. *Music from the South, Volume 1: Country Brass Bands*. Folkways Records FA 2650, 1955, 1961.

Redpath, James. *The Roving Editor: or, Talks with Slaves in the Southern States*. New York: A. B. Burdick, 1859.

Richet, Charles Robert. *Thirty Years of Psychical Research: Being a Treatise on Metapsychics*. New York: Macmillan, 1923.

Richey, Russell E. *Methodism in the American Forest*. Oxford: Oxford University Press, 2015.

Roberts, Blain. *Pageants, Parlors, and Pretty Women: Race and Beauty in the Twentieth-Century South*. Chapel Hill: University of North Carolina Press, 2014.

Rocha, Gabriel de Avilez. "Maroons in the Montes: Toward a Political Ecology of Marronage in the Sixteenth-Century Caribbean." In *Early Modern Black Diaspora Studies: A Critical Anthology*, edited by Cassander L. Smith, Nicholas R. Jones, and Miles P. Grier, 15–36. Cham: Palgrave Macmillan, 2018.

Ross, Marlon B. *Sissy Insurgencies: A Racial Anatomy of Unfit Manliness*. Durham, NC: Duke University Press, 2021.

Russo, Vito. *The Celluloid Closet: Homosexuality in the Movies*. New York: Harper and Row, 1981.

Sayers, Daniel O. *A Desolate Place for a Defiant People: The Archaeology of Maroons, Indigenous Americans, and Enslaved Laborers in the Great Dismal Swamp*. Gainesville: University of Florida Press, 2014.

Schechner, Richard, and Sara Brady. *Performance Studies: An Introduction*. 3rd ed. London: Routledge, 2013.

Schneider, Rebecca. *Performing Remains: Art and War in Times of Theatrical Reenactment*. London: Routledge, 2011.

Scott, Julius. *The Common Wind: Afro-American Currents in the Age of the Haitian Revolution*. London: Verso, 2018.

Self, Rico. "The Prancing J-Settes and Black Queer Feminist Worldmaking: 'Let's Set(te) the Scene.'" In *The Routledge Handbook of Ethnicity and Race in Communication*, edited by Bernadette Marie Calafell and Shinsuke Eguchi, 127–40. New York: Routledge, 2024.

Sender, Katherine. "Queens for a Day: Queer Eye for the Straight Guy and the Neoliberal Project." *Critical Studies in Media Communication* 23, no. 2 (2006): 131–51.

Silliman, Daniel. "An Evangelical Is Anyone Who Likes Billy Graham: Defining Evangelicalism with Carl Henry and Networks of Trust." *Church History* 90, no. 3 (2021): 621–43.

Silverstone, Roger. *Why Study the Media?* London: Sage, 1999.

Simpson, Mark. *Trafficking Subjects: The Politics of Mobility in Nineteenth-Century America*. Minneapolis: University of Minnesota Press, 2004.

Sorenson, Jacob. *Sacred Playgrounds: Christian Summer Camp in Theological Perspective*. Eugene, OR: Cascade Books, 2021.

Sostaita, Barbara Andrea. *Sanctuary Everywhere: The Fugitive Sacred in the Sonoran Desert*. Durham, NC: Duke University Press, 2024.

Southern University Dancing Dolls. East Baton Rouge Parish Library Special Collections, Baton Rouge, LA.

Spillers, Hortense J. "Mama's Baby, Papa's Maybe: An American Grammar Book." *Diacritics* 17, no. 2 (1987): 64–81.

Stevenson, Jill. *Feeling the Future at Christian End-Time Performances*. Ann Arbor: University of Michigan Press, 2022.

Stievermann, Jan. *Religion and the Marketplace in the United States*. Oxford: Oxford University Press, 2015.

Stoler, Ann Laura. *Along the Archival Grain: Epistemic Anxieties and Colonial Common Sense*. Princeton, NJ: Princeton University Press, 2009.

Stout, Daniel A., and Judith M. Buddenbaum. *Religion and Mass Media: Audiences and Adaptations*. London: Sage, 1996.

Stowe, Harriet Beecher. *Dred; A Tale of the Great Dismal Swamp*. Boston: Phillips, Sampson, 1856. Transcription accessed through Documenting the American South, University Library, University of North Carolina at Chapel Hill, 2025.

Strhan, Anna. *The Figure of the Child in Contemporary Evangelicalism*. Oxford: Oxford University Press, 2019.

Sundquist, Eric. *To Wake the Nations: Race in the Making of American Literature*. Cambridge, MA: Harvard University Press, 1993.

Sutton, Matthew Avery. *American Apocalypse: A History of Modern Evangelicalism*. Cambridge, MA: Belknap Press of Harvard University Press, 2014.

———. "New Trends in the Historiography of American Fundamentalism." *Journal of American Studies* 51, no. 1 (2017): 235–41.

Taylor, Herbert J. Papers. CN 020, Evangelism and Missions Archives, Wheaton College, Wheaton, IL.

Thomas, Harry, Jr. *Sissy!: The Effeminate Paradox in Postwar U.S. Literature and Culture*. Tuscaloosa: University of Alabama Press, 2019.

Tinsley, Omise'eke Natasha. *Beyoncé in Formation: Remixing Black Feminism*. Austin: University of Texas Press, 2018.

Tran, Jonathan. *Asian Americans and the Spirit of Racial Capitalism*. New York: Oxford University Press, 2022.

Trouillot, Michel-Rolph. *Silencing the Past: Power and the Production of History*. 20th anniversary ed. Boston: Beacon, 2015.

Turner, Cathy, and Synne Behrndt. *Dramaturgy and Performance*. New York: Bloomsbury, 2017.

Vaca, Daniel. *Evangelicals Incorporated: Books and the Business of Religion in America*. Cambridge, MA: Harvard University Press, 2019.

Van Slyck, Abigail Ayres. *A Manufactured Wilderness: Summer Camps and the Shaping of American Youth, 1890–1960*. E-book ed. Architecture, Landscape, and American Culture Series. Minneapolis: University of Minnesota Press, 2006.

Vickers, Jason. "'That Deep Kind of Discipline of Spirit': Freedom, Power, Family, Marriage, and Sexuality in the Story of John Humphrey Noyes and the Oneida Community." *American Nineteenth Century History* 14, no. 1 (March 2013): 1–26.

Vongerichten, Marja. *The Kimchi Chronicles: Korean Cooking for An American Kitchen*. Emmaus, PA: Rodale Books, 2011.

Warner, Samuel. *Authentic and Impartial Narrative of the Tragical Scene Which Was Witnessed in Southampton County (Virginia) on Monday the 22d of August Last*. New York: Warner and West, 1831.

Webster, Richard. *Art of Dowsing: The Art of Discovering Water, Treasure, Gold, Oil, Artifacts*. Edison, NJ: Castle Books, 2001.

Weimann, Robert. *Shakespeare and the Popular Tradition in the Theatre*. Baltimore: Johns Hopkins University Press, 1978.

Weisenfeld, Judith. *New World A-Coming: Black Religion and Racial Identity During the Great Migration*. New York: New York University Press, 2016.

Wenger, Tisa. *Religious Freedom: The Contested History of an American Ideal*. Chapel Hill: University of North Carolina Press, 2017.

Wimbush, Vincent, ed. *Masquerade: Scripturalizing Modernities Through Black Flesh*. Lanham, MD: Lexington Books, 2023.

———. *White Man's Magic: Scripturalization as Slavery*. Oxford: Oxford University Press, 2012.

Winston, Celeste. *How to Lose the Hounds: Maroon Geographies and a World Beyond Policing*. Durham, NC: Duke University Press, 2023.

Why Not Us: Southern Dance. 8 episodes. ESPN+, 2022.

Wonderley, Anthony Wayne. *Oneida Utopia: A Community Searching for Human Happiness and Prosperity*. Ithaca, NY: Cornell University Press, 2017.

Woodward, C. Vann. *The Political Legacy of the First Reconstruction*. New York: Oxford University Press, 1968.

Worthen, Molly. *Apostles of Reason: The Crisis of Authority in American Evangelicalism*. New York: Oxford University Press, 2014.

Wu, Ellen D. *The Color of Success: Asian Americans and the Origins of the Model Minority*. Princeton, NJ: Princeton University Press, 2014.

Yellin, Jean Fagan. *Women and Sisters: The Antislavery Feminists in American Culture*. New Haven, CT: Yale University Press, 1989.

Zarsadiaz, James. *Resisting Change in Suburbia: Asian Immigrants and Frontier Nostalgia n L.A*. Berkeley: University of California Press, 2022.

Zauner, Michelle. *Crying in H Mart*. New York: Vintage, 2021.

Contributors

Michael J. Altman is professor of religious studies at the University of Alabama and the director of American Examples. His most recent book is *Hinduism in America: An Introduction* (Routledge, 2022). His current research investigates the intersection of religious studies and professional wrestling in a project titled *Kayfabe!*.

Rachel E. C. Beckley received her PhD in american studies from the University of Kansas. Her dissertation focused on the connections between US evangelicalism and free market economics by examining the discourses of work and free markets. She is a multiterm lecturer in the Department of History and the Department of Religious Studies at the University of Kansas.

Ryne Beddard is a PhD candidate in religious studies at the University of North Carolina at Chapel Hill. He researches religion, race, and ecology in the US South. Focusing on the late colonial and antebellum Great Dismal Swamp as an unofficial sacred site, his dissertation explores the mechanisms through which racial and religious identities were produced and maintained in the backwaters of an emerging empire.

Judith Ellen Brunton is an assistant professor at Rice University's Department of Religion working at the intersection of religious studies, environmental humanities, and cultural studies of science. Judith's research and writing has explored how oil extraction influences contemporary imaginaries of the good life. Her future work expands on this to investigate broader cosmologies of land use in North America and the enchanted technologies they enable.

Dustin Gavin is a cultural historian and theorist of Black southern religion and culture. Standing at the intersection of Africana and Americana religions, queer of color critique, Black feminist theory, media studies, and performance and dance studies, Dustin's scholarship engages movement and gesture as culturally and religiously constructed embodied grammars. With reference to classical and contemporary works of Black anthropological and sociological theory, his work demonstrates how Black sociality and popular performance engage with the visual, political, and performative rituals, aesthetics, and sensibilities of Black religious thought.

Sarah Hedgecock is the Sawyer Seminar postdoctoral fellow at Tulane University. Her work engages the fields of religious, childhood, and gender studies, and she is currently at work on a book project about nostalgia, relationality, and white American evangelical girlhood from the Cold War to the present day. Her work has been supported by the Institute for Religion, Culture, and Public Life at Columbia University, as well as research grants from Billy Graham Center Archives at Wheaton College and the Southern Baptist Historical Library and Archives. Sarah received a PhD in religion at Columbia University and holds a BA in anthropology from Princeton University.

Kit Hermanson (they/them) is a PhD candidate in religion at Columbia University. Their dissertation, "Believing in Sex: Science, Religion, and Non-binary Sex and Gender in the Nineteenth Century United States," explores a variety of religious and cultural oppositions and innovations that emerged in response to the increasingly stringent regime of scientifically defined sexual dimorphism throughout the century. The Oneida Community is one of many queer-but-not-historical sites in the northeastern United States that they are passionate about investigating and preserving.

Mihee Kim-Kort is a PhD candidate in religious studies at Indiana University. Her research interests include Asian American culture and religion, evangelical Christianity, and gender and race.

Andrew Klumpp is the editor of the *Annals of Iowa*, the quarterly scholarly history journal published by the State Historical Society of Iowa. He holds a PhD in religious studies from Southern Methodist University, and his research focuses on the intersection of religion and Dutch and American imperialisms in the nineteenth-century global Midwest. His work has been supported by the Clements Center for Southwest Studies, the Van Raalte Institute, Agricultural History Society, and Society for US Intellectual History.

Jacob Lassin is assistant professor of regional and cultural studies (Russia) at the Air Force Culture and Language Center. He received his PhD from Yale University in Slavic literatures and cultures in 2019. His research focuses on the intersection of religion, politics, literature and new media in Russia and the former Soviet Union. He is currently working on a book project titled *Sacred Sites: Russian Orthodox Cultural Politics Online*, which explores how websites run by the Russian Orthodox Church and its allies reinterpret Russian culture to attract a new educated elite that supports the Church and the state.

Robyn Lee is an assistant professor in the Department of Theatre and Fine Arts at

Niagara University and a doctoral candidate at the University at Buffalo, SUNY. Her research explores contemporary Christian theater in the United States. She is interested in how the performances adopt and adapt new and old performance traditions, both sacred and secular, to create immersive, sensorial experiences that engage the spectator as participant.

Index